Jame

TWO TO SIX

BookSurge Publishing

ISBN: 1-4392-1388-7

CONTENTS

"There is no immortality but the memory that is left in the minds of men."

-Napoleon Bonaparte

The following is a true story. Names and identifying information have been changed.

1

The Call

"Who's this?" demands a shrill female voice on the other end of the line. My stomach, already unsettled, clutches up.

Another call and it's not yet 9:00 a.m. on Saturday morning. Still, I'm sufficiently annoyed to quell the anxiety and almost instinctively echo in counter-demand, "Who's this?"

"Lydia Cepeda," she answers without hesitation and with a challenge in her voice.

As it's not yet 9:00, I'm still in bed, but I'm awake. Mostly awake, at least, because of the first call which I answered moments—really only seconds—before this call. The first call, the one that wakes me, and leaves me a little queasy, is from a guy named Pablo. His call, I make an excuse and get off quickly. Though never pleasant, I've learned how to do that over the years. A forgotten tryst—nowadays almost always paid for—who must have asked for my phone number. As usual, that's all it took. But I tell him I'm going to Connecticut, and don't have time to "get together with him." All the while I am speaking to him, though, I'm trying to remember who, exactly, he is. Less than a week after I'd picked him up, and I can't really remember. Not good. But, again, not unusual.

"I'm Pablo's and Treat's mother," she continues, intruding on my thoughts with words that take away any of mine. The clutch in my stomach hardens into a knot as she tells me that she knows that both of them had been in my apartment a week earlier, knows it was me who had engaged in "sex games," not only with Pablo—who she says she cares little about, as he is already "lost"—but also with her other, younger son, Treat.

"He's too young," she says. "He's only sixteen."

As if seized by a vise, the knot twists in on itself. I wish I can come up with something, anything, to end this quickly. But I can't.

All I can think of is to deny—to pretend to be another.

"What are you talking about?" I say to her. "You must be trying to reach someone else."

I gotta know, though, what she knows, what she's thinking and, most important, why she's called. She doesn't sound like some crack-addicted street whore. She sounds like a mother, an angry mother.

My denial seems to set her off as, first, she dismisses it and, then, she begins to give me information—information I don't ask for and that doesn't help. Like the fact that Pablo and Treat spend the weekdays with their grandmother in Brooklyn because she, Lydia Cepeda, works. But, they spend the weekends with her.

With nowhere else to go, I assume my lawyer persona. I point out to her that she is claiming that I—or the other—was with her sons on the weekend.

"Which is it?" I demand. "You say they spend the weekends with you. Then you say they were here with me on Friday night. Aren't you contradicting yourself?" I almost taunt.

"Don't think I'm stupid," she warns. "I know what you're trying to do."

Of course, it can be both—with her, with me, just not at the same time. But I want to let her know I won't be so easily cowed. That I'm going to fight back—prove her wrong.

So, it continues. Again and again, she says, in different variations, "You were there .... You did it." And, in different variations, I say, "No, I'm not who you think I am .... No, I didn't." Through it all, the only thought I have in my head is, "What does she want?" Can it be simply to chastise me? No, of course not. Asking her, though, would not only be an admission that I care, but also a confrontation with a reality I can't even fathom.

Finally, with nothing left to say, it comes, "What's the point of this call?"

"Money," she responds simply.

A feeling of relief—almost anyway—mixed with confusion. If it's only money she wants, maybe I can deal with this.

"If you don't give me some money, I'm going to the police," she adds.

The relief disappears. But then, confusion again—would she really? Going to the police won't get her the money she wants. Going to the police would cause her all sorts of hassles too. Besides, what evidence does she really have that anything happened? Moreover, who'd believe them, and not me? Maybe she's just full of shit. Maybe she is some crack-addicted whore, trying to get money the easy way.

A little of the relief returns. I wonder, should I just hang up? With my nerve up a bit, I say to her, "Look, I didn't do anything. I don't know who you're trying to reach, but I'm going to hang up. You must be thinking of someone else," adding, without enough shame, "Lots of people use this apartment, including my brother. Maybe it's him you're trying to reach."

But she calls, or at least ignores, my bluff, telling me that she wants the money sent by Western Union. "Pablo can be in your neighborhood shortly," she adds, continuing, as if in warning, "and he knows you drive a Volkswagen," repeating to me one of the lies I had just told Pablo moments before.

I want this to end. But I want it to end with a neat and tidy conclusion—how? All I can think to do is ask for her telephone number, tell her I can give it to the one who may actually know Pablo and Treat. She's dismissive, but she refuses to provide her number. She becomes, for the moment at least, the one on the defensive.

Pressing the advantage, I ask, "Why not? The only way to resolve this," I say, "is for the two of you to speak."

"No," she replies, "I'll call him," adding, "when will he be available?" appearing to accept—again, at least for the moment—that another was the one.

It's become a stand-off. There's nothing left to say—neither of us is giving in. I don't even ask how much money—that, too, would be an admission. Apparently realizing I'm not about to hand over cash or write her a check, she says with her own final taunt, "This isn't the end. You'll hear from me again." With that, after a lifetime of minutes, the phone is replaced in its cradle.

The fear wells up in me again, unlike any I've ever experienced before. In over twenty-five years of living—and playing—in the City, nothing like this has ever happened to me. I had already gotten up out of my bed, and, while talking with her, had paced around the apartment, back and forth, as my mouth went dry. Now, I pace some more.

What should I do? Is there really anything to worry about? Then I remember another call, the one late Tuesday night—or was it Wednesday night?—only days earlier. The one I had swept from my memory, almost as easily as I had scoffed at the threat.

"You will pay us, or you will pay," a menacing, urban male voice had said in a voice weighted not with the authority of a mother's outrage but, instead, one weighed down with the prejudice of low expectations, easily dismissed as just another black guy trying to get something for nothing by scamming. I'd met a fair number of them and always felt I could deal with them.

I had said to him, "What are you talking about?" Then he had said, "He was only fourteen."

Did I even respond, or did I just hang up? A connection lasting less than thirty seconds has suddenly become connected to something far more ominous. But how? What sense does this make and what to do now, given this crazy woman who may very well not stop at anything to get my scalp, or at least my checkbook.

The instinct to flee sets in. I dress in minutes, without showering, slipping on what's hanging on the hook in the closet, unconcerned with whether pants match shirt, or even whether the clothes are clean.

White socks on. Sneakers tied.

I *will* go to Connecticut, I think. I head out the door almost as soon as the last lace is tied, carrying my down jacket. I get to the elevator and, feeling like one possessed, decide not to wait but to walk the nineteen floors down.

One flight down, I ask myself, "What if she does call the police?" Perhaps it would be best to take with me to Connecticut those scores of pictures—really scores upon scores of pictures—that I've taken over the years and have stored in that big expensive piece of Hartmann luggage which my father bought me upon my graduation from law school many years ago.

But again, the fear sets in. Pablo, or perhaps worse, the police are moments away from entering my building. Time to flee. No time to waste.

* * * * *

With the solid, muted latching of the car door, I relax a bit, taking comfort from its familiarity and austere German luxury. Outside, able to get away, I breathe deeply.

Wasting no time, however, I quickly depart from my reserved outdoor parking space, briefly wondering whether it's being staked out.

Pulling out of the lot on to Central Park West, I don't immediately head for the West Side highway. Instead, I drive around the corner onto 97th Street, park and open the window a bit inviting the air which, if anything, seems only further chilled by the pale November sun. I need to call William, my best friend, in Connecticut.

Over the cell's invisible transmission lines, I squeeze the essence of what has just happened into a fear-filled brief, summoning up everything with lawyer-like precision and with an almost obsessive need to reveal what's happened, as if sharing will dispel the nightmare.

"I'm coming up," I say.

"Of course," he responds.

I remain parked. I'm not sure why. Perhaps I'm waiting for Pablo to come alongside, to resolve what had not been resolved in the phone conversation. Perhaps I'm waiting for the fear to dissolve.

After about ten minutes, I figure, "Okay, that's enough."

* * * * *

As I get further away from the City, the paranoia and tension recede. It takes me almost two hours before I'm pulling into the lengthy gravel driveway of William's home.

He lives in Northwestern Connecticut, in Litchfield County, at the foot of the Berkshire Hills. He has a twelve-year-old house that he built to look like a 120-year-old French château.

William greets me at the door and walks me into the house as I immediately relive the early morning experience. He listens with a patient ear.

I've known William since we attended kindergarten together. When we were young, he was small and I was big. After many years of bench-pressing effort, he is now much bigger, somewhat taller and definitely darker, having inherited the dark hair, dark complexion and dark eyes of his Italian parents. When we were both 20, I told him he was gay. I think he knew, but by my telling him, he could at last admit it, at least to himself and me. That's the kind of relationship we've had, as close as one can be with another person, other than family or a spouse. So, I know there will be no judgment, just a desire to calm me and help.

We sit in his kitchen with its Traulson refrigerator, stainless steel countertops and six-burner Viking stove. For over three hours, we strategize, war-game and dissect, trying to put the problem in a box, trying to let normal life reassert itself.

Finally, exhausted, we decide to move on. We decide to go to church—Trinity Church, in New Milford, Connecticut—not to pray, but to do something cultural. We're going to listen to the American Angels. According to the notes on the program William hands to me, they are a choral group who sing songs of redemption and glory. Maybe it is a little like prayer. Whatever, it sounds like what I need.

* * * * *

Ten miles away and about ninety minutes later, I take a seat in a pew that feels so familiar. Hoping to be transported, I listen intently. I end up, though, being mostly bored. Yet we stick it out through the entire 20 hymns, sung by the American Angels.

* * * * *

Outside, after the performance, it's wintry. Big, puffy white clouds of snow have cloaked the denuded trees and virtually enveloped the church, a church which not only looks, but which is, 120 years old.

At the over-priced dinner at a restaurant with a view of Lake Waramaug, where my own summer cottage sits cold and empty, I joke, though not without a hint of foreboding as I grab the bill, "Let me pay this one, as it may be the last one I can afford."

He looks at me with eyes that say, "pshaw."

Separated by time and space from the unsettling events of the morning, I can almost agree.

* * * * *

On Sunday, I head back to New York. As part of the war-gamed plan, I leave my car at William's house. Making excuses to hitch a ride back to New York, I call my sister, Lisa, who is at her weekend home a few miles away. I figure that without my German sports sedan in its reserved parking spot, which had been mentioned in both calls yesterday morning, without that part of me that sits outside, exposed, in a public parking space, I, too, will not be there. So, I hope, neither will they. They will disappear from my life and it can go back to being what has passed for normal for so many years.

* * * * *

Traffic on the West Side Highway is horrendous, so I tell my sister to leave me off at the 96th Street ramp which is about a mile walk to my apartment. Besides, I have to implement another part of the plan. I am going to Radio Shack to buy a phone with Caller ID capability, so that if Lydia Cepeda calls again, I will know it is her and will not answer.

2

MY LIFE, MY LOVES

As I am riding the B train to work Monday morning, I consider how my life would be different, how things would change, if Lydia Cepeda really does go to the police. For one, work, for sure, would change. Or, more likely, disappear. What I've been doing for over 20 years, first, at a prominent white-shoe law firm in New York City; then—within two years—at a small but respectable midtown law firm with a long, proud history of serving primarily financial institutions, would be gone.

I think back to how I made "junior" partner in 1991. Even today, I remain a junior partner. I stay, nonetheless, because it's an easy-going place, and the work is okay, and the pay is greater than what most small town lawyers are paid. The paycheck covers what I really want to do—enjoy life.

And where I live—what would happen to that I think as the train pulls into the 86th Street station? Though small and further uptown than many—really most—well-heeled New Yorkers would accept, my home is a jewel box of an apartment, with great views of Central Park and midtown Manhattan. It is graced not only by a terrace where one can comfortably seat twelve for dinner but, far more consequentially, by a reserved, inexpensive parking space less than a hundred feet from my building in an outdoor lot unencumbered by any attendant. All I have to do is unlock the car, turn the ignition and the City's offerings are mine for the taking.

And there's family, of course. What would they think? From my observations after almost 50 years on this Earth, mine is as good as most. At least, that's the way I feel. The Cleavers and the Huxtables don't exist in real life. All things considered, we're fairly stable. We're all college educated and reasonably prosperous. None, other than my sister Lisa, are nearby physically, but all are nearby in ways that matter most.

Both parents, still alive, are living separately in Florida, though my father, a genetically selfish man, is barely alive to me or the others. My oldest brother, a judge in Arizona; the next oldest, a public school teacher in California; my younger brother, a culinary school graduate, with his most recent job as a chef at a premier country club in Palm Beach County. There's also Charlie, a vet outside Atlanta. In between me and the chef in age, Charlie proved my father's not terminally selfish. When, in Charlie's infancy, both his parents died in one of those unheard of accidents, my father—the brother to Charlie's mother—took Charlie in and treated Charlie like one of his own. He'd be my favorite sibling if it weren't for Lisa. Lisa, who they say looks like me except ten years younger and prettier, is a struggling musician with a talent and drive I envy.

As the doors of the subway open up to the 59th Street station, I think back to my arrival in New York in 1977 with my girlfriend from College, Mary, who was to attend Columbia Law School. Within two years of living in the City, I came out of the closet, at least to myself. I was young and good looking. Though I've always been a bit too heavy and a bit too formless, I am blessed with a nose, chin and cheekbones of just enough prominence. And, most favored, are the sparkling blue eyes rich and deep enough to invite the plunge. And plenty have plunged. I have used those eyes as my own personal weapon of mass seduction. All it seems I had to do was look deeply into their eyes, and say with my own, "I want you more than anything else." So many—no matter how beautiful—need and crave affirmation of their desirability. And for those that I want, there is no artifice in granting that affirmation.

"How can I give that up?" I think as I exit the train at 53rd and 7th. Of course, it's changed a lot from my early days. Back then, I got whatever I wanted. Or, so it seemed. Like the time when, on one of my many visits to the Gaiety Burlesque Theatre, I again confirm the existence of that energy field powered by sex and desire.

It was long ago, just after I'd graduated law school. I'd gone to one of their early evening shows on a Friday or Saturday night. I remember taking the spot I took a lot, towards the back of the theatre, standing in a doorway between the theatre proper and the lounge to the left. I walk in, between acts, so no one is on stage. As the lights dim and the heavy, throbbing, primal disco beat of the times surges through the pumped-up sound system, a dancer, Carlos, is announced, a name I didn't know at the time but have not forgotten since. He steps out onstage. He's new. He's stunning, absolutely stunning, like few I've ever seen. There's no way I can take my eyes off him as he strips down to his briefs during his first dance, and strips down to his shameless perfection during his second.

Classic Hispanic looks, a teenage Ricky Martin, Mark Anthony and Roberto Duran, all rolled into one. Only more perfect, and a body without match—trim, but muscled, beautifully muscled. I can't forget how, like the music, a jolt of electricity fueled by desire surges right through me, and from me directly into him.

Walking into my office building, I remember the next part, the magical part. The dance ends and within moments of his leaving the stage, he comes out of the dressing room and walks right towards me. And I look right at him, inviting him to continue. We talk and, at that time in my life, not of money. No, it's a talk suffused not only with the sexual energy we had both experienced, but with the sexual promise of that mad embrace we both clearly wanted.

The rest also happens and, as I ascend in the elevator to my office, I remember. Hard, smooth, chiseled, and with skin so taut that lying next to him, you believed that a mythic

Hispanic God, sculpted from finely wrought pale obsidian, had taken to life with blood flowing and parts throbbing. The only blemish on that boy's body was some overactive acne which was probably only trying to catch up to the rest of him. We met twice more before it becomes obvious that he was way too much for me to handle. No matter. I remember it like a voyage, however brief, through paradise.

That kind of beauty is still out there. I know that. Even though I have to pay for it now, how do I give that up?

As I sit at my desk, I realize that, except for what's going on in my head, it's going to be a quiet day. So I let my mind bubble and churn. It wasn't all promiscuity I say to myself. I was "good," too. I've had "real" relationships.

The first one happens early on. I am just beginning my second year of law school, less than two years after splitting with Mary. The night we meet is a glorious October evening in 1980. I drive to the Village, to go to Uncle Charlie's. The leaves on the trees, shadowing the former women's prison—now a library—at the corner of 10th Street and Sixth Avenue, are just beginning to turn.

Uncle Charlie's is then the new bar on the block, proudly displaying the latest in video and aural entertainment systems, the perfect counterpart to the proud displays of its patrons.

I notice him almost immediately, out of the corner of my eye—mostly because he is noticing me. Pale skin, pale blue twinkling eyes, softened Nordic features and a crooked smile that could steal your heart. However, I'm on the prowl that night, and he is a little too sweet and a little too soft. So I ignore him and survey the crowd for something harder, meaner, lustier. But he turns out not to be so soft. With a courage I rarely mustered, he approaches.

"Hi," he says simply, "My name is Greg."

That was it for the next ten years. And during those ten years, there are theatre and dinners too numerous to count, and summer weekends in Connecticut and trips to London, Paris, Mexico and Greece. And there is heartache and frustration and disappointment at my unwillingness to give all, or really to give up all else that I wanted. So one Saturday morning in April of 1991, over ten years after we first met, he gets out of my bed and, as he prepares for work, he says some words I had heard from him before. So, I do not believe. But that time, it is for good.

Even before the painful period of withdrawal is over, I meet another. I am suffering from sciatica, and, as a result, it is one of the very few times I am unable to go to the office. It is a coolly blessed, almost Spring-like July day when Sylvester, a Dominican boy I had met and seduced over a year earlier, shows up at my door with an angel, an angel from the East.

"Hi," the angel says, "My name is" –and he gives a name with too many 'Ns' and 'Gs' and 'Rs' all bundled together, though it flows melodiously from his distracting teenage lips. Focused just enough, I must look perplexed as he quickly adds with shy, downcast eyes, which distracts anew, "But you can call me Pi. 'P', 'I'," he clarifies, adding something about his father and a love of math.

Five foot seven—"and a half," he always corrected. His rich, brown, happy eyes are set in a rounded Asian face sporting an almost Western chin. And then there is his skin, skin so pure you feel you can inhale it. Within less than two months, Pi moves in and stays for the next seven years. Though almost twenty years my junior, I learn from him more than I teach him, more than I have ever learned from anyone else. Even more generous than Greg, Pi seems able to love me in a way that I almost can't understand, let alone fully reciprocate. Yet I love him with all of the love that I can muster. Still, though, it's not enough.

As I sit at my desk looking out the window, I remember that one impassioned argument where my cruelty erupts and I demand that he leave "my" apartment, rending in full throat the bond of love that is supposed to unite where there is no "I" or "mine," but only "us" and "ours."

He leaves, leaving me ill. I cry. He returns the next day, but it is over. His home country beckons now more than I do. He goes back in the fall of 1999 and, with his natural grace and beauty, he quickly achieves success as an actor.

I begin my life again, alone. Older, in my early 40s, the power to attract is slipping away. Impatience reigns and more and more, I buy what I want. I'd always done it a bit, but now I begin to do it in earnest. In New York City, even after Guiliani, finding boys ready to share their bodies for a price is easy. I figure that's my future for any physical relationship. They would be as disposable to me as I to them—a wallet and a good-bye.

But once more, and completely unexpected, it happens.

Late one evening in November of 2000—three years ago—I meet Robert on a dark Greenwich Village Street corner, offering not only his body, but also his affection, to passersby who are willing to offer not nearly as much in return. He's a young, black male dancer, studying at one of the premier dance institutes in the city. With a long, lithe body and with the whites of his eyes almost matching the brilliance of his smile, Robert is so beautiful and so accomplished in so many ways, and in ways so quickly noticed that I don't take him directly back to my apartment. Instead, we go on what is to be the first of many dates. That first night on our first date, we go to one of those precious dessert spots on the Upper West Side, serving up delectable sweets, as if in joyful premonition of what is to come.

There's no denying he's too many years my junior. But we connect in so many ways, as he, like Pi, is mature beyond his years. Even as I sit now in my office, I'm in a thrall. There's also no denying that. I have had enough doubts, though, to hold back. So I've opened my heart to him even less than I had with either Greg or Pi. There are just too many differences, too much time in between.

Still, I haven't let go, as I continue to quietly ache for him. And as he continues to quietly revel in that quiet ache.

Interrupted by my first phone call of the morning, I wonder, if Robert were to offer himself fully to me and I were to accept that offer fully, would I be able to give up, completely, the pleasure of the hunt?

For now, I'm going to follow the strategy war-gamed in William's house only two days earlier. I've got to stop, at least for a while, at least until the threat ends. Then, when I'm thinking clearly again, I can figure out just what it is I'm meant to learn by all of this.

3

December 12, 2003

As I wake up on December 12, 2003, the sky is a radiant blue with no hint of any threat in the air. The call and the fear of November 15th are on its way to being forgotten.

The day is chilly. So, as I leave for work, I put on my navy blue cashmere overcoat, made by Aquascutum. According to the label, Aquascutum garments are made by "appointment to her majesty, Queen Elizabeth, the Queen mother." The suit I select is a Gieves and Hawkes, the tie, something expensive from Barneys. And, as I'd been doing for the last few years upon the advice of the jeweler, I leave my "dress" Rolex Cellini watch in its cloth pouch and put on the Movado instead.

I catch the subway just before 9:30 a.m. and, after a ten-minute ride, and after buying my bagel and newspaper, I enter the lobby of my office building at around 9:45 a.m. I walk towards the elevator bank for the elevator servicing the 40th floor on automatic pilot, seasoned by ten years of doing the same thing, when two guys approach. Though taken aback by the interruption in my routine, I nevertheless notice that, close up, both are too casually, almost too crudely, dressed for a Sixth Avenue office building. With my legs weakening from the unrightness of it, they maneuver me into the corner of the lobby. The taller one asks me if I'm me. "Yes," I answer, my mind everywhere but on the answer. They identify themselves as policemen. My mind focuses and, inside, I gasp. I realize, almost instinctively, that it's not time to lose it. I look around and see no one from my office in the lobby. Good. Then, as if reading my thoughts, they say, "We don't need to make a scene, let's go outside to the car."

What else can I do? Again, instinct with its keen sense of self-preservation leaves no doubt that it's best to leave the building to deal with this, wherever it's going. Outside, in the morning sun, the taller one tells me his name is "Detective Dropt" and that they are in the "Sex Crimes unit" and that I'm being placed "under arrest."

My heart stops as my mind races. Good God. Fighting against my own awareness, I think to myself. Isn't a "sex crime" when you engage in sex where the person you are engaging is an unwilling participant and does not want to be engaged. Everyone I had ever been with had wanted it, though, for sure, some "wanted it" because of the money.

But that's not it. Of course it's not. At least not that alone. I know what it is. The reason they are here and the reason they are handcuffing me outside my office building and placing me in the back of their SUV is Lydia Cepeda and her son, Treat. For Treat, you can't "want it."

I scream silently. Is this for real?

I feel like I'm entering a twilight zone as I get into their vehicle with my hands cuffed behind my back. The other—not Detective Dropt—gets behind the wheel while Dropt gets in the passenger seat. The SUV is started and we head downtown. I'm in police custody. I gotta pay attention to what is said, to who says what. This can't be happening. I'm in police custody.

Detective Dropt tells me the other Detective's name is Detective Santini and that we'll talk when we get to the "precinct." Otherwise, neither offers anything and demands even less. This one is going to be "by the book," I think. They don't expect me to talk. It almost makes it worse.

Focusing, I ask where we're going. Detective Dropt explains that we're heading to some precinct on the Lower East Side, rather than the Sex Crimes Unit, where they usually work. I miss the reason why. It makes no difference. He might have said it's because they are painting their offices. Whatever he said, it doesn't register. I'm in police custody, with my hands cuffed behind my back.

Minutes pass. I need to make conversation. I don't know why. I guess it's because that's what human beings do, even in situations like this. I gotta remain human. I also want information. Information will help me survive. Of myself, I ask, "How can it be—how can it be that Lydia Cepeda has persuaded the cops to arrest a partner at a respected New York City law firm?"

I need to know more about Lydia Cepeda, to learn whatever it is they know about Lydia Cepeda. And her two sons. Were the cops listening in? What, after all, had I admitted? And, besides, she asked for money. Isn't that enough to condemn her and her motives? Would they really just come out and arrest me? But they have. What can I do? What should I do? I decide to act out. Can't wait too long to let it happen, though. So, with ten to fifteen seconds to work up to it, I do it. Exploding in a fit of manufactured epiphany, I demand, "Is this because of that crazy fucking woman who called me a couple of weeks ago? Are you aware of that call? Do you know that she wanted money?"

Detective Santini glances at Detective Dropt, who doesn't react. What does that mean? They must know of the call. That's why I'm here. Or, maybe not. Maybe Santini's just wondering why I'd say anything. Unable to stop, and certain I can't be wrong, I say to them and myself, "Who's the victim here?" I say it again, quieter though, realizing it has no meaning.

What's left to do? What's next? Screaming. Silently.

I realize, without admitting anything specific, that I have essentially admitted that there is an admission to be made by me. Stupid. But I can't believe this. It must be a mistake.

I'm not in Topeka. These are New York City cops. They know the ways of the world. Innocence is forfeited early here, with eagerness. They were prostitutes for Christ sake.

That's what I'll do. It's already out anyway. So, I'll also admit to that. Let me show them I know I did something wrong, but only a little wrong. Not worthy of all of this. Figure out what's happening by making an admission sure to elicit a response.

I say something, but as soon as the words are out of my mouth, I can't remember what it is I said. I think I tried to be artful, lawyerly, and it came out convoluted. I think I said to them "There is a kernel of truth in any big lie." Anything beyond the prostitution charge I want them to believe is a "big lie." Prostitution. It's the oldest profession in the world. You don't destroy someone's life because of it. Regardless.

Detective Dropt interrupts my thoughts as he responds to what I can't remember I said, "Look, I'll be happy to tell you all, everything, as long as you will do the same thing with me. But let's do this right. Let's wait until we get downtown, where we can talk face to face."

Real or not, I almost sense some sympathy. How can they not, I want to believe. Whatever age, the accuser is a hustler, working—not lured from—the streets. And that mother.

Detective Dropt adds, whether to verify, explain or excuse, "We're only doing our jobs."

I see it as evidence of further sympathy, so I can't resist asking "Is this worth destroying my life over?" He actually looks in his rearview mirror as he says, "Who says that's going to happen?" A trickle of relief, much needed, flows through me.

Seduced by what appears at least to be some ephemera of concern, I ask, "Why couldn't you have met me at my apartment building? Why did you have to arrest me where I work?"

"Were you even home last night?" he responds.

I just stare and think blankly, wondering at the significance of his question, confirming as best I can that I was home, as he adds, "I can't follow you all of the time."

Whoa...! He's been following me? Who has ever been followed by the police? My God! Am I that special? Am I that much of a threat? Me, followed? I go to work every weekday and go the gym, three blocks away, almost every day after work. Did he follow me to each? Did he really wait outside, until I leave? How long has this been going on?

If he'd been following me since that date, since that November 15th date when Lydia Cepeda called—or even since November 7th when I had "engaged" Pablo and Treat—then what had he seen? I think back to what I may have been doing. Out of town for five days for Thanksgiving, and for the rest, without a car and cowed from the call. So, without remembering specifically, he would have seen a lot less than he might otherwise have seen if it had been some other time.

My thoughts are interrupted as we pull into a parking space. We've arrived at the precinct.

* * * * *

The place is virtually empty of anyone other than cops. It's also noticeably clean and well-lit. It seems not unlike what one might expect of any small-town police station in America. Oddly comforting, as it's not a horror. My handcuffs are removed and I'm told to stand behind a white tape. No choice. Dropt and Santini do some paperwork at the desk. I feel myself moving into a mode of acceptance, to let the day play out, just see what happens.

What else can I do?

After they're through, we wander a bit searching for an empty room where we can sit and talk. Once settled, the talk is perfunctory. He reads me my rights. Bizarre. He seems so disengaged, it's almost as if he's either expecting or telling me not to say anything. Intently, though, he attends to the paperwork. For that, he needs details. Home address, work address, phone, fax and, to my surprise and some consternation, my internet service provider, screen names and passwords.

Finally, he reveals the charges, putting into words what has been left unsaid for over an hour, while I was handcuffed and in police custody. Two counts: Sexual abuse of a child; endangering the welfare of a child.

"Child." The word echoes. There it is. Out in the open. Treat and his mother have won. He then says, "We may add a third count later. Criminal sexual abuse in the Second Degree."

Why later, I think? What else is there to know? Why does it sound the same as the first charge? How is it different? All I can think now, though, is God bless and help me. With that benediction coursing through my brain, he reveals to me "And, of course, we have obtained a search warrant," giving them, I know, the freedom—by permission of the court—to pry, probe and rummage through all that I had always hoped—no, expected—would remain private. My home, my stuff, my things, my life, my pictures—are no longer mine. Treat and his mother have won, more than they may have expected.

Detective Dropt leaves the room as he tells me I can make my one phone call. I call the office. The office. Calling the office will assure that this will end, that things will return to normal.

"I'm not coming in today," I say simply. "Okay," she responds. The conversation with the Firm's receptionist lasts about five seconds. Today, I know, no one will miss me. I can miss today and return on Monday. No problem. I'm ready to spend the rest of the day in the custody of the police.

Things will—they have to—return to normal.

We move on. To take my fingerprints. It's Detective Santini's responsibility, as Detective Dropt disappears to take inventory, I'm told, of the contents of my briefcase.

Santini's not up to it. We stand alongside each other, as he handles my hands, palms, fingerprints—sometimes gently, sometimes not—whatever might work to get the machine to accept the prints. The returning Detective Dropt, with a mild rebuke, sends the frustrated Santini on to some other task, as Dropt completes this task with alacrity.

Fingerprinting, done. Next, on to photographs—mug shots. Face forward, face right, face left—done.

This will pass.

With other tasks to complete, they put me in a cell. The cell door clangs as it closes. The key turns. I'm not good in enclosed, locked spaces. Claustrophobia. I let them know that.

"There's nothing we can do about it," Santini says, "You'll have to deal with it."

This is the way it is. I'm under arrest. But, whether to keep me cool or out of genuine concern, he adds, "Someone will be right around the corner, if you need anything."

Need anything.

"Would you like a soda?" he asks, as he lets me know he's finished with me for now and it will be a while before he returns.

"Yes, please. Diet Coke," I respond.

Surprising myself, I don't scream out as he leaves. I'm coping; keeping my phobia in check, at least for now. I begin to do the only thing I can do—pace and think, pace and think. Common, ordinary thoughts. How long before this is over? What is happening at the office? Where's this going? Denying it's going anywhere worse than where it already is. I figure it'll sort out. This can't be real.

Dropt walks into the cell area, and asks, "Where are the keys to your Volkswagen?" "Volkswagen?" I reply. Then I remember.

That's the lie I had told to Pablo in that early-morning call on November 15, when he asked what kind of car I drove. "A Volkswagen," I had said. Does Dropt not know, after following me for whatever period of time, after presumably determining with at least some degree of certainty that the allegations made against me by a street hustler and his kin are credible—does he not know that the German sports sedan I drive is an Audi, and not a Volkswagen? I tell him I don't own a Volkswagen. He leaves, looking flustered. I wonder some more.

What does it matter, I figure. What does it matter.

After about an hour of pacing and thinking—but no soda—they reappear, apparently ready to move on to the next stage. Instinctively, I feel it would be best to remain where I am, not to move on. But there is no choice. Dropt unlocks the door of my cell and I leave with them, venturing out again into what my eyes and skin acknowledge is a beautiful blue, crisp December day.

We head uptown to a building I don't recognize in a part of town I'm only vaguely familiar with, where government offices are located—Federal, State and City. The building next to the one we enter is, I think, the Criminal Court building.

Once inside, we wander a bit again. I see, with eyes still not believing, a warren of efficient, characterless offices like those one would expect in any government office building in the country. The linoleum floors explain the smell of floor wax. But that other smell? Is it the burnt shavings of pencil shaved off in an automatic sharpener? Or are my senses just trying to distract me?

Dropt and Santini seem out of their element. Finally, though, they find a place, a large office which has within it a small cell—a cage, really. They put me in the cage.

What if I told them I wouldn't run? Would they let me sit in the office like a normal human being rather than putting me in a cage? With that thought, Dropt lets me know that he is arranging for others who look like me to be in a line-up—with me. A line-up. Santini sits nearby as I pace back and forth in the cage.

People wander in to view me. One guy asks of Detective Santini, "Is this guy a defense attorney in for contempt of court or something?"

My God, I think, I actually wish that were the case. Never in my wildest imaginings.

"No," Santini responds.

"Oh," says the inquisitor. The inquisitor then asks of Detective Santini, "So who are you with?"

"Sex Crimes," Santini replies.

"Oh," the inquisitor says as he leaves.

A dark-haired, 30-ish woman enters. She's attractive. She comes right up to the cage, looking me in the eyes, almost flirtatiously. She leaves. I wonder.

About an hour or more goes by before Detective Dropt returns. He says we're moving to another room. The cage is opened and we walk down a short corridor. Once there, it's clear it's the "viewing room." There's a bunch of seats, a desk in front of them and they're all facing an obvious one-way mirror, though I've never seen one before in real life. The room is bright, with fluorescent lights. My head spins slightly.

How much more?

"Where do you want to sit?" Dropt asks.

I think. "The first seat," I respond. Why not?

"Do you prefer to be viewed with your glasses on, or off?" he asks.

Again, I think, who cares? "Off," I answer distractedly.

I sit down. He leaves. Others, all white, all 40ish, wearing dress shirts and ties and no glasses, come in and sit down. We all sit for several minutes. A noise is heard from behind the mirror. In minutes it's over. The others in the line-up go back to their lives. Detective Dropt returns to the viewing room, saying nothing, but leaving no doubt that I had been the one selected from those behind the one way mirror. I can't help but wonder—what happened back there? Did he comfort them? Were they happy? Sad? Clinical? Vengeful? Bored?

Dropt interrupts my thoughts by saying to me, "There's going to be a third charge—solicitation of a prostitute." For some reason all I can think to do is point out, "That's not the third charge you had mentioned at the precinct." As if it matters.

Surprisingly, though, he looks flummoxed. Why, I think. It's as if they didn't know until after my admission in his SUV, or perhaps until after his meeting—presumably, one of many—with those behind the one-way mirror, that this had all been part of a solicitation.

What's going on? He didn't know I drive an Audi, not a Volkswagen. And he's only now charging me with soliciting a prostitute, as if he's just finding that out. How much more do they not know?

But, again—what does it matter? Can any of these errors, or inconsistencies or lies matter? No matter what, Treat was in my home. They have me. It's on to the next step. That's what matters now.

We leave again and get in his SUV, but this time, to go just around the block.

The entryway alone gives warning. It's stark and overwhelming. You can't help but feel like a cipher as the SUV pulls up, not to a door, but to a gate—a huge rolling, metal gate, leading to an alley big enough for several cars to park. In that alleyway, a steel door off to the side, providing an opening in the massive wall where me, Detective Dropt and Detective Santini wait in a small, filthy vestibule to be permitted access. A nod, a flash of a badge, a piercing buzzer, and we are beyond the first checkpoint.

We walk through a large, bleak corridor, with an x-ray light glare of fluorescent bulbs. Underfoot is gray concrete. All around are pale cinder block walls in need of another coat of paint. We seem to head downward, maybe not physically, but it just seems like a descent.

We arrive at another checkpoint at the end of a long, seemingly pointless corridor. "You need to be searched," a voice tells me. I'm not even sure who.

Just a pat down, I find. I'm not even asked to remove my Aquascutum overcoat. But the pat down seems thorough and professional, at least, to me. What do I know? Other than at some of those edgy gay discos in the 80s, I'd never been patted down before.

Detective Dropt lets me know that I'll have to undergo a "physical and mental evaluation." I almost breathe a sigh of relief. I'm going to talk to other professionals, ones with advanced degrees, talking to them as one professional to another. They will understand, maybe even empathize. Life's perverse, they know. They are separate from this, like me.

In the first room I enter—windowless, soulless—I'm asked perfunctory questions by a perfunctory person. The second—the same. Lives filled with completing the requisite forms while a clock on the wall marks the minutes. "No," I answer, "I'm not diseased mentally or physically." But, I think to myself, come back at the end of this and ask me again.

Then it's on to another set of mug shots. Who are these for, I wonder? No matter. There's no choice. These are taken by a short, squat, tough-looking female officer. How can she be otherwise, working only with cops and criminals and criminals-in-training.

"Do you consider your hair brown or gray," she asks.

Though my mind is in suspense, for a moment at least, this question edges through the fog. And, as it does, I'm slightly offended. It's brown, of course, though admittedly, with gray flecks. But my connection to the real evaporates. I shrug.

Detective Dropt offers, "It's brown, with a lot of gray in it."

Whatever. She writes it down. We leave, heading to the next checkpoint and then a few others. All relentless and bleak. Finally, we not only stop, but he sits me down in a room with some others—in uniform—near a row of cells. I say nothing, but my eyes are open so I see the cops as they read the *New York Post* and watch a tiny black and white TV with poor reception. I see that I'm in a room of faded yellow cinder blocks and wooden benches and a beaten, worn wooden table behind which someone in uniform sits and on which rests the TV.

I descend into a chrysalis of phobia, suspending thoughts too fearful.

Dropt appears from nowhere. Somehow I hear, "It will go easier on you if you tell us anything you know about others in your circle."

My mind reels—that's what I think he has just said—"Others in your circle." It's said, though, almost in rote, like when he read me my rights. Yet it cuts, again, through the fog, as it repels me. Not only am I repelled by the question, but by the fact I'm where I am, where such a question can be asked of me. But so it is. And there's nothing I can do about it.

Shortly after the question is asked and left unanswered, Detective Dropt leads me into another cell.

I need to know what to expect, how and when this phase of the nightmare is to end—and it seems like this is the time to ask So, questions begin to pour out. "When can I call a lawyer?" "When can I see a judge?" "How long before I get out?"

He looks at me, distant and professional, and then says, "There'll be a judicial administrator around soon to ask questions and to help out." That sounds positive, I think to myself. He makes it sound positive.

"And the Court continues its arraignments through at least 10:00 p.m.," he adds. "Look, it's not yet six. So it's likely they'll get to you before the night is over."

Before the night is over.

"But, of course, that can't happen until we finish our search," he lets me know. Then, I think, do it, do it quickly. Go to my home with the key you have taken from me and do it, so I can get out "before the night is over."

I look around. It's a private cell with a private potty, encrusted with caked-on defecation from multiple guests, modestly located behind a mini-wall, so that you could do your duty, unseen by the prying eyes behind the overhead cameras. And there's a phone. He sees me look at it. He tells me it doesn't work.

"You can understand why," he says. "Can't have you calling anyone before we search your apartment," he says.

My focus, though, has already switched. I notice that directly across from my personal prison gates, just beyond the narrow corridor, is another cinder block wall, as high and as bleak as the others that surround me on the other three sides. Unlike the other two cells of the day, there's no wide expanse, no room beyond, hosting the keeper of the keys. Just a wall. Impenetrable.

I know this isn't going to be good. I have lost all other control, so I warn Detective Dropt as he makes it clear he's preparing to leave to go to my home, that I might lose whatever control remained, whatever control that has harnessed that phobia which infuses me whenever I find myself riding elevators, planes or alpine trams. Never before having found myself a prisoner, locked behind bars, I know it will not be good.

"Is there no alternative to this place," I ask, nearly demand.

"No," he answers curtly, clearly on the way to losing that professional patience of his and clearly wanting to finish his day by finishing his search.

Given what I have just been through for the last nine hours, I feel no hesitation in responding in kind. So I amp up the tension level, wanting him to know that it can be bad, and he will be responsible. What dignity I have, I'm prepared to discard. Let them see a 48-year old white attorney break down in front of their eyes and let them deal with it. And he sees that in my eyes, hears it in my voice. So the soothing pro takes over again.

"Look," he says, "It's here or the hospital—Bellevue. But if we take you to Bellevue, you surely won't be arraigned and released tonight. And it may not even happen tomorrow. It will just delay the whole process."

Bellevue. Prison cells. The process. Don't want to delay the process.

"How about Valium? Can you get me some Valium?" I ask.

I had taken Valium a couple of times in my life. I know it works, and I know I had a couple left from a prescription I had gotten a few years earlier.

"Only at the hospital," he answers. I tell him about my stash at home. After all, he will soon be there, and can bring some back.

"No," he says. "Buck up," he says. "You'll probably be out in a few hours, and the judicial administrator will be by soon to help out. And besides, there are others within earshot."

He leaves. I buck up. As best I can.

I begin again with the pacing, pacing around and around. Watched by the ubiquitous camera. Waiting for my turn before the judge, who will let me out, at least for a bit. Again, with the pacing, the thoughts begin to flow. And again, I focus on the mundane. What is going on at work? Will they miss me? When will I get out?

Slowly, my focus changes. What about those pictures that Detective Dropt is certain to find? Twenty-five years worth of pictures. Lots of boys. Lots and lots of boys in lots and lots of pictures. Polaroid pictures. Boys picked up in the bars, in the discos, on the streets, at the booths. Boys filled with lust. Boys filled with greed. Boys filled with both. A good number in "scenes" or "posed" in ways certain to disturb.

But most disturbing, I remember, will be those two from the mid-80s, those two boys, those two frisky boys. Forget it. There's nothing I can do about it, so I pace. I consider the three charges already leveled. What else?

As I pace, I begin to recalibrate my life, my future, such as it is in this cage, in this moment. Perhaps this is my Red Sea, I think, to be parted so I can cross from the life I had been living to the next one. Maybe it's my time to move on, to change, to begin anew. Maybe I need this, a kick to the head, heart and groin, painful and momentous enough so that it cannot be ignored, to lead me to something else, something better. Fate working for me, not against me.

For over twelve years, ever since I made "Junior Partner" at my Firm, hadn't I been searching for something else, something better? For each one of those years, it had never been really good. I know that. I've not really been happy.

I begin to convince myself that maybe, moving on to the next phase of my life will be a good thing. After all, what have I been doing for more years than I can remember? Just the same damn thing, over and over again. Eating, sleeping, working in at the office, working out at the gym and imbibing – booze, cigarettes, boys.

Then I remember. Child sexual abuse. Endangering the welfare of a child. This is no way to move on. There's much worse to come.

I begin to fear that somewhere in the yellow pages of the next edition of the *New York Post*, there'll appear a story: "Lowlife Lawyer Debases Defenseless Black Boys." Or, perhaps, even in the sanitized white pages of *The New York Times*, its own story: "Counselor-at-Law Transgresses." A strange and different universe, unlike anything I know.

As if in preview of how different it may be, a jailer—starting with the first of three cells on my cellblock and working his way down to mine—offers up the evening's meal. It's a half-pint of whole milk and waxed paper sandwiching two pieces of white Wonder Bread, sandwiching not bologna—at least not bologna as I remember it—but a kind of ur-bologna.

I stop thinking about myself and look at the sandwich. I nibble at it. In it, is a bologna to put to shame any other bologna created by man. They seem to have taken the most disgusting lunchmeat ever devised and made it even more disgusting, not bothering to macerate the bits of bone, gristle and fat, but letting them reside on the surface to be endured, and masticated by the unfortunate diner who has nothing else to eat.

Fortunately, I'm not hungry. After one bite, I toss it aside, accepting it as simply one more element of a punishment too cruel and too unusual. I go back to the pacing, back to the thinking, with the phobia of enclosed, locked spaces never far from expression, but under control, at least for now.

Within thirty minutes of the meal, the "judicial administrator" promised by Detective Dropt, the one who will be by to "help out," arrives in front of my cell door with a question. Apparently not responding quickly or clearly enough, she barks again at me, "What's your name?" So much for the sympathetic advocate for my cause. Why should I have expected any differently? Like the rest, she's there to complete her rounds. I bark back my name.

She let's me know she needs questions answered for the judge, to present to him at the arraignment so he can decide, presumably, whether to let me out or keep me in. Questions are asked about my age; my address; how many years there; how many years at the address before; and questions about what it is that matters to most but have no meaning in here, among those questions, my occupation.

"Attorney," I reply. She looks up for the first time, not quite so separate. Or, perhaps, the opposite.

"Salary," she asks. I answer.

"Annual?" she queries.

"No, monthly," I respond.

A low, admiring whistle comes from the adjoining cell, a nod from the judicial administrator, acknowledging, perhaps, my difference, at least, with others she interviews, and making me feel here in this jail cell all the more special because of it. Then she looks at my suit, then at my Aquascutum overcoat, which I'd placed carefully on the narrow bench circling my cell.

She leaves. I begin again to pace and think. Thinking the same thoughts and feeling the same fears, except it's getting closer and closer to 10 p.m., when arraignments stop for the evening, and before which I know I'll need to leave in order to preserve my sanity.

My pacing becomes more frantic. I circle the cell like the caged beast I begin to feel more and more like. What else is there to do? I cannot think about the future anymore. It's all too horrible to contemplate.

But focus. I need to focus on the immediate, on the real, on the practical.

So I bring to the fore of my thoughts, who will I call, once allowed to make a call? Who to come take me from this cell? And, of course, I had planned for that, too—war gamed with William. Not thinking it could really happen, but saying to myself, if Lydia Cepeda does her deed, follows through, who will I call?

William, of course, who knows of the warning, so won't be surprised. Who, with his social tentacles spread throughout wealthy, patrician Litchfield County, probably has more contacts in New York City than I'd ever have, or want.

The other I'd call, a lawyer I know. Though Agnes is not a criminal lawyer, she's a practical lawyer who practices alone and who is not tied to the other lawyers I know, who can not know. I had met Agnes at the first law job I'd had, at that big Wall Street "white shoe" law firm. Though I had only been in touch with her intermittently over the 20 years since I had left that Firm, I remember each of those intermittent encounters fondly. Yes, she'll be good. Reliable and practical and, I trust, sympathetic.

But there is no working phone to use, and I'm alone with nothing to do but pace and think, and look at my watch, watching as it gets closer and closer to 10 p.m. As it does, I get more and more frantic, an entire night in this cell with a view of nothing more than four walls. A tomb. So, barely thinking to myself, I say "What else is there to lose?"

I can almost feel it. No more restraint. No more every day repression. No more dignity.

I begin to chant in a voice that gets louder with each chant, "I can't take it anymore! Let me out!"

I actually feel some small relief as I continue to chant, almost as with a mantra of one who seeks comfort through meditation. But as I convince myself of the truth of my own words, I get more agitated. The almost melodic, even-toned chant begins to turn into a high decibel rant eliciting, after a time, words of derision and commands to stop from one of the unseen cellmates to my left. But as the pure pathos pours out, I hear words from one of those cellmates, seeking to soothe and calm, making me feel all the more hopeless and pathetic and thus, through the grief, no longer even able to form words. Instead, only able to groan, I'm like a mortally-wounded animal facing an eternity of that which is unknown and, so, primally feared.

All dignity gone. I'm locked in a cage. My voice, with no words, echoes off the walls.

Eventually, three—possibly four, I can't really focus—of those men in uniform, no longer ignoring my intrusion on their peace and quietude, or concerned, maybe, about my state of mind or, more likely, about having to spend the extra time to fill out the extra forms if anything should happen, come down to my cell.

The one in front—older, almost avuncular—seeks to cow me into silence with semi-harsh words about improper behavior. But in this state, I'm not about to be cowed. I'll do the cowing. That is the least power I can exercise in this otherwise powerless position. So I virtually spit back at him that I can't take it anymore, that I have to be arraigned and released tonight, or I'll go crazy. As with Detective Dropt earlier, when I look him in the eyes, I know he understands. I'm on the edge. And it's on the edge of something he doesn't want to mess with, not unless he wants to pick up the messy, broken pieces.

He backs down, but promising virtually nothing other than to see what he can do to get me information that I want. He offers just enough to avert a crisis. And I realize there's nothing I can do, other than to seize another thread of hope to hold onto, however flimsy it might be. I quiet down and again turn my thoughts to the practical, to my survival.

I think of the Firm. I consider and dismiss each possible angle of cashing at least one more of those comfortably-balanced, monthly draw checks. The only possible—but really impossible—hope is that the wider world out there will not find out, at least not right away. Then, I'll be able to do something to add at least a little more to the future of no employment. After all, convicted—or even only charged—who would hire a child sexual abuser? No, even those on the minimum-wage, private security force patrolling my apartment complex need a clean police record. As one forever now sullied, regardless of outcome, I need to husband my current resources, to take stock of my stocks, bonds, real estate and law firm values, and determine if I can survive with nothing else, because all else is certain to be taken from me.

Money. That's what now is important. I think. I calculate. But, no matter how I compute it, it's not enough, not enough to retire with enough, at 48 years old, no matter how frugally I live. Maybe I should—for my own survival—go to the powers that be at the Firm and threaten, cajole or promise whatever it takes. Threaten to tell all to that wider world—and to tell sooner, rather than later. And with no P.R. filter, no spin, no artifice, no gloss—as if such a thing were even possible here. If they help me out, I'll do whatever I can to avert or, at least limit, the shame and stigma. Otherwise … .

But there is no game plan to plan. It's far too early in the game to do anything but speculate, leading only to further speculation, upon dizzying speculation—and then exhaustion. Reaching that exhaustion, the fear returns.

Not knowing or caring how much time has passed since the face on the other side of my jail cell door promised to give me information on my immediate fate, but knowing I can wait no longer, I again begin to chant and soon, again, to rant, all the while circling the cell in synchrony with the chant. This time, only groans from my neighbors, and no response at all from the jailers.

10 p.m. comes and goes and my rants grow even louder and more frantic. And then an additional hour passes, and I'm growing hoarse and have become anesthetized, robotic. Hearing and watching, they still don't respond. They no longer care. They do nothing.

Then, some unknown time and virtually non-stop ranting later, a multitude of bodies appear on the other side of the bars in that narrow corridor. Even in my state of suspended being, I see them. My own personal police, Dropt and Santini, with backup provided by the same three or four locals from hours before.

Admonitions pour from Dropt, "You've got to stop. This won't do." Or words to that effect. He, I no longer care to be admonished by. He, with the critical assist of others, has already brought upon me the greatest admonition I'll ever receive. And, having just gotten back from a field trip to my home, to ferret into my sexuality and lifestyle to help justify what he has done, I can hardly bear to listen to his voice.

But he's also the only seeming savior from, even if also the creator of, this immediate horror. I realize that, yes, he has to be there. He broke me, so he owns me. Somewhere, certainly, in the police code of professional responsibility, he's ultimately responsible to see that I survive for the remainder of my stay at the lodgings where he has interred me.

I can also tell he's not happy. He had probably expected to log in the unmentionables he has swept from my apartment, call it a productive day and go home to a good night's sleep, presumably alongside his wife of many years, knowing that whatever kids he may have, or hope to have, are safer. Or, at least they are if they hang out on dark urban street corners late at night, selling their asses.

That's the way I feel and I take fleeting solace in his displeasure. I have my own displeasures, multiplied manifold. The only escape is to insist on being taken to Bellevue. It's the only available treatment for my phobia, given that Night Court has closed and I'll otherwise be trapped there in this cell until Day Court opens. So I tell him.

He doesn't want to go. He again tries to explain to me why I should not want to go, but it's no use this time. It isn't going to work. Delay and arraignment be damned. Sensing my conviction, he capitulates.

"Get your coat and follow me," he says, curtly.

Dropt in front, Santini behind, we walk down the narrow corridor, passing my cellmates, who must be relieved to see me go. Through the playpen with the *New York Post* and tiny TV, where the uniformed locals pass the time, waiting and watching and reading—but only sometimes listening. Back into and through the cavernous, bleak concrete cinderblock halls. And then into a room I had not seen before. A big room, with several large and a few small cells on either side, some vacant, some overbooked, and with a massive oval desk, or really a station, in the middle of the room which, even at this time of night, is well-tended by men and women in blue and white.

As I begin to pass one of the cells, as if by design, another officer in blue—older, not unkind looking—opens the cell door of one of the cells and nods slightly towards the opening, as if expecting my arrival.

What to do? Is there really a choice? Am I prepared to insist and, if necessary, make a scene? This time, not in front a handful of officials—but in front of a stadium full of officials and their wards. In an eye-blink, in what is left of reason, I think: less delay, more space, less confrontation, less humiliation. So, in I go, and out go my consorts for the day and into the night, Detectives Dropt and Santini, who knows when to be seen by me again.

Another cell, the fourth of the day. It's large with an expansive space on the other side of the bars, filled with officers and other cells on the other side of the gate. I begin to calm down. As I look around, I notice that even at this time, on the near side of midnight, the cell I've entered is clearly overbooked with a faint sour smell of damp clothes and bodies.

It's about the same size as the living area of my apartment, perhaps eighteen paces long and ten paces wide. Stripped of furniture, it could comfortably entertain a dozen or so, but not if that entertainment includes a sleepover. There has to be at least triple that number clustered about, sharing my space. A butt parked on nearly every inch of a narrow bench circling the three walls except, as with any subway car, where some alpha male—and they are all males—has managed to spread other parts of his body. Surprisingly, however, there is no atmosphere of threat beyond what one might experience in a subway car, though admittedly a subway car traveling at about this hour of the night. I check out the crowd. I'm older than most, whiter than most, better dressed than any and totally ignored by all. Thank God.

I'm sure I'm also special in another way. What are they in for, I think. Subway offenses? Drug offenses? Minor bullshit. Not me. Child sexual abuse here, just recently having rejected my own private, protected accommodations, to share accommodations with the likes of those I had always previously pitied, avoided or taken advantage of. But no one knows or would know of the charge, or the pity, or disdain, while I'm here. So I'm safe.

It's late, and I'm tired. But I see the phone. Dropt and Santini have finished their jobs, so I'm free to call. The only hurdle—a line of others, and no change. I have nothing to do but wait in line, and I remember the Firm's phone card, still in my wallet. Even in the brief time I've had to acclimate myself to those in the room, I can tell that card might cause more agita than the charges against me, or the hidden feelings I have towards them. With unlimited resources to call—my resources—many would call more, and some would never stop calling.

Before I know it, it's my turn at the phone. No one is paying attention. So, I withdraw the phone card from my wallet, punch in the numbers discretely, the card number, the code number and the phone number—William's number—as per the plan.

No answer. Not in the plan. I don't bother leaving a message.

One more in the plan to call, but first must get her number from information. More numbers are punched, then numbers are remembered, and then the old numbers are punched again with the new number. She answers.

I'm connected.

Agnes is on the other end of the line. Outside. As she wakens from sleep, I reveal all.

"Where are they holding you?" she asks.

"Actually, I'm not exactly sure," I tell her. "It's by the Criminal Courthouse, downtown."

"Ah, the Tombs," she replies.

Of course, the Tombs, I repeat silently to myself.

She will find someone, she says. She will make calls, the late hour of the night be damned. She knows someone who is the aide of a former councilwoman and who will know someone worth knowing in this situation.

As we end the call, she says in reassurance, "I'll not abandon you. Call me back in an hour."

Finally, some small comfort in the midst of this totally distressing, totally surreal day, comfort given by assurances that she will find someone to help me out in a situation never to have even been imagined.

I hang up the phone and look around. Nearly every inch of space is taken so, what the hell—I have the phone, and no one is waiting. I have the card, unlimited resources. Can't tell the family or other friends. They cannot know. At least not until they have to. Besides, what can they do?

Still obsessive, and still thinking this may end with a return to normalcy, I call my answering machine at the office. There are a dozen messages from people obviously none-the-wiser for my situation. Some express concern for the illness I said I had when I excused myself in my call to the Firm's receptionist. At least one of those who leaves a message also leaves a second one, to let me know how important his matter is, and of how important it is that I return his call as soon as I can. Strangely, hearing about important deals and hearing how I'm wanted, I feel somewhat reconnected to the life from which I had been ripped not more than twelve hours earlier.

I then check my home answering machine. Then my cell phone's answering machine. One message. From my secretary. It's an odd message, hard to hear. It seems that she saw something this morning. But the message is almost whispered. Or perhaps, I don't want to hear, so desperate am I that she have seen nothing, so as to be able to reveal nothing. I erase the message after one hearing, not wanting to hear it again. But I do hear it.

She says she saw me this morning, coming in, and asks, "Should we call the mayor's office, or something?" That's it.

Like the message, our relationship is somewhat odd, at least in relation to those of the other attorneys and their secretaries at the Firm. We treat each other with decency and mutual respect, with an occasional brief interlude of friendly, if not intimate, revelation. Instinctively, I know not to reveal too much. For like offices across the City and beyond, gossip is the true currency of choice, the juicier, the more valuable. And my secretary undoubtedly enjoys and excels at collecting and dispensing it. If she saw anything this morning, then she has just been handed the keys to the vault. The only question is whether she will use them.

Oh, well, can't do anything about it now.

I hang up, turn around and know my phobia of enclosed spaces will not return, intimidated into quiescence by the presence of so many nearby. Crowded as it is, I find some space and sit on a dirty but not disgusting floor and bide my time until the next call to Agnes. Surveying the crowd, I'm confirmed in my belief of their minor offenses and almost buoyed by the small acts of consideration and gentleness I witness in a decidedly inconsiderate and ungentle environment. Even with the crowding, people making way without complaint and even if not needing to make way, making do quietly, without offense to others, regardless of the offense that has brought them here this night.

* * * * *

Only forty minutes have passed, but a new day has arrived and I can wait no longer. I go back to the phone and punch in all the magic numbers and she answers. She has the name of someone who can help.

"He's good," she assures, adding, "He comes highly recommended by my friend, the councilwoman's aide, and I've already left a message with his service." Though not absolutely certain he's in town, she believes he'll most likely be available for the morning arraignment.

"Most likely" isn't good enough, I think. "Call some others," I suggest.

"It's late, very late," she reminds me. Again, she repeats she won't abandon me. She will be there, at the arraignment, regardless—and it will be okay. She will make every effort to get a pro, but she will be there.

"Okay," I say with little real choice, adding, "If anything happens, leave a message on my home answering machine. Otherwise, I'll check with you around seven. Thanks."

It's settled. Now, I've got several hours with nothing to do except deal with the trauma. Yet, almost blessedly at this point, I'm overwhelmed by exhaustion.

My space on the floor is still open. I go back and lie, rather than sit, down. I roll up my cashmere overcoat and put it on the floor under my head to try to rest. Of course, it's impossible. It's better, though, than standing or sitting, or hoping.

Time passes. Around 4 a.m., inexplicably—as if in further punishment—the cleaning crew arrives. Again, a gentle, accepting response from the guests. No rebellion. No cursing.

The crew finishes applying their slightly dirty mops to a slightly dirtier floor in a process that begins to equalize the two. All wait for the floor to dry, then positions are resumed. Another hour passes and the breakfast service crew arrives. All are offered a mini-box of corn flakes, not the generic kind, but Kellogg's Corn Flakes. But dry, no milk. Better, though, than the pseudo bologna of the night before.

Again, however, I decline. Still no appetite.

After the empty Corn Flake boxes are collected, it's as if morning has arrived, hours early. Activity, expectant waiting and, within the hour, names are called to line up to whatever is to be next. One set of inmates is called. Off they go. Within minutes thereafter, another group—including me. I line up, as if in camp, a particularly militaristic, unpleasant camp, with the camp counselors dressed in blue and white, with badges, clipboards and orders barked out at us. We march in single file down a long corridor.

"Stop," they command. We are counted again. Then we are marched into my fifth pen of the last twenty-four hours. Again, it's crowded. Although darker and more confining than the previous cell, it's also closer, I know, to my freedom. So the panic is held at bay.

There are three cubicles on one side with large sliding shutters which, presumably when unlocked, open to the other world. The world I have left one way and will be entering a new way. Now the crowd is antsy, more expectant, each waiting for release, if not freedom.

Someone begins to stir more restlessly than the others, then begins to make a scene. He's white, tall, thin to the point of emaciation, seemingly Southern and, older than any including, God hopes, me. He's apparently still not dried out even after a night in jail. At least that would give him some excuse.

His voice gets louder and louder. He goes into a rant and a rave. A rant and a rave of how he has been mistreated all of his life and how all others deserve to eat his shit because of it, especially the "niggers." I can't count the number of times the word "nigger" passes his lips.

And I think, here I am, here, where they want me to be, communing with those that they feel I should be with and maybe become a part of.

Looking at and listening to the asshole, I think to myself "fuck him." After too many minutes have passed, the others in that jail cell do just that, in a way. One of the "niggers" trips him as he walks by, and another or two kick his arrogant white face and ass as he lays spread out on the cell floor. But not, unfortunately, in a way that silences him. Enough, however, in a way that I feel is right. And enough that does, fortunately, diminish him, so that for the most part he can now be ignored.

After it quiets down, I think to myself, "When was the last time I've seen anything like that?"

I want to call Agnes, but some big, unhappy looking guy is hogging the one available phone, saying, from what I can tell, nothing of consequence on it. Once he finishes talking about nothing, he guards it as if reserving it for his sole use.

As time passes, he loses interest. So, I remove the magic card from my wallet, punch in the magic numbers, and catch Agnes just as she's about to leave her apartment to meet Max, which I learn is the name of the guy who is supposed to help.

Agnes says, "I've talked to him, he's coming down."

Thank God.

"He's handled some major cases," she adds. "He's black," she then notes pointedly.

Yes, I realize in the back of my mind, this is in part about black and white. They are black, and I am white. In this world, then, this will be in part about black and white.

I wait. In less than an hour, a window shutter in one of the cubicles slides open, and what I believe to be Agnes's voice calls out, "Jim," expecting me to be the only Jim on the other side of an impermeable wall. She cannot know that her Jim, whom she has known for years and whom she has always seen only in the most respectable of environments, is now in a pen with multiple miscreants, who are to be addressed with the pretend dignity of "Mr." to separate one from the other.

Waiting to hear her voice again to make sure it's her, I don't respond. She quickly repeats my first name, this time followed by my last name. And there it is. The relief floods through me as, for the first time in almost 24 hours, a human being is here to see me whose intent and purpose is to help, not hurt.

I move to the cubicle with her voice. I see her and feel the sympathy and concern in her eyes. I already feel a little better as we turn to the business at hand. She has signed in as my attorney of record, but expects Max to be here soon. It appears that they will arraign me on the three counts and release me, and that it will be happening in less than an hour.

Though a litigator, she's obviously out of her element in Criminal Court. With an air of calm confidence, she suggests that she go and check on Max's arrival. I concur and then wait, and within minutes he arrives.

He comes to the same cubicle window. He's my age. Not strikingly but comfortably handsome. Though sitting, he's clearly taller than me. Solid, with Afro-American, not African, color and features. His shaved, bald head, big full lips with matching white teeth and deep brown eyes draw my eyes. A bowtie and hat—one of those old-fashioned dress hats with a brim and a band around the middle—complete the picture. When he looks at me with an engaging, comforting smile, it's as if he's inviting me to join him in his certitude.

In this moment, at this time, a soothing, commanding presence, in whose hands I'm fully prepared to hand my fate, feeling he's here to use his talent and knowledge to attempt to level the playing field in this all too real game where I'm the quarry.

In a steady, deep, almost sonorous voice, he essentially repeats what Agnes has already told me, but with a bedside manner infused with a force of personality which I can only hope has been molded by the courtroom and the many battles fought therein.

We finish. The shutter closes. I move back and the space becomes free for the next inmate to confer with his counselor, a counselor unlikely to have been recommended by a councilwoman's aid as "special" or committed enough to his client to come down to the jailhouse on an early Saturday morning on very short notice.

In what seems like only minutes—at least in comparison to the rest of the night—my name and those of others are called. We are escorted to a door just outside the cell, which leads directly into a large, sun-filled but otherwise almost empty courtroom.

It looks so civilized.

Agnes, a friend of Agnes's and a few others sit in the bleachers reserved for the spectators, none seemingly carrying a notepad or wearing a hat with the word "Press" printed on the front. Notwithstanding one of my fears, freedom for me this morning will also, apparently, mean freedom from the press.

The inmates, several of us, are seated in what would otherwise have served as the jury box—too incongruous to contemplate. Even more incongruous are the words of one of my companion inmates as I pass him by. With nothing other than what seems like genuine concern, he asks if I had survived the evening okay, apparently being one of those unseen other cellmates in that cellblock where my phobia had reigned. I glance at him, nod and mutter an affirmation with whatever distracted appreciation I can muster. I then swiftly return my attention to the center, to the judge, to the lawyers and to the beginning of decisions by others which may now rule my life for God knows how long.

First up are two cases involving people caught up in subway misdemeanors. Quickly disposed of, they confirm my suspicion of the petty nature of the offenses of those persons with whom I had shared the evening.

My case is called. The charges are read. For this morning, at least, they seem to garner no more attention from the bleachers than the two previous subway misdemeanors. With a question directed at me by the judge, "Not guilty" is the answer that Max whispers in my ear, which is repeated to the Court by me. A time and place for the next proceeding is set.

It's done. I'm out.

I turn, walk through a small gate and proceed out of the courtroom with Max, joined by Agnes and her friend as we pass by the bleachers. We continue through the lobby and out the courthouse door into the morning light beyond, which is shadowed by a not quite permeable tissue of wispy clouds, as if in perfect counterpoint to my state of mind. Even without the press to report the offenses of which no one is presumed innocent, I know for sure that I step into the dim morning sun with my life dramatically and permanently changed.

And then we talk. And oddly, the certainty of that change in my life becomes far less certain. First off, Max points out that there is no press and would not likely be press on an early Saturday morning. So, my case is already old news. And he reminds me that the State does have to prove its case. And that this does involve a process. That, I hope, will be more rigorous than the process involved in throwing me in jail for the day.

"Take the remainder of the weekend to recover," Max says, "and go back to work on Monday."

This is a plan not included in the dramatic scenarios considered by me throughout the previous night. But, as he says in both warning and comfort, "We have to take it one day at a time."

I realize I need to get a sense of Max's background. If he's to be the warrior on my behalf then, given how easily and brutally the State gets to exercise its power, he better be a warrior with successes and the battle scars to prove it.

I ask whether he has handled similar cases before. He's cocky, as he almost snorts, "Only if they also involve more serious offenses, like capital murder." Quickly recognizing either the arrogance or irrelevance to me of his words, he shrugs, essentially dismissing the words which had just passed his lips, and says, "Yes—many times."

As he looks at me with those reassuring eyes, I feel, "Good enough." At least for now.

We talk briefly of the facts. He mentions that the prosecutor inadvertently let him see papers that indicated the complaining witness is a convicted prostitute. Not news to me, I tell him, as I briefly explain the event and the phone call from Lydia Cepeda. I then tell him what worries me—the search, the pictures. There are easily in excess of two hundred Polaroids, taken over almost twenty-five years. Many will offend. Nothing hardcore, or even approaching hardcore, but nudity for sure, with many depicting S&M games with young, mostly Black and Hispanic males. And, based on the charges against me, there is at least one who would have been best not to have been there at all.

Max is comforting. "Pictures, everyone has pictures," he says. "They're like the dog that doesn't bark. You forget about them." In other words, I guess, the words not said again, "Take each day as it comes." There is nothing that can be done about it now. The police have them, and the police and the State will decide what to do about them.

Too exhausted to continue, we exchange cards and shake hands for the first time. His big hand envelopes mine so that mine feels completely absorbed when he wraps his other hand on top of both of ours. He says he will call me Monday.

I leave with Agnes and her friend who, I discover, is also her neighbor. He had generously driven Agnes down from her Upper West Side apartment, and is now driving both of us back uptown.

I look out the front window from the back seat of his mini-van, noticing that the wispy clouds had thickened to further dull the light of the morning sun. I can't fail to notice that the mini-van is filled with children's playthings. Sickeningly, for what I realize shall surely only be the first time, I wonder what this stranger, this friendly neighbor, must think—how does he feel about having an accused child abuser in the back seat of his family mini-van?

Fuck Detectives Dropt and Santini. Fuck the State. Fuck Lydia Cepeda and her two sons.

As we head towards home, the neighbor acts as if it's not even a consideration. Instead, the conversation is filled with what one might expect between a concerned friend, now also acting as a counselor at law, and another in distress—some facts, some figures, some explanations, some descriptions. But no accusations, either said, unsaid, implied or threatened. Perhaps Agnes's blessing is enough to keep a parent's outrage in check.

We reach my apartment building. Agnes and I get out. I go to the concierge, Eddy, who hands me the extra key to my apartment, not knowing it's to replace the one taken from me by the police.

On entering my apartment, I notice that, other than a bedroom cabinet door, unhinged from what were already weak hinges, very little seems to have been disturbed from however many hours Detectives Dropt, Santini and company spent in my home the night before. The only thing missing is a large, expensive piece of Hartmann luggage.

I see that the computer remains on the desk which was bought to hold it. "Get rid of it," I was told. "But nothing's on it." I had said. "Just get rid of it," it was repeated. "Yeah," I say to myself as I hang up my cashmere overcoat. Surprisingly, the coat at least, looks no worse for all the wear and tear.

Agnes and I talk a bit as I order out breakfast for both of us and write her a check for what she has done and for what I expect I may need from her in the future. We finish. She leaves.

I'm exhausted, but wired. It's just after noon. Agnes is only an acquaintance friend, at best, and I need the real thing. But not family, not yet. There's two I know I need to call. One, William, of course; the other, Pi—in a land so far away, I could only wish I were there.

It's half-a-day ahead where Pi lives, in the deepest morning. I know he'll be awake, and even if he isn't, I know it won't matter if I awaken him. I dial his phone number. He's there, and awake.

"Oh, no!" he gasps after I tell him. "You've always been so fucking careless," he virtually yells at me. Hearing the catch in my voice, his anger against me dissipates.

Closer to the tradition and dealing with challenges of a homophobic society, Pi has definitely grown more spiritual. And, right now, that's what I need. So, we talk for almost three hours. Nothing is held back. Finally, twenty-some hours later, to an ear that's listened to and heard so much, I cry. It's a cry so deep and profound it seems to go beyond the indignities of the last day to include all those I have ever suffered. And, perhaps, all those I have inflicted.

Pi, too, cries out. His cry, though, is without tears. Instead, his is in defiance of those who have caused mine and in support of my battle, and their ultimate defeat. As we talk, I feel as close to him as I was when I first fell in love with him.

It's approaching the very early morning for him and the late afternoon for me. My voice is fading fast due, in no small part, to the high decibel usage from the night before. It's time to let him go. We start our goodbyes at least thirty minutes before we actually hang up. Maybe this can go on forever, I think, reveling in the comfort I'm taking from his call. But no, time intervenes, we say a final goodbye, and we hang up.

I'm exhausted but I have to call William. In what is, perhaps, a blessing, he's not at home. It'll wait. I feel myself separating. I remain seated at the granite counter top dividing my kitchen from my dining area. My mind won't stop running, but it can only run in circles.

It's dinner time and, finally, I'm hungry. Mindlessly, I order out Chinese food, open a bottle of red wine and, while I wait for the delivery, take a long, hot shower, soaping and shampooing away the grime and the grit, if not the shame or the threat, of the day just passed.

* * * * *

With dinner and wine consumed, and the edge still not dulled, I remember the Valium. I find the plastic bottle with an issue date of over three years earlier, and three tiny tablets of the ten dispensed remaining. Wondering about their continued efficacy, but certain that whatever potency remained would be enhanced by the bottle of wine I had just consumed, I wash a tablet down with New York City tap water. For the first time in almost thirty-six hours, I lay down—not on a hard, filthy, prison floor, but on a clean, virtually new, luxuriant Dux mattress.

The drug kicks in and, for a while, I feel like I'm surfing through a kaleidoscope of stars towards a rendezvous with my favorite aunt. She, perhaps, would have, if not the answers, then at least a guidepost to those answers. After all, I reason in my hopeful state of drug-induced reverie, she has passed, she had loved me and, in her new state of divinity, she will know and will tell me what to do.

But no such epiphany occurs. Instead, I pass into a drug-induced torpor of restiveness. Throughout the night, I toss and turn. In the early hours of the morning, I redirect my energy into getting up, opening another bottle of wine and pouring it first into a glass.

I feel the need to connect to one more. I need to talk with Robert. Is he a symbol of, or a savior from, my dysfunction? I don't care. I dial his cell. There's no answer. In what remains of my voice, I leave a brief message. A message of veiled despair left at 3 a.m., a message which, if he has any sense, he won't return.

* * * * *

On Sunday, William calls around mid-day, interrupting my pacing. I tell him. The nightmare we talked about has come alive. What more can we say? Just before we hang up, he tells me of the big news of the day, the news that Saddam Hussein has been captured, and is in the custody of the American authorities.

4

Return to Work And To Family

It's Monday, December 15, 2003. I leave for the office early, unable to sleep. Other than by the demons in my mind, I make it in unmolested.

Exiting from the elevator, I walk through the reception area and from the reception I receive from Grace, the receptionist on duty at this early hour, I can tell that no alarms have been raised, that my secret remains secret. For now.

I enter my office, which is large and airy with a view of other office towers on Sixth Avenue. I listen again to my voicemail messages from Friday, this time in familiar surroundings.

Today, in addition to responding to the dozen or so messages, I'm going to spend most of the time working on a new version of a deal that I had been involved with for years. Something familiar. Also a distraction, as the transaction is a soap opera in itself. A bank I represent has lent a lot of money to collect lots of interest and fees, but having—in the process—to get into bed with the dysfunctional family of a dead visionary. Now, a child of that dead visionary is dead himself, having committed suicide by excess—to many drugs, too many serious drugs. For the first time, I understand. In another way, though, if only I had that kind of money. Nothing goes wrong with that kind of money.

* * * * *

At around 2:30, I pick up the ringing phone. It is a Miss Spear. I don't know her name. The knife edge of fear, dulled for a few hours, returns razor sharp and my mind freezes. She tells me she's Max Rosario's secretary, and that she wants me to deliver—it seems personally and immediately—a check for $1,650 to cover his appearance in Court on Saturday morning.

To leave now would create suspicions, suspicions I just can't handle. With the address unknown to my secretary, a messenger will also arouse suspicions. She will wonder, and her wonder will be added to the mystery of my Friday absence. Given the frenzy of the day, we've barely spoken. But I can already feel them arising—subtle, newly-erected boundaries, protecting both of us. Whether she doesn't want to hear or doesn't want to intrude, I feel it.

But the check to Max Rosario has to be delivered.

With all of today's activity, including multiple documents being emailed, FedExed and couriered, she'll just have to convince herself to "not hear" or "not intrude" again. There's nothing else I can do.

The check goes out by messenger charged to the deceased heir.

I finish this first business day after, by billing fourteen and a half hours, catering to clients, and having lunch and dinner catered by the clients' money. And by not thinking.

* * * * *

Wednesday, lunchtime, is interrupted for a trip to Max's office on Vesey Street with Agnes. He keeps us waiting fifteen minutes in his modest reception area in the even more modest building housing his small, timeworn suite of offices.

My initial impressions of him are confirmed, only more so, as soon as he ushers us into his office. Still the bowtie. Still the reassuring manner and confident eyes and smile, which are echoed by a carelessly messy but decently-sized office. There are pictures not only of Malcolm X and Thurgood Marshall, but also oversized, framed copies of his profile in New York Magazine and colorful renderings of his court room performance in one of his most high-profile cases, a case that caught the attention of both the media and the public. Impressive.

Today, it's all very business-like. He lets me know how much it's going to cost. A fixed fee of $15,000, in addition to his Saturday morning fee of $1,650, for everything up to trial, which by demeanor and voice tone he suggests is highly unlikely.

We talk of the details left incomplete at our first meeting on Saturday morning. In answer to my unspoken plea, he leaves little doubt that this process isn't going to end soon—that we have to take it one day at a time. He then hands me, and I get to confront for the first time, the Complaint report which gave the police the right to arrest me. It is set out in neatly hand-written script.

Reading through, it is as if the hard and, admittedly, less than innocent kernel of truth has germinated into some nightmarish popcorn, filled with hidden crevices of unseemly consequence. Most disconcerting, it's not what I remember. Even the day noted as the day of my crime is wrongly identified. How can that be? First, they didn't know about the car. Then, they didn't know about the prostitution. Now, they don't even have the right day.

One day at a time, I tell myself. Out loud, though, I note the discrepancies. Max nods and writes them down. By way of explaining some of them, I tell him they're after my money. So, of course, there are going to be discrepancies—people like that lie for a living. This time he just nods. I say it again, and ask how I should protect myself against the extortion. He says simply, "That's not my area. That's for you and Agnes. I'm here to deal with the criminal aspect of this."

I nod.

"Look, we obviously have to figure all this out," he says.

Having, essentially, just met me, I realize these words have a different meaning for him than for me.

"As part of it," he continues, "I think you should hire a private detective. There's a guy I know who's good. He's an ex-cop, twenty-five years on the job. His name's Pete Santoro. I think you'll like him"

I nod again, this time feeling better—a step that we're taking rather than waiting for them, a step that should get us closer to the truth of what's going on. The fee I will negotiate separately, Max lets me know. I nod once more.

"Ultimately," he says, as he lets us know he's finishing up, "you'll have to decide how to proceed. Going to trial and losing would almost certainly result in jail time. Preliminary indications are that the DA's office is prepared to accept a plea with no jail time."

I look up, apparently with enough alarm that he quickly adds, "I'm just bringing that up to let you know that, at this time, that's the worst that can happen. We still have quite a ways to go, but I want you to start to think about all of the options. We can talk about it more fully next time, after I get a better read on the Assistant District Attorney who's handling your case, and once Pete's had an opportunity to do some digging."

"Accept a plea," he had said. Before I can even begin to think about it or ask any questions that are already beginning to bubble up, Ms. Spear walks into his office as if secretly summoned. He fondly introduces her. It's clear she's the keeper of the gate and, as I learn, with him for over twenty years. Magnanimously, he tells her that my calls should be considered important and promptly connected to him. Otherwise, he lets us know we're dismissed.

"Accept a plea." My questions will have to wait.

* * * * *

At the end of seven days, of days busy with work and nights thinking about "accepting a plea," dulled with not-such-fine wine, I'm on my way to Florida. I had long been scheduled to be with my mother, my brother, the chef, and my sister, Lisa, for Christmas. No one will know this Christmas time. It isn't necessary. It's too early for even me to know much. So what can I let them know? I'm just going to try to relax. Fortunately, the double-aisled plane has just enough empty seats, including one alongside mine, to quell the phobia which had so recently run rampant.

* * * * *

There is warmth and sunshine and mom at the airport to greet me. The tension and the reality of a thousand miles away begin to recede. Driving to her home, we plan a dinner, just the two of us, for later that night.

* * * * *

We choose a big, airy oyster bar, well-appointed with lots of mahogany and beveled glass, for a light dinner and a bottle of Pinot Grigio. After a couple glasses of the crisp, white wine and a dozen briny oysters, I actually relax. Feeling the essence of what I'm about to say—so without artifice or guile—I tell her that I'm becoming more weary of what I'm doing, and am seriously considering a change.

This is not so new. I've said it before, if not quite so determinedly, so she looks at me sympathetically. She has, after all, made major life decisions of her own that were bold, that had challenged convention, divorcing my father when she was in her forties, at a time, in 1975, and in a small town in Connecticut, where such things did not happen.

"Maybe you should consider moving down here to practice law," she says.

Not unexpected, but not what I wanted to hear. So I mutter something about "making bigger changes than that." She looks at me. I know she senses something. I continue on, not really knowing what I'm saying but feeling it, feeling the change that's almost inevitable.

"Well, you're still young. You've got a lot going for you. Whatever you decide I'll support you," she says, wrapping it up as we move on to talking about preparations of another sort, the ones for the up-coming holiday.

* * * * *

It's Christmas Eve day. With the Florida sunshine eager to prove its glory, I take one of my solitary bike rides, heading south along the Atlantic Coast Highway, A1A. I know it's inevitable that I'll see it, but I choose that route anyway. My other route is to head north, to patrician Jupiter Island, with its tasteful barrel-tiled, seaside mansions.

When I get there, they, of course, are there. Yep, here, in sunny, stripped-down Florida, a thousand miles away from my trauma, the beach is packed with beautiful surfer boys of all shapes and sizes. It's too weird, beautiful bodies conjuring up images of crime and punishment. It actually makes me nauseous. I turn around and head back.

* * * * *

As we sit around the tree handing out presents on Christmas day, I know that my gifts are noticeably less generous than in years past. Nobody, though, says a word about it. But there are looks from my brother and mom. And there's the silence from Lisa. Mom must have said something to them. What do they think? At a minimum, they must know my life is changing. But they can't possibly know why—or we wouldn't be doing this.

Towards the end of the gift opening, the talk turns to how to make my cottage in Connecticut, which everyone loves, even more inviting than it already is. Without thinking, I almost bark that the cottage will likely be sold. I tell them that I'm intending my life to be simpler, not ruled by possessions or driven by attachments.

With that outburst, the "why" of my change can't possibly look happy. I can't worry about it, though. There's nothing I can do. Nothing.

5

RE-ENTERED

As my eyes focus in on the Polaroid picture and the bold-faced type of a formal-looking notice, my knees buckle and my head goes light.

It's Tuesday, December 28th. I've just flown back from Florida and am entering my apartment. It's bitterly cold outside. I'm back, but I had not expected my reality to confront me so soon, and with such force.

They have been here again, in my home while I was away. I can't believe it.

As the notice reveals, under the official heading of "Search Warrant," they came five days earlier, on December 23rd, two days before Christmas. They came to retrieve, as the warrant states, "any computer, computer diskettes, compact disks; any media capable of storing digital and electronic data; any software," and on and on, to make sure they cover it all, let nothing get by.

I look at the blurry Polaroid picture of what they had confiscated. There seems to have been nothing of import, from what I can tell. Of course, how could there be, as there was nothing left after their first visit. Not even the computer.

What it looks like they did take was a dozen or so zip disks that I knew Pi had loaded with several of his projects while he was at studying design in the late '90s, and which I'd all but forgotten.

Although certain of the innocence of whatever they might find on those disks, my gut registers that they are making every effort to disprove mine. From the search warrant and from what they took, it's clear that, if they can, they want to get me on internet pornography. There, from what Max had told me on that Saturday morning after my arrest, sentences start at ten years. They want to throw away the key. They won't stop until I'm completely destroyed.

Struggling to retain my presence of mind, I call Max on his cell. He answers and tells me he's traveling back from his weekend home in Pennsylvania to his apartment which, I learn, is in the nearby Morningside Heights neighborhood. After a brief but intense blurt of the situation, he tells me to call him from an outside payphone. My paranoia shoots through the roof. Max is seasoned at this and even he's worried. Good God, will it end?

I put on a coat and go back out into the frigid night air and dial his cell from the corner payphone. Hearing my distress, he says he will call me in about 45 minutes, when he expects to be back in New York. He'll come to meet me outside my apartment building, he tells me.

I go back up to my apartment to wait. While waiting, I pace. An hour passes before he calls. I hang up and go back downstairs, with the search warrant and the picture they had left behind.

Within minutes, he draws up to my building's 100th Street entrance in his SUV, alone. Alighting from the warmth of his vehicle, he immediately says as he shakes my hand, "Let me see what you have." Reviewing it in the icy glare of the SUV's headlights, he inquires if there is anything they took which may be of concern.

"No," I answer simply.

"What does this mean?" I ask. "Are they never going to stop? Is my office next? Are my phones tapped? Are they still following me?" I demand in rapid fire.

Still cool and collected, at least compared to me, Max tries to allay my fears, halfheartedly, though, it seems to me. He doesn't have the answers, so what can he do. Then I realize he also doesn't really know who I am, what I'm capable of. Numb, and with little left to say or do, I'll just have to take whatever comfort I can in his weak words of reassurance. Paranoia returning, I suggest that perhaps I should purchase a phone card and use public phones. He quietly agrees. My God.

"Listen," he says in an attempt at some reassurance, "The police rarely devote significant resources after an arrest, except in extreme circumstances which, from what I know, is not the case here."

From "what he knows," I repeat in my mind. Well, I know everything there is to know. What do they want from me? Do they want to dig and root around and track my sex life from when Mary and I split twenty-five years ago?

One day at a time, I think. One day at a time.

Max promises to call the ADA's office to see what he can learn. That's all that can be done for now. I shake his hand again and head out of the cold, back up to my apartment. I open a bottle of wine and drink myself into unconsciousness

* * * * *

I spend Wednesday night discarding the boxes and boxes crammed with Pi's school books, school projects and innocent but innumerable magazines that he had accumulated and that I'd previously ignored. Pi is a pack rat and this is the evidence. I had abhorred that quality in him. I have never been a pack rat. Except, as now is so frighteningly clear, where it may count most, except for the Polaroid pictures. Evidence which can no longer be discarded. Evidence which is now in the hands of the police.

Sweating as I carry and heave those heavy boxes into the huge outdoor dumpster in the chill mid-winter night air, I begin to wonder about the next phase of my life where, it is likely, possessions and the past will no longer matter.

6

LETTING GO

"You've got to just let it go."

That's Max's advice to me on this last day of 2003, the end of the old year and the cusp of the new. Vaguely familiar, I recall, from recovery groups. I think they say, though, "Let go. Let God."

I never really understood what they meant. But now as I think about it, how can the two not be related? To let go, at least to let go of those things that have previously been all that had mattered, you need someone to catch you, and something to take its place.

It has been less than three weeks since my arrest. Time filled with obsessing about the practical, about making plans, about coping, defending, surviving. But with Max's admonition, to "let it go," I realize, as I had not before, that I must begin to confront the long-term. With that, I , too, need to "let God" and to explore the inner, what motivates, what I have been ignoring or subjugating to the pursuit of the momentary pleasure for too long.

I have taken the day off from work and the gym, figuring I've worked and sweat enough this month. Besides, there's not a lot to do at the office. So, I go retrieve my briefcase, taken from me by the police, which contain the keys to my home, my cell phone, some gym clothes and a New York Times dated December 12, 2003.

At One Police Plaza, I wait in a short line with others who presumably also had their belongings confiscated. I fill out some forms and my stuff is returned to me by a not unfriendly cop, wishing the other cops who are hanging around a Happy New Year.

It's crisp and bright outside, helping me to ignore this additional police building, and these additional police people.

I make my way over to the Trade Center site, a place I had visited only twice since September 11th. A chain link fence enforces its emptiness. Needing a connection, and with Max's office right alongside the site, I call him.

"I'm finishing up a brief," he says, "but come by at 3:00."

I walk around some more, going to and through Trinity and St. Paul's Churches. Quiet and peaceful, but temples I can't relate to, honoring a God that seems to me not a part of one and forgiving, but apart from one and judgmental.

Then I walk to and through the true temple of our times, Century 21. As has been the case for the past three weeks, I have no desire to partake and consume, or even to browse.

3:00 o'clock arrives. I go up. Max greets me gently. We talk a bit, only a little about the case. He must be able to tell that I need more today. He says how he considers himself a spiritual person and how it sustains him. Desperately wanting something to sustain me, I listen desperately.

We leave his office to walk to J&R Music, so he can buy some CDs. It's on this brief walk that he says, "Just let it go." Kinda like what Pi had said—with "surrendering to that which is," internal peace is achieved.

"Isn't there something you always wanted to do?" Max asks.

"Write a book," I say to him, not unhappy with the diversion from thoughts which demand too much.

"That's good. Do it," he replies encouragingly.

Not really, though, I think. I just want to continue to live the small, comfortable existence I've been living.

We get to J&R Music. He looks at me with those friendly, supportive eyes and engaging smile. We say goodbye, unable to refer to a new year that is unlikely to be happy, at least for me.

He goes in. What to do? It's New Year's Eve.

I start walking north, the only way you can walk without hitting a body of water within a mile or two. And it is towards home. My mind is not empty, but swirling with so many thoughts as to be effectively empty of any useful thoughts. And then the words, "Just let it go," followed almost intuitively and instinctively by the corollary "to God." "Just let it go to God."

"Who is this God and where is this God," I wonder.

I had been raised a Catholic. God is Divine and above, who issues, in stone, the Ten Commandments. His Son, having suffered through the Stations of the Cross, instructs us on the inevitability of that suffering. If God's Son himself cannot avoid it, how can we mortals? And, in the world of the Catholic Church, not only is it inevitable, it is deserved. It is a world full of judgment, hell, purgatory and sin—both venial and mortal—all warned about and administered over by nuns and priests. Is it that to which we are to surrender?

But, of course, there is also the redemptive power of confession.

Confession. Your sins will be forgiven. What did I use to confess? I remember vividly that a part of confession, at least a lot of the difficult part of confession, involved sex. Should I confess that I touched myself? That I masturbated? And what did I fantasize about while I masturbated? Was it boys even back then? Well, by sixth or seventh grade it was.

Never spoken about, of course. But almost anything having to do with sex except, perhaps, sex between a husband and a wife, I knew to be a sin.

No, religion, at least as I experienced it, wanted for me not to be redeemed, but wanted for me to deny and condemn that which seemed so intrinsic and undeniable. If only I could have been inspired by whatever grace, magic or mystery so inspires others to renounce, if not even transcend, those desires deemed so corrupting.

Crossing Houston Street to the underside of the NYU campus, I confirm in my mind that, by high school, I had left religion behind. And, shortly after I settled in New York, I had left the guilt and the shame behind as well. If there were a God who, after all, never seems to make an appearance, He must have put us on this earth to enjoy ourselves. After all, just look at all the pleasures He's given us—including sex. The only thing we shouldn't do is hurt anyone. That's what I began to think anyway. And that's the way I was living. At least so I thought.

Still, I remember one religious, or I should say, mystical experience. Passing by buildings dedicated to science and reason, I recall it well.

It was the spring of 1982, in Central Park, the end of my second year in law school. I was young. I was beautiful. I was powerful, with no worries before me and a future assured.

For a long moment that beautiful spring afternoon, in the Sheep's Meadow, I connected in a way I had never done before, or since. Connected, I felt then, and for a long time after, to a source that is both a part and beyond me, connected to others and to all. Mystical, transcendent, New-Agey, perhaps, but deeply comforting—an experience, to me, embodying Pi's words and those of others I've read and heard.

That particular late spring afternoon in Central Park, I sat in a favorite location and lit up a joint to more fully enjoy the beautiful weather.

Most likely it was the joint. But, who cares. As I lay back on the lawn, I simply seemed to diffuse. That's the best word for it. I felt diffused, the particles of my being, seeping out and joining with the rest of that from which we all come. Yet, at the same time, completely, intensely in the moment, as passing white cottony clouds became an extension of my will pausing to provide shade until granted leave to move on and permit the sun's rays to once again shine through to my uplifted eyes, protected only by the shimmering leaves of a familiar tree.

Delusional? Or transcendent? Who knows? Maybe it only works when you are high. Or when you are young and beautiful and powerful.

I hope not.

As I approach the Fifth Avenue shops, there's one thing I know for sure—that we are all trying to connect, perhaps even to be united in one. Isn't that at the core for any of those going to church, temple or wherever people gather—a yearning to share? One in the body of Christ, it is said.

With dusk turning to darkness, I look around. The crowds, going this way and that, appear backlit by the dazzling holiday lights and even more dazzling storefront displays. Feeling so distant from them all, I wonder if I'll ever again be a part of whatever it is we are all meant to share.

7

EASTER COMES EARLY

I didn't know whether to expect Robert to respond to my early-morning message of December 13th. Would I have, if he had left me a message like the one I left him?

Notwithstanding that we met because of money, we have, over the three years I've known him, formed a different kind of bond. In addition to the theatre and the dinners out, and a few weekends in Connecticut, we've had conversations, many conversations; mostly honest, and almost always affectionate. We are not afraid to confront the reality of the chasm caused by the differences between us and how that not only complicates but saps the vitality of a real relationship. For almost a year after we met, we are together often, pushing and pulling, seeing where it will go. Guiding us through is the conviction that we should relax and enjoy the moment, not obsess about the chasm or complications, or even the need for a "real" relationship.

Very early on, money stops passing between us, at least in any obvious way. It becomes more traditional, the way an older guy snags a beautiful young thing. You need something? I will buy it for you. You want to enjoy life? I will show you how. But because there is so little of that, and so much more of so much else, I fall in love, at least for awhile.

He makes so few demands. I offer, and give, but seldom more than just enough to test the strength of his affection. The compulsion to test, let alone the reality of our differences, guarantees that, eventually, the push would overwhelm the pull.

My hesitation to share too much is good for him too, I tell myself. Otherwise he will end up resenting where his dependence might lead him. And, I have no doubt he "needs" no one—that, with effort, he can be strong on his own. So, when he accepts a summer job in Virginia after his third year at school, the separation begins.

We stay in touch, however, sometimes more intensely than other times. I, intensely enough I discover, that in my hour of greatest need, I barely hesitate to call.

And in the ultimate rebuke of my doubts and suspicions, on the Thursday following my call, he calls me back.

I tell him not everything, but enough, so that he understands. The conversation is brief but plans are made to talk again in early January, after my return from Florida and his return from Puerto Rico.

When I reach him on January 7th, I can tell he's hesitant. I begin to feel guilty. What right do I have to draw him into this trauma? What can I offer him now? I know that he can offer me a sympathetic ear, shock at the extremity, if not the injustice, of it all. And mostly, what I truly want, physical, tactile comfort. I need someone to hold without embarrassment, a full connection. And that is possible only with someone you have held before with love.

We talk some more. Still, I hold back from offering all the details and all the emotions as his hesitation remains palpable. He must be absorbing it all, too, and wants, or needs, to do it slowly. I can almost hear him struggling with his doubts as to what he should do. He promises to call me back within the week.

Three days later, he rings me at home, after work. "I can be there in half an hour. Is that okay?" he asks.

In my gut, I feel the beginning of a sense of warmth and calm I have not felt for weeks. "Of course," I say.

* * * * *

As I open my apartment door, I drink in the sight of him. He's so beautiful. Adding to the luster of his beauty, I marvel at how he gets clothes of such different colors and styles to match so well, at least to match him so well. He looks like a chocolate Easter bunny, shrink-wrapped in shiny, multi-hued foil, ready to be peeled.

Perhaps, in a situation where no thing is taken for granted, all things are seen as if for the first time. Everything about him looks so clean and fine and perfect. Skin, lips, eyes, especially the eyes, warm and caring, with a hint of the resolve at the decision he's made. As it appears from those eyes that there could have been no other decision, it hits me how close we've become.

He comes in, and we kiss lightly.

He peels off the first layer, with furry collar which, nonetheless, is far too slight a layer for a mid-January evening. The madras sports coat underneath offers no more protection, other than to defend his fashion status.

"Okay, tell me everything," he says firmly.

The fourth to know, after Agnes, William and Pi. The only one—Agnes doesn't really count—in person.

He stands on the kitchen side of the granite pass-through countertop. I, on the other, pacing back and forth, as I have done so much lately, recount in full, everything. Nothing is left out, including invective, interpretation, despair, anguish, fear, contrition and, ultimately, powerlessness.

With few interruptions, he listens. I finish, weak from the effort. I must have gone on for almost an hour. He comes around to my side of the granite countertop, simply shaking his head. What can he say?

For the first time ever, he takes my head in his hands, and pulls my face close to his and looks into my eyes with such sorrow in his, that tears begin rolling down my face, both for my own plight and for his ability to grieve for me. He, grieving for me, after all that he has been through and overcome. Not only up from the streets of Harlem to a world-renowned dance institute, but rising above the tragedy of having a drug addicted mother who abandoned him at four, an older brother in jail more often than out and too many relatives and classmates who shunned or mocked him because of his homosexuality.

In a few short years, he has proved that I have been right about him, stronger even than I could have believed. So, unashamedly, I draw on that strength. We hold each other, tighter and tighter.

Reluctantly, I draw away from the embrace as he quietly asks me, "Is that everything?" After I nod, he continues, "This is strange. I don't understand. I fooled around with older guys at that age. And so did others I know—and no one ever even thought of gabbing about it, at least not to the cops." With a delicious, prim, mock self deprecation that I've so often chuckled at in the past, he adds, "And to think, I wasn't even smart enough to be getting money for it."

The sparkle in his eye turns too quickly to a sigh as he says, "I don't know. Something else must be going on here. If they were out for the money, it doesn't make a lot of sense. And I can't believe that the cops, crazy as they've become, would be interested in this. Christ, by sixteen, I'd moved out on my own. In fact, by sixteen, I think you're legal in a bunch of places, aren't you? No," he says with my weariness in his voice, "No way they're going to fuck you up over a sixteen year old with a fucked-up mother."

It's my turn to sigh. That's all that can be done—at this point, there are too many discrepancies and unanswered questions. I slowly let go of the immediacy of worry and give him a look filled with what I hope confirms that it's joy, not fear, which prompts me to ask if he can stay for the night.

* * * * *

With my body cupping his and with my arms wrapped around his perfection, I indulge in a fantasy of time standing still, frozen in this moment of the simple pleasure of affectionate human contact. I look over at his sleeping form, then, given the power that comes with feeling alive, I'm able to finally let myself go. I close my eyes and drift off to dream again, at least for one night more.

8

Two Meetings with Max

On the afternoon of January 16th, I check my cell phone voicemail. Max and I had agreed that's how he would reach me. There's an unexpected call from Ms. Spear. My heart races as I dial Max's number. He wants to see me the next afternoon at lunchtime in his office, she says.

* * * * *

I arrive at the appointed hour. His demeanor and tone are sober, yet soothing. He has spoken to the ADA, whose name I learn is Antonia Strauss. She explained to him that the second search was simply a matter of "crossing t's and dotting i's."

Whatever, I think. Not much I can do about it now. It almost seems as if it were years ago rather than a mere three weeks or so. He comes to the point, "She seems prepared to agree to a plea that doesn't involve jail time."

"Whether to accept the plea," he had said at our last meeting. He, at least, seems pleased with this news.

He continues, "If we accept her offer, you'll have to plead guilty to at least one felony."

At a minimum, I know there goes my license to practice law. Years of education and many, many more years of life—gone. One of the consequences that had consumed me during my twenty-four hours in jail. And, ever since.

But wasn't it Max himself who told me on that Saturday morning when we met that "The State has to prove its case." Well, I guess, Treat was in my home. Case closed.

But that's not all.

Having to finally confirm even though I really already know, I ask him "What about the sex offender list?"

"You'd have to register," he answers quietly.

What more can I lose? Self-pity sweeps through me. Pablo the prostitute, his crusading, extorting mother and the legally innocent Treat have achieved, if not their goal, then at least their revenge.

Interrupting my purposeless reverie, Max, as if in challenge to that reverie, tells me that "Nothing," which he repeats, "Nothing has yet been decided. We're going to take this one day at a time and see where it goes." As part of that, he lets me know that he has contacted Pete, the private detective he had recommended at our earlier meeting.

I think, why are we even talking about a detective if, as he seems to be suggesting, a plea to at least one felony with all the consequences that such a plea entails—other than jail time—may not be the only course but, perhaps, the better course.

Well, I guess it's this roller coaster of "one day at a time." It's not over until it's over, and it's best to be prepared. So, a detective it is. Maybe this detective can actually flesh out some of the squirrelly facts blurring my vision of the complete picture.

"Good," Max says, interrupting my thoughts again. "I will arrange a time for you to meet him. He knows his stuff and what questions to ask, etcetera. So I don't think I need to be there. I'll fill him in on the details I have."

I thank Max and go back to work.

* * * * *

On January 28th, about a week after I meet with Detective Santoro and hand him a check for $2000, Ms. Spear leaves another message on my cell phone's voicemail. Max wants to see me again. It's important. Can I come down at noon?

This message is far more ominous sounding than the one twelve days earlier. Barely able to think, with my heart in my stomach, I return the call immediately. "Of course, I'll be there at 12:00," is all that is said.

I arrive, but he's not there. Ms. Spear says that he is out meeting on a Federal case and should be returning shortly. The small waiting area in his office is too confining, so I go out to the elevator lobby to wait and pace, and wait and pace some more. Ms. Spear comes out to offer brief words of comfort and a glass of water.

Four days ago, on Saturday morning, I quit smoking, just stopping cold. I have welcomed the small cleansing that has already occurred. But, in this agitated state, the temptation to buy a pack arises. I dismiss it, at least for now.

Thirty minutes, an hour, an hour and a half goes by. Finally, Max arrives. With that warm, inviting smile, his presence enfolds like a down comforter. He apologizes for his tardiness, suggesting by way of apology the importance of his prior commitment and letting me know that he had been apprised of my agitated state. Just happy to finally see him, he's already forgiven.

"Rest your shoe leather," he says to me, "And come into my office."

Crowded, as before, with unopened and partly-opened boxes and files, I take a seat in the faux leather armchair facing his desk. I say nothing, waiting for him.

He pauses, and then says quietly, "The ADA has decided to hand down an indictment."

I blanche. Can't be, I think. This is not what was supposed to happen. At worst, a plea deal, a plea to a felony, for sure; one resulting in the loss of my license to practice my brand of law, one placing me on the "sex offender list," but not an indictment.

"It's just politics," he adds quickly as if that should appease. "The DA's office needs so many of this type of crime, and so many of that type of crime to proceed to indictment. Unfortunately, your type of crime is the one they need this month."

I look at him skeptically. He doesn't blink.

With little alternative, I tell myself on the way to being convinced that, perhaps, that's all it is. After all, he should know. He offers some further words of reassurance, noting, most pointedly, that the ADA is continuing in her position that they are not seeking any jail time and that he believes the indictment will be based on the three charges in the criminal complaint. But he acknowledges that this is an important development and that's the reason he wanted to tell me personally. He also notes that no options have yet been foreclosed, that all avenues are still being explored.

Questions about these options intrude on my consciousness. Questions that might bring back some semblance of control. Has he learned anything more about the accusers? Has Pete, the detective, learned anything at all that might shed some light—like on those telephone calls? No, he answers to both questions, seemingly not really wanting to discuss it further now. Again, the mantra I have yet to internalize, one day at a time.

More to the point, I ask "How long will it be before the indictment?"

"Soon – this week or next," he responds. I blanche again, and my insides settle lower, shutting me down, as they draw blood from the rest of my body.

I sit quietly for awhile, just looking at him, seeing however only a shadow, as my eyesight fades. As I sit, my past passes in front of me. But it's in a fog, a fog made even more opaque by the realization of the loss of its meaning to the rest of my new life.

How different it could have been. When was it? 1980? Intrigued by my criminal procedure class, hadn't I briefly considered a career as the one who hands down indictments? But, then, does nineteen years of education lead to working a lifetime of sending people to prison, where "success" is measured by the destruction of one life in the vindication of another's? Not for me. For me it was a different path, one providing more money and the less egregious power, and whatever happiness, that money provides.

I focus again on Max's eyes, filled, as always, with what appears to be empathy. Does he feel it too? That this isn't fair. With a need for affirmation, I ask a question I've asked before, "Who's the victim here?"

He nods, as if in understanding, and says, "You are."

What else could he have said? And, as before, what meaning does it have?

I struggle to rise from the chair, consumed with the enormity of it. Bitter and resigned, I offer myself up, saying to

Max, that if that's what the State wants, let it have it, do as they will, feeling almost self-righteous in my conviction that any excess of mine has been trumped by their own. Can one be crucified for one's own sins? Clearly, the teachings of the one who was crucified for the sins of others will not protect me now.

Before I leave, Max says, as much to himself as to me, but with what to me is an untimely confidence, "I know it's not what we had hoped for, but my experience has been that the system treats guys like you better than most. It'll be okay. It'll work out."

Somehow, I find the energy to return to the office to complete the truncated day. As soon as I arrive home, I call Rich at his office, not allowing time which now, all too readily, is filled with tearful regrets and the alcohol that keeps those regrets bearable.

9

A Brother and A Sister

"They're scum. That's what you have to remember—they're scum." So says Rich, almost as soon as I finish telling him the facts. What else had I expected him to say?

When he picks up the phone, before I am able to begin, I say to him, I love him. I have never said that to him before, in almost twenty-five years.

Rich and I met in Law School in 1980. Both of our names ended in "C", so we met in Law School. He, I and Ted "C" formed a study group.

We definitely were the best of the "Cs", and better than a lot of the rest of the alphabet. The three of us ended up on Law Review. For those few years, and a few years after, Rich and I are soul buddies, spiritual buddies. We remain connected and, likely, forever will.

Of course it is him who is there for me to recount my first spiritual "trip" in Central Park, that lazy, late spring afternoon in 1982. Not only to hear about it but to understand. He is also the one who gives me the book, *The Celestine Prophesy*, where the protagonist vividly describes an experience eerily echoing the one I'd had in the park.

For sure, there are probably more differences between us than there are similarities. Yes, he lived on the edge sexually and otherwise during our time in law school, and for a few years beyond. But five years after law school, he moves to La Jolla, near San Diego. And, instead of becoming a California asshole, he meets Alice. And she changes him, giving him everything he wants. He does the same for her. Three beautiful kids and a beautiful home in beautiful La Jolla.

As the years pass, we speak less and less often. Now, knowing that I'm going to be indicted, I have to call. I need his strength, his ferocity, his intellect.

We connect over the telephone wires. Just before I say I love him, I ask him if he has time to talk. He hears the sound of my voice. "Of course," he says quietly, with the catch of hesitation of one who believes grief would never pass between us.

Now I am telling him that the guy whom he has known for so long, the guy who, less than a year earlier had been out to his home to celebrate his first born's Bar Mitzvah, is being indicted on charges of child sexual abuse.

Put to a test surely neither of us ever thought possible, I can feel his love as he listens to me without embarrassment or judgment.

Trained as a lawyer, but born a litigator, we move on to the other reason I had called him. After I outline the facts and answer more questions asked of me than by Max and Agnes combined, the first thing he says is, "You've got to fire that attorney, whoever he is, and hire the best—so what if it costs you five or six hundred thousand. Your lifetime earnings potential is at stake and that dwarfs that amount by many multiples."

"Compared to fifteen thousand," I think. Fifteen thousand.

Able as he is to read my mind, Rich continues, "Look, I know you don't want to hear this, but with the piddling retainer this guy's asked you for, he's either bush league or he's treating your case like its bush league. Either way, it's not good. I don't have to tell you how important it is to have the best in your corner. Remember, that ADA, she couldn't get a real job with a real Firm. We both know the only decent Government lawyers work for the Feds. If you get your rocks off busting balls—or even sneakin a 'get out of jail free' peek at unformed ones—you become a U.S. Attorney, not some local yokel D.A. And that's true whether it's a D.A. in Podunk U.S.A. or in good ole New York, New York. Up against a real lawyer, she'll crash and burn like a tight-ass girl scout competing with a Tijuana whore."

"If only," I think. Then I think, "Half a million bucks—for what, for who?"

Again reading my mind, he interrupts, saying, "Listen, I have a contact who can put you in touch with Roy Black. There's no better. Do I have to say this? O.J.'s walking around free because of his lawyers. There's a reason that people with money hire the best. You know it and I know it—

we've seen it in our own work. Mark my words, it'll happen with Michael Jackson too. Your case is easy compared to those two. Jim, whatever the discrepancies, one thing's for sure—he's a prostitute selling his ass on the street. So, even with nothing else—and you can bet your ass there's plenty more—your so-called victim is completely and utterly compromised. And that's me using every effort to ignore the bizarre business with the so-called mother."

I raise counter–arguments, including the simplest—Treat was in my apartment. He pooh-poohs that, as if a good lawyer can call into question even the most basic facts. "Still," I think, again without saying, "A half-million dollar roll of the dice."

With Rich, it takes nearly another hour before we're ready to hang up. Just before we do, he repeats, "You've got to remember—they're scum. And, you've got to be strong. We'll get through this. I'll be there whenever you need me and we'll get through this."

Buoyed, I call William whose reaction is the opposite of Rich's—quiet, contemplative. I look at my watch as I get off the phone—it'd be early morning.

"Fuck them," Pi says, after I tell him. "Leave. If they want to destroy someone who is good on the word of someone who is not, then take off and let their rotten world rot some more."

How easy he makes it sound.

Then, more quietly he adds, "You remember our trip to Greece?"

"Of course," I respond, as my eyes are drawn to an end-table where a picture of us taken by another tourist in front of the Acropolis sits in its onyx frame.

"Santorini. You could go to Santorini. Better yet, Rhodes, it's a real town, yet still beautiful and quiet. They'd never find you in Rhodes," he adds, trying, it seems, to convince himself as he tries to convince me.

But it's a dream both he and I know before he even finishes. We talk for another hour before we say our good-byes.

Exhausted, I go to bed, knowing it is time for the family to know, at least part of the family. I'll call Lisa tomorrow, I decide, even if it is just before her birthday. I can't wait any longer.

* * * * *

The announcement of Lisa's next performance is in the mail the following day when I return from work, inviting response, an unsettling reminder of my intent to call.

"Okay, just do it," I think.

She picks up and almost immediately senses it—that I have a purpose I'd rather not have. "Okay, what's the matter?" she asks. "What's going on? Everyone is worried, especially mom. We don't understand what you're doing, talking about leaving your job and moving to Florida or wherever. It makes no sense to anybody."

It's too quick. I'm unable to say anything. Many seconds pass as she waits. As the seconds pass, it gets even tougher to say anything. But it's too late not to.

"Come on, tell me—whatever it is, it's all right," she coaxes with softened voice. My eyes well up with tears, as sharp, jagged inhalations of my breath betray me. My nose is clogged as I suck in air to retain my composure.

"You can tell me," she repeats even more quietly.

"It's nothing," I lie without conviction, still not yet ready. She listens, hearing beyond the silence as only one who loves can do. That's all it takes.

I begin to sob, quietly at first, then uncontrollably. She speaks to me with words I barely hear—but I feel her. It is as if she is next to me, stroking my hair, while I lean my head on her shoulder. My anguish increases, as I begin.

When I finish about fifteen minutes later, it's almost as if I can hear her sigh with relief. Then, with both a question and an exclamation in her voice, she says, "Sex is what this is all about? I don't believe it—this kind of thing must happen all the time in New York. Those gay boys are like that. Once their dick can get hard, they want to use it."

A sob-filled chuckle emerges from deep within me, knowing, however, that her dismissal doesn't matter. To her, though, it does, as she continues, "God, the way you sounded, I thought you had killed someone. That in a drunken stupor, you had run someone down, or something."

Having filled her with the fright of a possible mortal sin, I guess this lesser sin seems to her almost as if no sin at all. But if not a sin, it is a crime. I should've put her on with Rich, and then she'd know that too.

"This is crazy—I see those teenage boys, young teenage boys, parading up and down Christopher Street at all hours. And you know it's not to window shop, at least not for clothes. I don't know what the hell is going on in this City. It all started with that friggin' Guiliani. There's not enough locks and keys or fascist, fearful sex police to stop it. And this one—the little piece of shit—trying to extort money from you besides. Aren't there enough real sex crimes for them to concentrate on, for chrissakes."

My uncertainty as to whether I'm supposed to add to this in the silence that follows is answered as she continues, "I just don't believe they want to destroy your life for this. That's too fucked up—that's not how it's going to work out. You've worked way too hard to get where you've gotten to. But if you focus on the worse-case scenario, it'll happen. So you better start fighting back—and stop feeling sorry for yourself."

As the reality of it begins to sink in with her, though, she shifts to what can be controlled, asking me, "Are you going to tell Mom? Maybe you should. Maybe you should also talk to the judge," as we refer to our brother in Arizona.

No good. I can tell, without her saying, that she thinks that maybe his power or influence can reach across the borders to protect me in New York. But it's not going to, it can't, happen, and I'm sure she'll realize that. So, I say nothing

Instead, I reply, "Let's see what happen. Right now, there's really nothing anyone can do, so there's no sense at this point in causing any more pointless grief and anxiety."

Just before we're ready to say our goodbyes, she asks, finally remembering him and knowing I would have called him first on something like this, "What did Rich say?"

With just enough energy for a brief recap, I can almost hear her nod as she takes his side. Clearly, I'd conveyed his pungency, as she says, "Typical Rich. I bet there was even a drum-roll flourish at the end." To my silence, she adds, "No matter what, you just be sure to keep him closer than you ever have before, you hear."

With it unnecessary, I don't bother to respond. After a few more words of reassurance, the conversation ends but not before I promise to go to her show the following evening, on her birthday.

10

In Between

Other than keeping my promise to Lisa, and dragging myself to work, for the rest of the month of February, I live the life of an impoverished and celibate hermit, waiting for the letter summoning me to the Court to be indicted.

By the default of inaction, I also make a decision—to stick with Max, at least for now

Reflective of the way I make that decision in the odd, inverted universe I now inhabit, I take control by withdrawing. No more calls to develop potential clients. No more nights out. No more spending money. No more living.

Survival instincts kick in. Even with no one to support and making a good living, I had always fretted about money. Now, I just basically stop spending it. Fanatically, I seize on the advice I read in one of those popular "how-to get rich" books, sure to make more money for the author than for the suckers who buy them. As the author argues, don't spend money on frivolous things, like café lattes, or any designer coffee for that matter, and you'll be surprised at how, "over time," it can add up. The key words being, "over time." How much time do I have?

* * * * *

Time, however, does pass—one week, two weeks, three weeks—with no summoning letter from the State telling me where to appear for my indictment. As time passes, lunacy grabs hold. I begin to think that, perhaps, the State has forgotten, or is no longer interested, or has privately acknowledged its error in judging. Max, after all, had said, "Soon—this week or next."

In the warm, senseless embrace of this lunatic hope, I actually begin to relax, reverting a bit to being a sensate creature again.

In this state, I find myself sufficiently aware during one of my visits to the gym at the end of February to notice, in the gym's lower level spa area, a tall, slender adorable looking black boy, with rounded angelic face and roving eyes. Those eyes seem to latch onto the shadow of the cornered glimpse of my own as I briefly survey those few preparing to shower at the end of a workout.

Though charged by the vision, I say to myself, this is not the time or place. So, offering no more than that glimpse—charged though it was—I proceed directly to the steam room where the tropical heat pumped to unnatural excess has always been my reward for the admittedly slight and undemanding exertions on the gym floor above which my simple routine demands.

Given that most of the gym's members are, like me, middle-aged and tired, or too-fast approaching, the steam room is not a reward—other than in rare circumstances—because of those who enter. No, I love it because of the simple and primal pleasure of sweating and sweating some more, drawing out the toxins and washing them away in the chilly water from the shower head contained within that steamy box.

Moments after I sit and begin to yield, however, he enters. We are alone. He takes a seat, out of sight of the clear, though fogged-up, glass door. Almost immediately, he undrapes the towel circling his waist. We feel each other's eyes on each other's bodies, and I see his erection growing. Two fingers beckon. I can no longer resist.

Deprived of sexual contact with any other than Robert since at least December 12th of last year, I get up and move to his corner. As I place my hands tentatively on his body, and welcome his on mine, we whisper to each other. I learn he is a guest and not a member, twenty years old and recently moved to New York. His eyes invite; my lips brush his, as I continue to hold on to what he has offered. Subdued, though, I stand up.

"No more, I gotta go," I say. All he can do is nod.

I can't do it. Not just because I can't remember the last time I've done it here, or because I'm worried about who might enter, but because sex is the problem. That drive has taken me to a place without light.

I shower and leave. When I arrive home, my mailbox contains an envelope with a return address from the State. In it, a calendar notice advising that I am to appear on March 4, 2004, at 9:30 a.m., and that if I fail to do so, "bail may be forfeited and a warrant for your arrest may be issued."

11

Surrender

Two days later, three days before my indictment, I meet again with Max at his office. "As we discussed, this was expected," he says. "Let's talk about where we're going from here."

Where I'm going from here, I rejoin inwardly.

"Let's consider what the ADA will accept and what we are prepared to offer, should we decide on a plea," pushing me there, even though couching it as a choice.

"Losing at trial can result in jail time," are words needing nothing further. Inexorable, it has become.

"We don't have the indictment," he says, "but I have no reason to believe the charges will differ from the criminal complaint. So, we have three counts, one for sexual abuse of a child; one, patronizing a prostitute; the last, endangering the welfare of a minor."

We talk. Or, rather, he talks—and I listen. It's all about pleading out. Regardless of anything else, Pablo and Treat were in my home. Or, more to the point, Treat was in my home.

Before I can bring myself to 'accept a plea' and destroy my life, I have to ask him, as if, perhaps, there's still some possibility of deliverance, "What about the extortion threat?"

I can't even tell if Max believes me, but he confirms, again, that it's irrelevant. As for the private detective? Well, other than having run what was probably an internet search on Lydia Cepeda—something I had already done myself—the $2000 paid to him looks like it was wasted.

Maybe Rich's half million dollar legal team with Roy Black in the lead could wreak havoc on the credibility and motives of those who accuse. But they were there, in my home. That, and a birth certificate, is all that counts, regardless of almost anything else. Besides, I'm tired. In a lot of different ways. Exhausted in fact. I can't go through the Tombs again, not even for another twenty-four hours. It's time to live the lesson, to let go, to surrender.

I just can't think about it now.

After a few more words of no import, I tell Max what I can tell he wants to hear, that I will 'accept the plea.' But I tell him I will agree to plead guilty only to the last two charges, not the first. Both of those are felonies; both—I think at least—enough to extract that pound of flesh.

Max tells me that I might also have to accept an "attempt" with respect to the first charge, an "attempt" to engage in sexual abuse of a child. He asks if that would be okay, saying the punishment won't change, still no jail time.

I nod.

It's over.

Max looks satisfied, if not pleased. After all, he is well on the way to tidily wrapping up another case with a fair degree of ease. The way I see it, though destructive of my life as I know it, it saves me from the unknown devastation of what might occur with time behind bars. And, I'm tired. So, it's over.

I rise from my chair. As I do so, he says in caveat that now all is settled, "I've not yet heard from the ADA, but I expect to before the court date and will let you know when I do." One more hurdle, but portrayed, by the tone of his voice, as nothing more than a formality.

Suddenly fatigued and queasy, before leaving I get the key to the lobby bathroom from Ms. Spear. Unlocking the door, I sit by an almost clean toilet. After a minute or two, in the time it takes for me to turn my head toward the bowl, my stomach heaves, expelling all that is inside me, all that I have taken in.

Drained, I sit. After five maybe ten minutes, I get up, wash out my mouth and leave. This time, I do not return to the office. Why bother? I head home, but will call no one. I can't. I'm too tired. And I don't want to think about it. I'll tell everyone later. The only friend I want now sits silently in a kitchen cabinet. Aided by its warmth, eventually, I'll sleep.

It's over.

12

POUND OF FLESH

"I don't want to alarm you," are the first words Max says to me after Ms. Spear connects us. It's way too late for that. It's March 3, 2003. One day before my date in Criminal Court to be indicted. Alarm me? My only solace at this point was in the expectation that he would call to confirm that the ADA had accepted the terms of my defeat.

Receiving a message from Ms. Spear on my office voicemail to call Max when it had been agreed that we would communicate through calls to my cell phone, mere alarm would have been a reprieve.

With my gorge rising, I ask weakly, "What's going on?"

"Listen," he says, with what seems a forced tranquility, "The ADA is not agreeing to negotiate on terms I can accept." Offering me no time to think, let alone ask why, he gets immediately to the point of the urgency of the call. "Can you get some money, as you probably should bring some cash tomorrow?"

Distracted from focusing on the reasons or the significance to focusing on the details, I ask, "How much?"

"A few thousand… around 3 or 4," he says. "Cash."

It's after 3 p.m. and I'm pretty sure I can't take that much out on my cash card. I go to the wallet in the pocket of my coat, hanging in my office closet. There's a check in it.

"Okay," I say.

"Good, we'll talk tomorrow, when I see you," he responds.

Not so quick, I think. "Why?" I demand. Sensing my need, and perhaps even my entitlement, to know, this time there's no characteristic dismissal to another day.

"It's the pictures," he says simply.

A breath, and then another, to quell the dizziness. "So what's going to happen?" I ask between breaths.

"I don't know," he answers. "She, the ADA, was brusque when I spoke to her. She called me just before we called you."

I can tell he is not holding back and, even in my state, suspect it happens too often between prosecutors and defenders, positioning to strike, parry and, ultimately, win. But it only happens in battle, and this wasn't supposed to be a battle. I had caved, accepting my defeat. And now, apparently, it isn't enough.

In a bit of his own positioning, Max says, "Look, we can deal with this. We'll talk tomorrow."

With tasks to accomplish before me, I hustle out and go to the nearby Citibank branch, hand the teller a check for $4,000, and, as he hands me the cash, I look over his head to the clock above and see that there is fifteen minutes before they are to close. I pocket the crisp, neatly folded $100 bills in an amount I've never carried before, but carry now as a shield to assure, if need be, that I'll be able to purchase my freedom, however temporary.

Somehow I remain calm enough to return to the office. I know, though, that this is the time. So, I click on the Internet Explorer icon on my desktop computer and, several clicks later, and with information complete, I book a flight to Florida, to depart in three days—on the 6th. Two days after my indictment.

Then, with a deep breath, I dial my mother's number.

She answers.

Surprising myself, I successfully suppress the desire to reveal all to elicit the comfort of what I know would be unconditional love. Instead, acting as if I've succumbed to her multiple entreaties, I tell her that I'm coming down to attend the Tuesday night birthday party she was planning for Charlie, who was driving down from Atlanta for the occasion. She seems to accept my sudden generosity of spirit, probably because it feeds into her constant demand for the presence of her children. Her obvious happiness adds an unsettling counterpoint to the darker reasons for my trip.

Reverting to type, she asks how long I'm going to stay. I tell her a week, knowing it will never be long enough to satisfy. "Well you know, if you are moving down here, you should really take more time, so you can look around at some property," she responds. What usually annoys, this time reassures. So, I relax a bit, and we banter for another fifteen minutes before we hang up saying we love each other and that we will see each other on Sunday.

* * * * *

Once home, I prepare dinner and eat restlessly as I down a bottle of wine. I set the alarm and call Lisa to tell her what has happened. She is quiet and we both agree that it is best to wait to talk to Max. One day at a time. I ask her to call me in the morning, as a back-up to the alarm, before she leaves to meet me at court.

I take the last of the dated Valium, preparing myself as best I know how to face that for which no preparation is possible.

As I drift off to sleep, I wonder, maybe it just wasn't meant to end so quickly, maybe there's more to learn. I'm not sure, though, if I can take any more lessons.

13

INDICTMENT

9:30 a.m., March 4, 2004. Room 1113 at the Criminal Court in New York City is filled to near capacity.

Lisa and her girlfriend, Leslie, are there when I arrive.

We had all greeted Max, outside the courtroom, as I surveyed the corridor with nervous eyes, fearing reporters or others who might expose. Before passing through the courtroom doors, Max had said to the three of us, “Remember, after the charges are read and the plea is requested, just say ‘Not guilty’. It will be over quickly. We will be one of the first called. After that, we’ll talk.”

Now, sitting directly behind Max, who is in the row reserved for attorneys, my senses are heightened but distorted. The lights appear unnaturally bright, voices disturbingly loud and the movement of bodies exaggerated. It is as if everything has an echo. When I turn my head or refocus my attention, what was seen, noticed or heard before continues to fill my brain, even as the new reality intrudes. I feel like an observer, not fully in the dimension of what I am observing.

To ground myself, I close my eyes and breathe deeply. Lisa grabs my hand.

Fifteen minutes after the appointed time, the room settles as the judge enters and the court is gaveled into session.

Activity surrounds the bench for the next five minutes or so. A case is called; not mine. It's ignored, neither heard nor seen. It is over in minutes.

From the front, I hear my name. It echoes through the chamber, unlike all other echoes I've experienced this morning. Lisa and Leslie shift, and Max gets up. I follow him through the gate, separating the officials from the others, and stand alongside at the table reserved for the accused.

Max withdraws a pen and paper from his jacket pocket. I do not move, staring straight ahead, focused on nothing. Someone begins. It's not the judge, nor the prosecutor. Whoever it is, it's a male voice and he is reading my indictment. I strain to listen, but hear only words. Words like "criminal sexual act," "sexual performance by a child," "forcible touching," "prostitute," "sexual abuse." Words, even as I stand, I know will become my identity.

Max scribbles on his paper. Then, I swear that I hear from him a sharp intake of breath. Mercifully, the reading ends. When asked my plea, I respond as Max has instructed, knowing it means nothing to any who listen, other than a signal that the battle has begun and that whatever the lore, the burden is on me. Looking at Max, he nods, affirming it is over for now.

I leave as quickly as my brain can register the movement of my feet, with eyes straight ahead, passing by all the strangers made intimate by bearing witness to my humiliation. This is how it's done; to me, it appears an act as perverse as any I may have committed.

I glance at Lisa as I head toward the door, letting her know, by my eyes that I have no intention of stopping to retrieve my overcoat or briefcase. I make it to the corridor, unmolested, even by stares of shock or disgust. My only relief as I stand in the wide, unforgiving hallway outside the courtroom is my awareness that there are no stray reporters ready to pounce on a sex crime and the disgraced lawyer who committed them.

Max follows Lisa and Leslie out the door into the hallway. We move away from the courtroom, heading towards the stairway.

A brave face. I've heard the expression, but never before really experienced it, not where it was so raw or where it meant so much. It's the best I can think of to describe Max's face.

Leslie and Lisa are glum. I'm still in partial shock. The three of us wait for Max's assessment.

"Okay," he says, "Now that we know where they're at, we can start planning our defense."

Having heard only words, I ask him to spell it out, to go through the charges.

"They have indicted you on seventeen counts," he responds.

"Seventeen counts." It barely registers. I can't help resisting. It can't be, as it had gone by so quickly. I say something. I'm not sure what. He tells me that when there are multiple counts based on the same offense, they are combined into one. Ten counts on the pictures, three of sexual abuse, four others—seventeen becomes six. Max's gasp must have come when "ten" was read. I don't bother to ask him, gasping myself at how three charges have now exploded into seventeen. It sinks in that ten of these counts are related to the pictures. And, there is little doubt, that the four new ones, even if supposedly there to vindicate Treat, have also been added because of those pictures.

I wrack my brain trying to recall twenty-five years worth of pictures, remembering as I had the morning of December 13th, when I first met Max, only the multiple pictures from one time, long ago, now almost out of time. Any others would be too easy to raise doubts.

I ask if all ten counts can be the pictures of only one. He doesn't know or, at least, doesn't answer, and he acts as if it makes no difference.

Taking charge, he says, "Here is the first thing we are going to do. I am going to put you in touch with a woman I know named Florence Sisters. She is a forensic social worker. I have worked with her before. She is good."

Anticipating my queries, he continues, "She is going to do a profile of your life, make you human in a process that rarely bothers to look. Here, we're in luck. The judge is a good man, willing to look beyond, to the person, and prepared to make judgments independent of the D.A.'s office. So we are going to give him something to look at. A reason to listen to our side, to do what is right."

Whether it's only a straw or something more, it doesn't matter—at this point, anything to hold on to, anything at all is better than nothing.

Aware that I'm leaving for Florida in two days to finally inform my mother, he invites us to his office to call Florence to arrange for a meeting.

"She'll fill you in on exactly what she does," he says.

We trek the several blocks to his office to draft another into the battle—this time, on my side. On the way, Leslie hands me a book written by a woman named Glenda Green, entitled "Love Without End."

14

“Shit Happens”

“Shit happens” is the pithy response that spills from my brother Charlie’s lips, as he dismisses the possibility of there being any grand design or even the possibility of there being mystics, sages or prophets able to make sense of—or, perhaps, intermittently predict—the chaos that seemingly surrounds us. Infected with the AIDS virus more than fifteen years earlier, his cynicism is earned.

Not wanting to accept that trauma has no purpose, not even to enlighten, I mutter quietly, “I don’t want to believe that,” adding, with an unchallenged ambiguity, “and I will tell you why later.” It’s as if I am trying to convince myself that my trauma trumps his, and that his conversion to believing in something, anything, depended only on his faith in my salvation, regardless of any faith in his own.

There are six of us sitting around my mother’s dining room table in her home in Palm Beach Gardens, Florida, having just consumed our fill of steak and cake. We’re celebrating Charlie’s birthday.

The morning before I had boarded the flight to Florida, resolved to relax and let go. Buoyed by a conversation with a seat mate who claimed to be happy living a peripatetic, hand-to-mouth existence as a musician, I choose to believe that the crystalline sky and radiant sun greeting my arrival is nature's tender of further salve for, if not even gentle admonition of, my troubled soul.

Now, sitting around the dining room table with my mother, Charlie, my other brother, the chef are the Pulaskis, two of my mother's dearest friends—a pediatrician and his wife.

Notwithstanding Charlie's glum response, a festive mood prevails. For the evening, I've actually reverted a bit to my old self, engaging in spirited discussion. As is usually the case when the Pulaskis visit, the conversation had turned to politics, sure to ignite, as they are dyed-in-the-wool, true-blue—or is it red?—Republicans. That sin, though, has long been forgiven, as they are truly good people, prepared to forgive the foibles and tolerate the differences of those they care about.

Charlie's invective is prompted after I steer the conversation from the political to the spiritual, selfishly seeking affirmation of divine purpose, impending apocalypse or mystical revelation. Something, anything, as significant as the events which have overwhelmed me.

Surely, if divine, life's twists and turns must have a purpose; good must be intended to come from bad, and lessons taught—if accepted with an open heart—must result not in crippling pain, but in redemption. To "surrender," to "let go" is to invite God, not His opposite.

But if it's to be something dark, let it be dramatic—environmental catastrophe; or global war between a god-driven East and an ungodly West; or power, unleavened by wisdom and compassion, wreaking destruction on itself . Why not.

What I really seek, though, is the impossible—assurance that life is not a series of meaningless or banal coincidences. That if we look with greater care, we will see "signs"—if not miracles—pointing a way toward an answer, or at least a glimpse of the shadow of the divine.

Unlike Charlie, the others have not succumbed to cynicism, at least not so openly. In probing the mystery life presents, however, the talk turns not to scripture, clergy or religion—which rely on faith in miracles. Instead, it turns to psychics—who promise proof of miracles. If the future can be predicted or untold secrets revealed by one so seemingly separate, then chaos cannot reign. Our "separateness" must be a myth. If such a power exists, then might not anything be possible?

I have heard stories from both Robert and Pi, offering some inspiration for hope. But it is my mother who begins. She recounts two experiences; one I've heard, in part, before and another, newly revealed. The one which is known occurred about ten years earlier. She had traveled with a friend on a day trip to Cassadaga, Florida, a town virtually percolating with soothsayers and clairvoyants. Mostly, my mother remembers that the psychic she engaged knew not only of

Charlie's illness, but also foretold of his strength to surmount. Overwhelmed with emotion at the time, she recalls little else except that she paid the woman for an additional session.

The second experience, previously untold; a story from before the lives of her children. My mother was only sixteen and sought guidance as to whether she should marry my father. Traveling to the nearby city of Hartford, Connecticut, she was told not of the rightness of her choice, but that she would have seven children, and would divorce and remarry. Amazing. Almost right, on the second prediction. Divorced, for sure—but, at least as of yet, no remarriage. Truly amazing, however, as to the first prediction. If two had survived childbirth, she would now have seven children.

Continuing the theme, I tell of one of Robert's best friends, who had an abortion when she was only a teen. Devastated by the experience, she held a mournful commemoration for years after, on the anniversary of the event. Informed by nothing other than the presence of her young seeker, her psychic knew the story, and gave her the advice I've now heard so often—telling her she had to "let go." Robert had no doubt that the session helped his friend to adjust, as if her spirit had been cleansed in absolution by a higher power.

I then relate Pi's story of an arsonist, the owner of the damaged building and a psychic, who named a name which, more than a year later, was proven true.

Four anecdotes; two personally experienced by the teller—and two by a teller twice removed. But, there's more. I have one, final story.

It was the day after September 11, and I had received a call from Pi. Of course we talked a lot about the event—the enormity and significance of the attack. At some point in the conversation, he asked, "Didn't Nostradamus predict this?" I scoffed. "Really," he said, insisting, "You should check it out in the book I gave you."

Later that evening—actually, in the early morning hours of the following day—unable to sleep, I'm watching the around-the-clock coverage on television. Restless, I remember Pi's admonition and look for the book of the Nostradamus prophesies, which I had probably opened only once or twice in the years since he had given it to me. With hundreds of verses, I check the index and find only six identified as related to New York City.

I read the first five, unimpressed. The last one, though, grabs my attention. Quatrain X.XLIX reads, as I recite it to the congregants:

> "The Garden of the World
> Near the New City
> In the Road of the Hollow Mountains
> It will be Seized
> And Plunged into the Tank
> Forced to Drink Water
> Poisoned with Sulfur"

To me at least, I argue, it isn't hard to accept the Trade Center as "the garden of the world" nor, especially from the perspective of a sixteenth-century mystic, the skyscrapers surrounding it as "hollow mountains." And the depiction of it being "seized" seems pretty evocative.

What had sent a chill down my spine that early morning, I tell them, is that while I was struggling with whether the words "forced to drink water poisoned with sulfur" had any application to the devastation eight miles away from my bedroom, I was watching on the TV screen as streams of water from untold fire hoses poured onto the smoldering site.

If that weren't enough and what really clinched it for me was when I read in *The New York Times* two days later a description of the area carved below the Trade Center to support the buildings as "a bathtub," equally un-poetic, so a fitting solution to the remaining puzzling words of "plunged into the tank."

If inclined to believe, this prophecy may be the most enabling. And, by the charged quality of their silence, it seems the others agreed

Tales and verses imbued with an undeserved significance? Probably. To me, though, they have become more satisfyingly otherworldly than unanswered prayers to a traditional God, or the self-proclaimed salvation of the "true" believer. Now, in my current state of near exhaustion, they are tales offering a kind of mystical sanctuary, however temporary or flimsy, from a world no longer indifferent.

It's getting late. Charlie and I are staying with my other brother at his home several miles away, so we begin our goodbyes. As I'm planning to tell my mother what I have yet kept secret at dinner tomorrow, I'm resolved to tell my brothers tonight. They can offer support when I pull away the pillars of her dreams for her middle child; dreams not merely dissolved or unfulfilled, but inverted to a scape she should not have to travel alone with me.

Outside, the warmth of the day has lingered into the night. Unnatural shadows are cast by artificial light, and the faint citrus and palm-like fragrances are inhaled with senses no longer burned by the southern sun.

Getting into the back seat of my brother's Mercedes wagon, I realize this is not the time for small talk, or to delay or make more awkward any transition to what I have to say.

"Listen," I begin, as we back out of my mother's driveway, "I have to tell you something."

The back of their heads staring me in the face stiffen just a bit at the neck to conform to my tone, waiting silently for more.

"I was arrested back in December," I say straight out.

A weak, "Oh, no" from one, and a disbelieving "Huh?" from the other. More of the same from each as I continue, reliving again what I will no longer live without. Questions and comfort complete the short trip.

Standing in another familiar Florida living room, in a meager effort to shift focus and lighten the gloom, I apologize to Charlie for ruining his birthday. With a tilt of his head, a look in his eyes and a couple of words, the focus returns to me.

Charlie comes close and says simply, "It will be alright."

Knowing it won't, I break down in his arms as we hold each other like we have never done before, grieving even more as I realize this, shamed to have failed to hold him when his first lover died of AIDS, or when he learned shortly thereafter that he, too, was infected with the same deadly virus.

Giving voice to this part of my grief, he holds me even tighter, saying, "It's okay," as tears stream down his face.

15

Mom

A thousand-mile separation, a March sun that enfolds and my brothers' love all help me to relax, at least a little bit. To further help to prepare me for that evening's meal and a conversation for which no preparation is possible, I take my customary bike ride, avoiding, however, the boys on AIA and, instead, heading north to Jupiter Island. For this ride, the only high I want is the one nourished by the pumping blood that rewards physical exertion.

The chef returns home early from his job as a chef to prepare the final meal my mother will taste before adding another heartache to those she has already endured in her seventy-three years. By my acts, a pall of unforeseeable dimension is now certain to descend over whatever increasing pleasure she has had in her life since she left my father and established a career as a successful real estate agent, only recently to semi-retire to enjoy the fruits of her labor and the always too-infrequent visits of the children she loves.

Never a complainer, she's revealed little to us of the difficulties of her early life. In fact, it is only long after the passing of her stepfather, who had often been invited to our home as a welcome member of the extended family, that we learn that his reputation as a curmudgeon was really far too forgiving. Even then, abusive of a nature not fully revealed, is where it was left.

In her mid-teens, she escapes into the arms of a man who loves life so much that there seems no reserves left for those closest to him. He philanders and they rage, with some of my earliest memories filled with the detritus of that rage—a broken door to their bedroom, the sickening sound of a slap against undeserving skin, and the occasional unhappy appearance of my mother's mother, all four feet two inches of her, to intervene and protect.

Her kids bring her comfort, and she stays with my father for over twenty-five years, in part to assure ours. Just after their 25th wedding anniversary, with all, other than Lisa, away at college or starting a career, she leaves him. The struggle in the years that follow is mirrored by the various places she lives. All, however—regardless of size or fashion—feel reserved as a refuge for any of us in need. Now, at a time in her life when I should be offering the refuge, I bring her this instead.

* * * * *

It is hard to claim that any one of my brother's meals surpasses any other, but the one tonight is as good as the best—a thick-cut piece of tuna, seasoned and grilled to perfection, accompanied by a homemade citrus sauce, with creamy polenta set against crispy green beans.

An unusual chill keeps us inside, and thus deprives us not only of the company of the patio's tropical plants swollen with colorful bloom from love and sunshine, but also from the soothing gurgle of the oversized, free-form hot tub commanding its far corner.

We talk, surprisingly at ease, about nothing. Eventually, though, but far too soon for me, we are finishing up the bakery-fresh tart. I lay down my fork and feel the heat of the attention from my brothers.

Though a task he'd normally disdain, the chef gets up and carries an armful of dishes to the kitchen. Charlie diverts his attention, pushing back his chair, as if to follow, but doesn't. I look at my mother. Her face, one I share, one I would never do anything to harm, is already tensing and draining of color. She senses it.

"Mom," I begin, "I have to tell you something and it's very difficult. Just remember and believe me—no matter what, everything will be okay."

I rush through with enough detail to convey the essence and gravity.

Ashen faced by the time I finish, and with eyes momentarily frozen, drawn inward—whether to relive a past now so separate from the future or to consider that future—I don't know. What I do know is that it is about me. Unlike any other I have told, her thoughts, I know to my core, are all about me and helping me through. And that thought riddles my core with holes.

She sits quietly for long, unendurable seconds. Then she begins shaking her head back and forth, ever so slightly. She looks into my eyes, "I knew something was wrong. I just didn't know what." Admitting now to myself the questions in her eyes and voice since my last trip to Florida, I have no doubt.

"I'm glad you told me," she says, "It's bad, but now that I know, we'll get through it."

I breathe deeply, and wonder. I knew it would happen this way. I knew I would be forgiven my sins by the penance of confession, forgiven the pain I have brought into her life by the willingness to share it with her. As if by the telling I have not wounded, but healed. By her love and strength, forged of a suffering I could only previously imagine, I am assured she will withstand whatever happens. Whatever shame may come will be the shame others assume, not her own, shame assumed by those unaware of that love and strength, or shame demanded by those motivated by their own shame, because of their failure to compare.

We get up and hold each other. No questions are asked—just acceptance and resolve passing from mother to son. The tears are soft, quiet and brief.

With her, maybe I will get through this.

* * * * *

The remainder of my trip, too sober to be called a vacation, is quiet. A couple of walks with my mother in the park nearby her home, uninterrupted, other than by our shared presence and that of her most faithful companions, Cartier and Gypsy (a Shiatsu and a Pomeranian), both adorable and both certain to be her antidote, if only partial, to the hovering gloom.

I also begin to read "Love Without End," the book given to me by Leslie on the day of my indictment, a book I previously would have disdained, premised as it is on a conversation with Christ. But as the author herself says, "You need not feel compelled to believe in the events of this or any other story to discover the truths within it."

In my current state, disbelief is not so much suspended as abandoned. How can I not want to believe that Christ actually revealed to the author that "judgment was the original sin?" And that "the Hebrew word for judgment … actually refers to redemption and vindication—not to opinion or condemnation." Where Christ chides mankind for using "the power of condemnation and punishment to support its destructive agenda," instead of applying justice "with the intent of restoring brotherhood, and not dividing or diminishing it."

How can I not want to believe that?

16

A Conversation With Florence

"I was expecting your call," Florence says to me, in a tone more gentle than I had expected.

It's 5:00 P.M., Monday, March 15th, one day after my return from Florida. Having passed an uneventful Monday, I'm now making my planned call to Florence Sisters, the forensic social worker recommended by Max,

"Max told me quite a bit about your case but we should meet."

She wants to come by my home to see how I live, and the sooner the better, she says. So, we make an appointment for the upcoming Saturday, the day after my next court appearance.

* * * * *

Court on Friday results only in an additional invitation, not to be spurned, to court on the following Friday. I leave, humbled again by the power of others over my life to command my appearance at their whim and fancy, without regard to my own.

On Saturday morning, I prepare myself to meet Florence. To assure her comfort, I move my car to a vacant space on Central Park West so she can park her car in the space reserved for decades for mine.

I watch as her car pulls into the outdoor lot and as she parks. Within minutes, she knocks on the door. Her gentle phone presence is matched by her physical presence, and I know I'm going to like her as soon as she steps into my apartment.

Younger than me by at least ten years, and moderate of stature, she nonetheless exhibits a calm self-confidence. As we say hello, there's no judgment in her eyes and, right off, her easygoing, soft-spoken manner soothes and relaxes and virtually invites the sharing of secrets.

After she accepts a glass of juice, we settle into seats in my living room.

"Let me know all the details of your case, and then we'll get into your personal history," she starts off, after explaining to me that her job is to prepare a report on 'who I am and where I come from,' so that those who are making decisions about my life can get to know me as a person, humanize me. In this effort, she would like to talk to as many people as possible who know me well, especially family, preferably after I have told them what's going on, and then to get all or some of them to write a letter to the judge.

"I don't want to give you any false hopes," she says, then adds—underscoring why we are here—"But this type of report has been known to change, or I should say soften, some minds, resulting in a satisfactory disposition of a case without the need for a trial."

Knowing all this, I tell her I am preparing a list with contact information and will give it to her the next time we meet.

"Okay," she says, "Max's told me a bit, but it's important for me to get your version of the crime itself."

Fifteen or twenty minutes later, she says, "Alright, let's move on to your early life. We'll go for three or four hours today and, at our next meeting, hopefully, we can finish up."

She begins by asking questions, lots of questions; many—I've got to stop and think. Others—I'm embarrassed I can't answer. Questions like, "When did my mother's mother die?" "Who is my favorite aunt and what is she like?" "How many cousins do I have?" "What were my relationships like with them?" "Who was my primary caregiver?" "What are my early memories of my father? … my mother? … my siblings?" "What year did I start kindergarten?" "What about the family pets?" And on, and on.

And then she gets to questions about abuse.

"Abuse?" I respond quizzically, feeling dismissive but knowing this is where we have to go. So, I give her the short answer, "There was none, at least not physical, except, of course, unless you count when my older brothers—particularly the teacher—would lock me in the wine cellar. It was kind of an easy step, if you will, to go from there to claustrophobia."

I know that's not what she really wants, though, so I continue, admitting that there was what one might call "psychological abuse from my father, as he was distant, couldn't be bothered."

"And, perhaps," I acknowledge, "a therapist with the dense insight or imagination of a Freud could argue that my maternal nurturing was somewhat lacking, as my mother, too, had to cope with my father's evanescence, and a house full of kids. But I always felt loved by my mother—my mother would do anything for me, for any of her kids. There wasn't a lot of touchy-feely stuff, but she was always there for us. Given the less effusive nature of that generation, she was actually quite affectionate."

Though a "poster-boy for emotional reserve," I do recall for her my father's one weakness—how his eyes would get teary when he would watch a sappy movie. I also tell her how he would beam with pleasure when I entertained his golfing or drinking buddies by playing the piano.

"Bottom line," I tell her, "My father was a good provider for all of my physical needs, paying not only for my private secondary school, but for my college and law school." Pausing, I add more in the nature of what I know she wants to hear, "Only once do I remember him raising his hand to hit me. That happened when a broom I was balancing on my fingertips fell on his head. As soon as he saw the terror in my eyes, he wigged out."

Florence seems unwilling to accept that I wasn't abused, looking a little disappointed or frustrated or skeptical, or perhaps all three. Maybe she thinks it's too painful or embarrassing for me to discuss, or so deeply repressed I can't recall, or it's one of those forgotten memories which can only be unlocked with the right questions.

So, she prods. "What about others—did others abuse me?" ... "Am I sure?" ... 'Could this have happened, or that have happened?'

Just as I'm realizing that, so far, the word "sexual" has not yet been uttered before the word "abuse," Florence says, "And, just to make sure there's no question here, I'm including whether you were ever sexually abused or taken advantage of?"

Feeling comfortable enough not only to match her specificity but to unleash my innate sarcasm, I respond, "Not only did no one ever do to me sexually what I didn't want done, but I have to admit that, even though I was exploring my sexuality at an age before my home state of Connecticut would let me choose to offer sex, I never chose to make that offer, other than to my peers, that is." I pause and, seeing nary a blink, add, "Do you consider that sexual abuse—groping with other pre-teens and teens?" Before she can respond, I continue, "And even that was extremely rare and done only in the most furtive and repressed manner."

Whether or not following the Psych 101 playbook, she just looks at me. So, per the playbook, I fill the silence with an honest-to-goodness instantaneous memory which actually fits the bill. "There was that time when I was around ten or so. I had come to New York City with my parents and some old guy—at least that's the way I remember him—in the men's room off the lobby of the Hilton Hotel was clearly trying to, quote unquote, sneak a peek. Creepy," I acknowledge to her, "And, apparently, at least somewhat memorable. But not exactly a psycho-sexual death blow." Pausing, I can't help but add, "Those were saved for the nuns."

Even with my sarcasm in full bloom, she says nothing. So, with that about the extent of any "abuse," I continue by dismissing the pervert and engaging what some might consider the perversion, "How could it be other than furtive and repressed?" I ask. "I'm not sure if, according to the nuns and priests in my Catholic parish, it was or wasn't considered a sin to touch yourself sexually. I am positive, however, that it was a sin to let others touch you or for you to touch them. But sin or no sin, it wasn't ever talked about. No, it was treated as dirty and shameful."

"Look," I say to her, getting to what I believe to be the crux, "We're talking sexual abuse. I'm charged with sexual abuse, not because he didn't consent but because he couldn't consent. He's too young. So, the real question, at least the question I would think everyone wants answered—including myself in some ways—is do I like boys who are, quote, unquote, too young? Or, to put it more graphically, am I some sort of pedophile predator?"

Still nothing, other than a raised brow—perhaps at my convenient phrasing of "the question."

Undaunted, I continue, "In one way, that's easy to answer. Pre-pubescence is a turn-off. It does nothing for me. It doesn't make sense. It's not as appalling as murder or incest, except, perhaps, when not considered in the abstract, when you realize that the act requires the presence of a pre-pubescent."

Unsettled, as if by a too-real ghost, I wrap it up, stating, "Of course, in the other way—the way of the law—I realize that's not a satisfactory answer."

With that, I feel free to blurt out, though without much enthusiasm, some words expressing my disdain for the hypocrisy of a society that privately salivates over Calvin Klein ads and all manner of teen sex-pots, while ostentatiously expressing outrage at the very perversion which so titillates them.

She nods, but then says none-too-gently, "Nonetheless, when it's acted upon, there are all sorts of legitimate issues about power and control and feelings of sexual inadequacy. But I don't want to get theoretical; I want to get back to your life, your childhood." With my hide suitably tanned, she queries, "You were raised a Catholic, right?"

Given the headlines, I don't need a compass to know where she is headed. So, also ready to forego the "theoretical," I concede to her, somewhat wryly, that not even the priests who populated my childhood—Father Graziani; Father Caldo; Monsignor Botticelli—abused me. Or, to my knowledge, any of the other boys. Too many Italians in my parish, I tell her. The priests knew better, even if they had been otherwise so inclined.

"Okay, fine," she says, as if in reluctant surrender. "More generally, then, why don't you describe for me some of your early sexual experiences."

Here we go, I guess. "Well," I tell her almost impishly thinking back to my childhood desires, "I definitely had a crush on Tony Tantino, who was a classmate of mine in grammar school. A couple of the other boys were also kind of cute." Tony was special, though—blond hair and blue eyes—unusual for an Italian. Athletic, which I wasn't. Having a body to match, which I didn't. And even kind of smart, which made the rest of it better.

Florence seems satisfied that we're back on track, asking me, "And when did that crush start?"

"I can't remember for sure," I reply, curious at just how far her curiosity extends, and more than willing to go along to find out. "Certainly, it was in full rage by the seventh or eighth grade. Maybe it started in sixth grade. What age is that?" I ask, tying the two, sex and age, together again.

"About twelve," she replies.

"Uh-oh," I say, half in jest. She looks up, almost shrugging, as if to say that this is what it's about, at least in part, what she needs for a "full" report.

I wonder what she'll write. Maybe it'll say, "The subject is not at fault." Instead, it will argue, "Faced with the explosive, youthful sexuality of one Tony Tantino, the subject became helpless, a fixation developed. And, as any enlightened psychosexual forensic social worker will confirm, you cannot blame the victim of what is surely an unfortunate disease."

"What did you two do? I mean, sexually?" Florence asks, interrupting but not ending the reverie—instead, just encouraging me to relive the details out loud.

"I wrestled with him when I visited him at his house. Once."

Yeah, I admit to both of us. Not much happened, nothing at all, really. But, with body pressed against body and with hands roaming, it got the hormones flowing. Unfortunately, he let me know that his mother, who was apparently watching from the kitchen window, told him not to do that anymore, at least not with me. To myself, I chuckle, remembering how I got back at her. If she had known, she probably would have been the first mother to have been mad at me. I recall it well and, with Florence asking, "Is that it?" as though she is reading my mind, I tell her the story.

It was the day of my long-planned pool party, after eighth grade graduation. Tony was the only one I invited to change in my bedroom instead of the pool house. Of course, I had to show him where my bedroom was and, or course, it simply made sense for me to stay. What I don't tell Florence was that it was worth it. He was well past puberty. In fact, so far past, I could only dream of catching up with him which, unfortunately for me, I never did. I do tell her, "Other than seeing him naked, nothing happened."

"How did you feel at the time?" she queries, in a tone lacking the voyeurism some might see as permeating the question.

How was I feeling at the time? Truth be told, Tony Tantino, in a way, is at the root of at least some of my "issues." As William has said, "Don't we desire what we envy?"

Bringing thoughts I've previously had into words, I tell Florence "For the most part, I was usually placed on a bit of a pedestal when I was young because I was always a little smarter, a little better looking and, until I went to a private boarding school, a little wealthier than most. Problem is, as a result, expectations were high and, as an athlete, I didn't "measure up," the way Tony Tantino did I remember without saying. "Frankly, that caused me a lot of shame and embarrassment when I was a kid."

We briefly get into how feelings of inadequacy—this time in a discussion not quite so "theoretical"—likely lasted throughout my adult life as well. But Florence still seems fixated on my other youthful sexual experiences, as she asks, "Anything else?"

"Furtive encounters, really quite inconsequential—at least in terms of the physicality of it—with some neighborhood kids," I tell her, letting her know there was a cousin, once or twice removed. And, after I got to boarding school, a classmate or two, or three," thinking especially of one I would have liked to have groped, that charity case tough black boy from Harlem, Sporty Shea.

Yep, that was the age of raging hormones, as I recall how I had wanted Tony and Sporty and some of the other boys.

"If society weren't so effective in instilling that gay-guilt thing," I say out loud, "then, like it was in 7th grade with the first girl I ever went out with—Cindy DeRicco—I would certainly have been far more likely to have rounded a base or two with some of those boys, to use the lingo of the times."

Sex with boys. Sex with girls. Then I recall the over-keen interest of a couple of my high school male teachers. But it's another high school teacher not so easily brushed off—even by a fourteen year old boy from the sticks—as pathetic, who brings back the most vivid memory.

"You know, in my freshman year at that Jesuit boarding school, I had this old, cadaverous-looking priest who, as the first question on the first test given in that class asked, 'How does the human equation vitiate objective reality?'"

At this, Florence, whose impatience or skepticism, I've noted, is signaled by raised eyebrows, raises those brows higher, presumably expecting me to come to the point. Or, perhaps, to answer Father Grogan's question.

Sex. And Reason. And that vitiating human equation.

All I can do is shrug in semi-response to her silent question murmuring, "I just wanted to show you the varied challenges I faced as an adolescent, what with having to simultaneously navigate the shoals of a confused sexual identity and some Jesuitical objective reality. Oh, and by the way, I got an 'A' on that test," not telling her how I had also celebrated the trashing, by those Jesuits of course, of some of the worst of the mind-warping religious superstitions dear to the hearts of my grammar school nuns.

"So, as a young teen, you had girlfriends?" She opens with, as she seizes on one 'objective reality.'

"Yeah, but deep down I knew I wanted the boys," I close with manifesting the "real" 'objective reality.'

"But there were girls," she repeats as might a Jesuit intent on challenge or, more likely, control.

"With little or no connection psychically even if there were somewhat more physically," I respond, adding, and demonstrating why, perhaps, Father Grogan gave me and 'A' on that test, "Mary, when I went to college, was the first real girl, if you will."

Accepting the well-timed diversion/compromise, Florence says, "Okay, I may want to go back to your high school years, but what about Mary?"

By the time I met her, I tell Florence, I had settled into my heterosexual years. In fact, I remember only one guy who I was attracted to in college, and that was in my freshman year. And, I never saw him again after I became a sophomore.

After about twenty minutes, Florence says, "We'll complete your college and the later years in our next meeting," effectively wrapping up our almost three and a half hours together. "In the meantime, I'd like you to see this psychiatrist I know. He's very well respected in the field of forensic psychiatry and, from what you've told me, I think he can be very helpful in your case."

Prompted only by my blank look, she explains, "He does a lot of work with sexual dysfunction. There are actually tests out there that can identify pedophiles and it would be worthwhile for you to have an evaluation, as a clean bill of health would be good for your case. And, from what you're saying and from what I can tell, I think that's likely. But, regardless, the test results will be yours alone, if you don't want to share them. "

"Really?" I ask, genuinely intrigued. "A test?"

I guess I should have expected it. What can't be tested or quantified nowadays, I think—even perversion—without, presumably, the need to do anything perverse. I actually feel some release and then a little annoyance. Why hadn't I been told about this before? If I can't clear the charges, I can at least clear the stain, the psychic wound, by presenting proof of my near-normalcy by the report of a "well-respected forensic psychiatrist." This is what I want, what I need—almost more for me than for them.

"Good," I say. "Let's do it."

So, together, we call the office of Dr. Burell, the therapist, and set up an appointment for me in two weeks. We also set another appointment for the two of us this coming weekend as I write a check for the full amount of her fee—$2000.

I say goodbye, realizing, again, how much I like talking about myself, especially when the listener appears interested. I don't even feel pissed about the money. Nothing I can do about it, anyway. It's all a part of the process. Besides, she just spent a few hours with me. We have a number of more hours to go. She's going to interview several friends and relatives, arrange for some letters and then write a report. I'm actually getting a bargain, I think. And, in the scheme of things, it's peanuts.

So, I feel no qualms in spending more money by ordering out Chinese.

17

Gone

Sitting in my office a few days after my conversation with Florence, I get a call from Walter.

Upbeat, entertaining, always good for a laugh, I've known Walter for more than twenty-five years. I met him when I myself was just a "pup," newly-minted in New York City. He's always acted the sophisticate; well-dressed, seven years my senior, born and bred in New York. Back in 1978, he seemed certain to be a success at the real estate company where we both worked and where we first met.

For all the years that I've known him, I've probably talked with Walter more often than anyone else, averaging—I'd guess—almost once a week. Yet, we've never gotten really close, evidenced most clearly by the fact that we've never even talked about my homosexuality. It's been hinted at, and he certainly suspects, if not knows. But we do not talk about it.

I hang out with Walter because I marvel, almost revel, in his ability to remain upbeat through good times and bad. He makes it easy to feed off his optimism and the joy he takes as a consummate materialist, as he chats breezily about the sexiest car, the trendiest Manhattan night spots, the most glamorous vacation locales and the most gorgeous "wool." Yeah, he has a way of talking about women like they are objects—"meat," "fur"—with each body part dissected and examined. And the younger and more virginal the body part, the better.

Eventually, our conversation turns to a discussion of life options, like retirement, even if that means living modestly, perhaps even living abroad in Costa Rica—things we've talked about, on occasion, before. This time, though, I know I'm sounding more serious, on my mind as it is. As he is sensitive enough to realize that it's not quite the idle musings we have engaged in for years, but more real, more immediate, he asks, with what seems like genuine concern, "What's going on? Is the Firm finally on to you and about to dump you?"

"No," I reply, "Something else."

He persists. I think, "Yeah … why not?" It's time to tell him. He, too, should talk with Florence—write a letter—let those who are anointed to judge that I'm at least as normal as he is. If there is anyone who appreciates the beauty of youth, and who isn't shy about it, it is the Humbert Humbert of the real estate brokerage business, Walter Moses. Besides, my world is now consumed with this, and if he is to be even a small part of it, even an hour-a-week chat buddy, then it can no longer be hidden. So I say, "Let's meet."

And, as he has been for some time, down on his luck—no, he hasn't yet achieved that success—I tell him I'll buy.

* * * * *

It's gloomy and cold as I walk to the Italian restaurant in Rock Center that we have been to a number of times before. It's busier this time than the others when I arrive—not really conducive to stark, disturbing revelations.

After being seated, he makes a big show of staring at the waitress' butt, as if it is the most enticing butt in the world, acting worse than the stupidest, most pathetic frat jock. I begin to wonder, how had I always put up with this? As we sit waiting to order, I swear though, it's more egregious than usual. Maybe it's just my mood.

* * * * *

Halfway through lunch, I've still said nothing about what I came to say. About to fill a pause in the conversation with the point of the lunch, he interrupts what's not yet said, asking me if I know a photographer by the name of Jock Sturges. I don't. He goes on to explain that this photographer takes pictures of young girls, "really young girls, naked." I've heard enough. I tell him to stop.

It is likely the first time in over twenty-five years that I cut him off so abruptly. He stops, but not without looking somewhat wounded and annoyed; also quizzical. He doesn't, however, pursue the reason behind my command. Instead, he effectively undermines any of its significance by again flirting with and ogling the waitress, almost challenging me to respond, which I don't. Deciding, though, that I had made a commitment to myself when I invited him to lunch to reveal all, and as I continue to think he remains concerned enough to want to know all, I say as a way to confront yet postpone the reason that we are here, that we'll talk outside, after lunch. We finish.

* * * * *

Outside, the day continues in its misery. Bundled up against the icy wind, we walk up Fifth Avenue, chatting pointlessly for a block or two, looking in the storefront windows.

I begin to edge toward seriousness.

He interrupts, not for the first time today. "You know what works for me?" he says.

"No," I respond.

"I'm aggressively shallow," he answers. "That's how I remain happy, or at least content."

"Aggressively shallow." Good Lord, he just doesn't want to know. With words I probably won't ever forget, he's telling me he doesn't want to hear or share in any of my misery on this miserable day.

Awkwardly, we walk a few more blocks together. On separation, I say that maybe I'll visit him again at his home in

Long Island that weekend to talk, not yet fully wanting to believe that he does not want to hear.

It is not until I get back to the office that I reflect, and realize the distance between us. So I do nothing—no call, nothing.

* * * * *

In my office three weeks later, Walter calls. He says he is checking in; says that is what "friends/acquaintances do"—his words. I thank him, tell him that "things" are the same, and, thinking, "he's called, it still might be a good idea for Florence to speak with him—she has, after all, said the more the merrier—and, I have, after all, known Walter for more than twenty-five years. So, I let him know that a friend of mine who is helping me out may call him in three to four weeks to talk to him.

There is a pause. A sound, perhaps, of breath being swallowed. If I could have seen through the phone lines, I'm sure he would have looked like the proverbial deer in the headlights.

It's then that I fully absorb that I probably won't call or hear from him ever again. Maybe his pathology, being so much worse than anything I can imagine, let alone live, he's meant to vanish, to disappear as soon as I even hinted to him of the real-life trauma I'm facing, unable, I guess, to face anything that might trigger his own demons.

As I hang up the phone, I wonder how many more like Walter there will be.

18

Just Another Day

I turn my head and look at the radiant dial of the alarm clock. It's 6:30 a.m., and the phone is ringing. It didn't waken me, though, as I've been tossing and turning, half-awake and half in fitful sleep, most of the night—and for the past hour or two, mostly in fitful wakefulness.

It's Wednesday, March 24th, and I'm supposed to appear in court. Who can be calling at this hour?

Imperfect as it is, I don't bother to take the time to check the Caller ID name and number on the Radio Shack phone I'd purchased to give warning of those calls that can seize your life. Knowing that consternation can turn to terror in that time, the phone passes my eyes and goes directly to my ear to know without doubt and without delay who it is.

A sound, like a mechanical hyphen, on the other end of the line. Then a click. It's on. A recorded voice. Male, bloodless, without any inflection, other than that of authority, demanding you to listen.

"This is the Manhattan Criminal Court," it begins.

I can do nothing other than listen.

"This is a call for ...," and my name is spelled out, slowly and distinctly. It asks me to confirm it's me by pressing a number. I comply. It then tells me what I must do and when

I must do it. That is, appear at 9:30 a.m. this morning, in Criminal Court, at 100 Centre Street. It also warns that if I fail to do so, a warrant may be issued for my arrest.

It asks me to press another number if I understand. I do so. It's over. I breathe. Then I get up. I shower and shave and, in affirmation of my dignity, I put on my best suit, an Italian black pinstripe from Barneys, my Cellini Rolex dress watch and my navy blue cashmere Aquascutum overcoat. I head for the subway.

* * * * *

The court appearance itself is a non-event. Another postponement. The ADA doesn't even bother to show up. "That's a good thing," Max says to me. "It means it's not important enough to her."

Small comfort, I think. Of greater comfort, the next court appearance isn't until May 6. All of April for me. More than six weeks before I have to return to this ugly, stark, and bleak building.

With a mind now less distracted than during my prior visits, I wonder how this building ever got built, this building where the law, which at its best, is noble, even majestic, is applied. And applied not to determine who gets the money, or how many angels dance on the pinhead of this or that constitutional right. But applied to determine who gets to live how. And even, if some get their way, who gets to live at all. Not only does this ugly building fail to radiate any nobility, or any respect for its mission, it mocks it. As, leeched on to its massive confines is a jail—a Tomb—equally massive. Joined, not as a harmonic whole—the punishment yin to the redemption yang—but rather, I fear, as a warped one-way wheel designed only to crush.

As I get further away from that building, the morning appears brighter and bluer, and I feel on my skin the faint breath of spring for the first time since winter's fall. I walk slowly to the subway, soaking up the brightness.

* * * * *

Even with the time spent in court, I bill seven hours to clients. I have to admit I'm beginning to do what I'd really done very little of all my career, but which is a time-honored practice in the legal profession, at least in big-time, big-city practice. I'm padding. What the hell. Some lawyers believe it is perfectly acceptable to bill even for dreaming about a deal. Not to mention that time spent is always rounded-up, and sometimes it's rounded-up in increments where the minute-hand has been forgotten. With all I've got to deal with, there's just less time to deal with work. And I don't need any questions from the Firm as to why I'm billing less. Besides, I tell myself, my clients can well afford it.

* * * * *

It's around 6:30 p.m. by the time I settle into the seat of the Exercycle at the gym. With no *New York Times* to read, I grab a copy of one of the freebie magazines the gym keeps stacked for its patrons. This one is called *New Life Expo*, a pamphlet about—really an advertisement for—a "New Age" event to be held this weekend at the New Yorker Hotel. Fifteen dollars for a day-pass gets you a gaggle of speakers, chock-o-block full of self-proclaimed mystics, sages and soothsayers.

Yeah, I figure, why not? Maybe I should go to see if there's anything more to this "New Age" stuff. Pi and Max's nostrum to "let it go," or the uncanny accuracy of various psychics or the prophesies of Nostradamus, or even my faded memory of a decades-old visitation of the divine in Central Park, are no match for my fear that Charlie is right—that "shit happens," that there is no greater purpose for what I'm going through other than that I got caught.

Besides, I think almost whimsically, there are all these little coincidences virtually demanding that I attend. If I'd had my newspaper, I would never have picked up this pamphlet. It dealt with a topic I've always been intrigued by, and have started to more seriously explore. The event is cheap, cheap enough even for me not to feel put off. And, although I'm supposed to see Florence on Saturday, our meeting is not until 4:00 p.m., sufficiently after the scheduled time of most of the lectures and panel discussions. And, in the eeriest coincidence of all, the New Yorker Hotel is located directly across Eighth Avenue from where I was and where it all began on November 8, 2003.

19

HARMONIC CONCORDANCE

"And of course, you all remember where you were on the day of the Harmonic Concordance," repeats Sean David Morton, one of the paranormal luminaries gracing the New Age Expo, and the host of the premiere kick-off event, billed as a panel discussion of wondrous occurrences past, present and yet-to-come.

The panel includes a gaunt husband-and-wife team, clad in white robes, who exude so much tranquility and spirituality you have to wonder how Sedona is faring in their absence. Also, clumsily at the dais, is a folksy, backwoodsman's type who, but for his creation of a celebrated tetrahedron out of native timber, seems even more misplaced and uncomfortable than the ghostly couple. The reason for their discomfort is that the other two panelists filling the remaining seats on the dais seem determined, like their host Mr. Morton, more to titillate the audience with tales of prophetic revelation and personal mastery over the domain of the magical, than to offer any serious path towards enlightenment.

One of those remaining two—a big, loud, fat, theatrical black person, of uncertain gender, appears to me as nothing less than a shameless huckster. But, judging from the reaction of some in the room, s/he's one with a following ready to believe claims of astral transportation and communion with fairies.

The host, having had some success with predictions in the past about the then-future, is afforded the deference due accuracy in a field where random chance is the only possible measurement, at least for any with a scientific bent. Clearly, in the crowd overflowing the confines of the smallish assembly room, there are no scientists. Some skeptics, for sure—for I am one. I can't get over feeling that Mr. Morton reminds me of the grown-up version of the kid that everyone shunned in grammar school. Now, at last, he has found a way to ingratiate himself. Claiming to be endowed with gifts that even the coolest kid would envy, he gets everyone to forget that he's always been a little too goofy looking, a little too animated. Well, gets almost everyone to forget.

But I, too, want to believe. So I dismiss the antics of the black huckster, strain to understand if the scant offerings of the woodsman are wisdom or wanderings, and listen with only half an ear to the gently-offered, but soporific advice about the importance of contemplation and compassion from the saintly couple.

It's Morton and the other proclaimed psychic at the dais—a middle-aged woman, respectable-looking enough but for the blond dye job done up in a 60's Jackie-O fashion—who fascinate, who, for all my skepticism tinged with disdain, I don't want to dismiss. Yeah, now that I'm in their midst, I want these psychics to prove to me that they have, at the least, a nodding acquaintance with mysterious forces which pervade the universe. That would be magic, and what better antidote is there to fear than magic.

When Morton advises the audience to avoid Washington D.C. and, apparently for good measure, New York City, on the coming Fourth of July, I find myself actually hoping that something, a momentous something, will occur. The Black transgender breathlessly seconds Morton's vision and dramatically trumps with a warning of his/her own that, "It could be worse than 9/11." The blond quietly demurs, and the other three just seem appalled. For me, it's a place-and-date test. Good, I think. Now I'll see if other-worldly realms can be harnessed.

Seeking confirmation that true prophesies have occurred before and to wash away the stain of the failure of the prophets on September 10th, I resolve to ask a question, probing for documented predictions from the past which turned out to be true. If I'm not too tongue-tied by my phobia of public speaking, I plan to offer the assembled multitudes one of my own, that of Nostradamus and "The Garden of the World."

Being one of the few hands raised, I believe it is to me when Morton points my way. Instead, the guy directly behind me stands up. Beyond my annoyed relief, I hear as the interloper asks, "Of the two—the Harmonic Concordance and the Harmonic Convergence—which is considered the more powerful astrological event, and why?"

The crowd shuffles restlessly, as Morton and the other panelists had already discussed the "Harmonics" at some length. The Convergence had occurred in the late 80s; the Concordance only last fall. For that, Morton had led a group to Peru and had attempted—I guess from Vulcan mind-melding telepathy or some such—to contact on that date similar groups of pilgrims who had journeyed to Egypt and, more locally, Central Park, in search of I-don't-know-what. In the earlier encounter by the panel with the topic, I had vaguely recalled not only the more recent event—which, after all, had been heralded by a total lunar eclipse—but also press coverage in the mainstream press of the decades-old Harmonic Convergence. That coverage I remembered as being unusually engaged.

My attention to that earlier discussion had waned, however, when it turned to talk of "paradigm effects," "the ascent of individual God-consciousness" and, even more obliquely, "energetic stargates to the ascension of Mother Earth."

Nevertheless, when Morton once again, in response to the interloper's question, expectantly demands each of our recollections as to where we were that fateful day last fall, I focus. Though it must have been the second or third time that he mentions the date, I hear him say as if for the first time, "It was on November 8th."

My head jerks slightly to the left, as if I'm turning to him my right ear, to hear him better. But I've heard, and it's registering, as both my focus and the pit of my stomach to my lower intestines goes soft. Tripped into uncertainty, I regroup to confirm in my mind the date. This can't be, I think. Or do I want it to be? A major astrological event to give witness, if not even perhaps to serve as mid-wife, to the seminal event of my own afflicted rebirth.

With this whirlwind of coincidence—this time seemingly more divine than banal—jumbling my brain, I hear nothing else until we are asked to leave to make room for the next panel.

Jazzed now, I check the schedule to check out what other presentations I can attend before having to return home to meet with Florence. Of the multiple choices available in the next time slot, the offering of the same blond psychic from the just-ended panel seems the most promising, billed, as it is, as a "how-to" session to develop one's psychic abilities.

* * * * *

The room is small and overflowing. Even with the hairdo, she's comfortably ordinary with bright eyes and a sunny, engaging personality to match. But, uncomfortably, she requires audience participation.

"Introduce yourself to your neighbor, relax, open the mind and exchange some general chitchat, and then quietly focus attention on each other for the next several minutes, until I tell you to stop," she orders us. "While focusing that attention, open your mind and accept the energy flowing into you. Then talk to your neighbor to see if you have picked up any psychic messages."

Not without trepidation, my elderly neighbor and I give it a shot. Her insight that I'm "looking/searching for something" seems a pretty safe bet for all in attendance. Mine, stated diplomatically after observing her fidgety annoyance with all who intrude on her personal space, that she "seems distraught, a bit on edge," is accepted graciously, albeit obscurely, as she admits she's been attending these Expos for a number of years in what appears to be a futile search for some yet undiscovered relief from some unidentified malady. I leave it at that.

"How did you do?" the blond psychic asks her audience.

She points to the eagerly raised hands of a 30-something Asian guy and his neighbor, a somewhat younger Caucasian girl. "Well, it really is rather amazing," the girl says with a gush which makes me wonder whether she's a plant. "I told him nothing about it, but he knew I'm a writer and that I'm seriously involved with someone. In fact, I just got engaged."

Convinced her enthusiasm is that of a convert, the crowd—and I—murmur and stir, as would be expected after a good little shake. The instructor looks pleased as she maintains that some are definitely more gifted to "plugging in" than others, but that all can be made more sensitive through training.

* * * * *

Ten minutes later, I'm settling comfortably into a sparsely peopled room for a presentation by a self-proclaimed channel of the Archangel Gabriel. Other than being laced throughout with a verbal tick of "So it is the Word," which I find unexpectedly endearing, this particular channel is all fuzzy lines and no clear picture.

It's then on to a packed audience for the grandson or grand-nephew, or some sort of descended relative, of the late, great Edgar Cayce. This relative spends most of the allotted hour apologizing for the failure of most of the master's prophesies. Next, it's a tuneful symphony of crystal orbs to meditate by. My day is topped off by a woman who does absolutely astounding things with her voice, which, if she so chose, I am sure, could probably include shattering the eardrum. And a welcome bit of relief it would have been.

Fearing I'll be late for my appointment with Florence, I hurtle out of the New Yorker hotel at around 3:15, pausing only slightly to glance across Eighth Avenue. With that unsettling reminder, I have little doubt that the highlight of the day was the Harmonic Concordance and me. The way I see it, a portent—even if an accursed one—is better than none at all, better than being alone in a world that seems to promise nothing else.

20

A Conversation With Florence, Part II

Mom, Charlie, the chef, Lisa, Pi, William and Rich are all on it. Walter, not only off it, but forgotten. Those unresolved, my other two brothers—the teacher and the judge—and Greg, my lover of ten years, and with whom I haven't spoken in even longer than that.

My father? Florence would like to include him on the list of those to write to the judge on my behalf. But it isn't going to happen. He hasn't been involved in my life for the past twenty-five years, if he ever really was. So, it's not going to happen now.

"What about Robert?" I ask.

"Who is he again?" Florence responds.

"The dancer," I answer.

"Oh, yeah, let's think about that some more," she replies. Yeah, she's right. Let's think about that some more.

With the names of three other friends close enough to be told rounding out the list, I hand to Florence all of their phone numbers so she can call to interview them, to fill out my life, to present a sympathetic portrait to a judge who is to decide my fate.

Pi, I tell her, has offered to call her at 11:00 a.m. on Wednesday at her office, so she can avoid the cost and hassle of making a call half way around the globe. With that, we move on to complete my version of my life.

"We left off with you beginning college and hooking up with a girlfriend. What was that like?" Florence begins.

"Yeah, Mary Nocera. I gotta admit, even from the beginning, I was a bit restless, if you will. But, as I mentioned to you last time, for the three years we spent together in college, I really had pretty much settled into the straight routine. We had sex regularly, enjoyably, and everything else. At least in my opinion."

Florence flashes me a look, as if maybe Mary might be available to provide her own letter to the judge, to give a side of me that's long since disappeared.

"Don't even think it," I say. "It was a different lifetime. Last time I heard, and that was a couple dozen years ago, Mary was on the other coast, living the life of the well-paid L.A. entertainment lawyer."

"How did that end?" Florence prods.

"In New York City," I respond, figuring I didn't have to say anything more. But I do. I go on to tell Florence how the ending began. How I had moved to New York with Mary when she entered Columbia Law School and how, somewhat over a year and a half later, I had picked up in Times Square what was to be the first of those many young Black hustlers, this one brought up to the Columbia-owned apartment I shared with Mary.

Once I began, I admit to Florence, I couldn't give it up. I was out constantly in search of sex. And it's not like I was out there fucking and sucking away, because I wasn't, I tell her, using euphemisms. I'd almost surely be dead now if I had been. It was just the excitement of the game itself, and the control games I often enjoyed once the prey had been snared. In the very beginning, it was a hustler or two or three, to ease myself into a new life, the gay life, a life of pleasure without commitment. Then, realizing how easy it was to do for free, it was trolling the bars with only an occasional hustler, when I was particularly horny or lazy.

I tell her not only about the Gaiety burlesque but give her a brief preview of the bars, among them Uncle Charlie's—Chelsea beefcake; the 9th Circle—young college boys; the Works—the crème of the Upper West Side; Cowboys—the crème of the hustling boys; and Rounds—Cowboy's replacement. And then I preview the clubs, including those known to all, like Studio 54. With my sarcasm arriving far too early in the session, I portray it as a venue of sinfulness and sensuality where, with mock horror, I let her know I brought my sister when she was just fourteen. Proceeding on to those clubs known only to the select few, I try my best, with spare words, to describe the likes of Ice Palace—imported Spanish beauty from beyond the bridges and tunnels; The Saint—THE gay disco emporium of hard bodies and hard drugs; the Copa—a Fort Lauderdale extravaganza of sunny stripped-down

Florida boys; and Crisco Disco—slightly seedy refugees from everywhere else who couldn't or wouldn't go home and didn't mind, or perhaps even enjoyed, being frisked at the door. And that's before I even get to the '90s.

I tell her about some of the boys I picked up over the years—nothing, I let her know, too long-lasting, other than Greg, Pi and, kind of, Robert. "Them," she says, "we'll talk about later," continuing, as if two weeks had not passed, with the relentless, "How old were the guys, the younger ones?"

"Look, there were teenagers, no doubt," I respond, with the clipped tone of one explaining to a child what's been explained before. "But I didn't generally ask for an I.D. Like I told you last time, criminal and/or perverse—sweet sixteen and never been kissed has an appeal to me. Frankly, anyone who's beautiful and full of life, energy and possibility has an appeal. Where decay hasn't yet set in, then, for the most part, neither has bitterness or fear. Perhaps I was just trying to steal a bit of their youth and beauty to delay my own decay, and bitterness, and fear. But I can tell you that by seeking the eternal within those boys, they also saw it within themselves. Given how briefly that feeling lasts for most, maybe I even bestowed a blessing," I say, with my sarcasm apparently unlikely to alight any time soon.

To cast aside the snide, I repeat to her how, in actuality, my arrogance masks my insecurity—something we had touched on briefly last time. "If it were a quote, unquote 'transaction' not involving money," I admit to her, "I would hold back. Often, if I waited long enough, they would come to me. And, I needed, wanted them to want me badly enough that they would come. That way, they'd have no right to be disappointed. That's not to say I never made the first move. But, it was rare and, then, only when the cues were unmistakable."

"Well, since you've made it sound like you didn't miss out on many transactions—quote, unquote—I'm actually kind of surprised to hear this," Florence observes.

"When I really wanted it, I didn't often miss out," I confirm. "But there were a few memorable times when I did—some because I held back; others because the cues weren't strong enough. And, a few, I'm sure, because they weren't interested." I tell her of a curly, blond haired bartender at that 80's era hustler bar—Cowboys who fit the "no-interest" category. And the dark haired beauty I circled round and round with at a street fair on Columbus Avenue who I "held back" on. "The one, though, that I remember best," I continue, "was the roller-blader. He was stunning—perfect, pure, innocent sexuality."

"Innocent," she says with a question, exclamation and accusation all rolled into one in her voice.

Figuring I might as well tell her the whole story and really probably wanting to, I begin, "It was springtime, at the end of my first year of law school. As usual, I was constantly on my bike in Central Park. I'm not sure when I first saw him or exactly how many times. For sure, it was only a few but I'll never forget the last time."

"Back then, behind the café at the Sheep's Meadow, where they now store Park equipment, a boom box would blare the disco tunes of the era and the young park denizens who had taken to rollerblading, which was then a relatively new phenomenon, would blade dance. He was there. And boy could he blade dance. It wasn't just his beauty that makes him so memorable—though he was definitely in that just-blossomed state of full perfection."

I see Florence's eyebrows rise once again, presumably at the words "just-blossomed." Well, too bad. She can wait to hear the whole story.

"He was my height," I continue, "with longish, tousled jet-black hair, sparkling blue/grey eyes—oh yeah, I remember—a complexion unblemished other than by the ever-so-slight fuzz of an incipient beard, and a body toned as would be one which had emerged dancing from the womb. Oh how he could dance. Every movement seemed as if it emanated directly from his libido, yet a libido still filtered by a grace and innocence that only hinted at having been compromised. I couldn't keep my eyes off him."

I look at Florence and wonder, is it my imagination or does she seemed more engaged than usual. Perhaps it's her imagination. Catching my eye, she nods and says, "very poetic."

"He inspires me still," I say with no better answer. I return to my story.

"It was the last time I saw him. As I watched, along with the usual coterie of less talented admirers, a female voice to my left broke through my reverie with 'Isn't he gorgeous.' Who else could she be talking about, I figured. Then to her companion, she said, 'He's my brother.' I turned to look at her—there was no choice. She was a normal, almost frumpy, looking teenager and every part of her being, other than her hands, was pointing directly at him. Who else? Before I had turned my head completely back to look at him once again, I hear her say, 'He just turned sixteen.'"

I don't even bother to look at Florence.

"I wasn't surprised, and I know that I didn't even have to know that for sure for it to have an effect on what happened next. There I was with my bike and the rest of the voyeurs, once again transported to a different world, one filled with sensuality and beauty. Then, he slowed. Then, he slid up on those roller blades to within a foot or two of my face and asked me, in a voice so naturally calm I knew mine would squeak in comparison, 'Do you know what time it is?'"

"Why? Why did he come up to me and ask that question? Was it a cue? It didn't matter. I just couldn't handle it. I don't know why—too perfect?—too young? No. In a club, it would have been different." I pause in expectation.

"Why?" Florence asks. Expectation fulfilled.

"Well, I guess when you come right down to it," I respond, "He just seemed too innocent—there has to be more than a hint of compromise in that innocence for me not to feel—I don't know—a lech?—pathetic?—inadequate to the task or, at least, frightened of it? In a club, though, you're compromised. In a club, it would have been a done deal."

"Okay," Florence summarizes, "I know what you're attracted to and your general modus operandi, if you will. But let's talk some more about the street hustlers. Just because it's so—I don't know—dramatically different from what most people do, including, I'm certain, most gay people. For one thing, surely you must realize that you've been taking quite a chance. It must be dangerous, and bad things must have happened to you all the time," she observes.

"Actually, not," I say to her, unbothered by her obsession or her judgment. "There have only been a handful of incidents in the twenty-something years I've been doing this, and not a one really scary," I pause, catching myself. I wish it were only chagrin that I feel, but it's the wave of nausea that overwhelms. "Well, obviously, that's not quite right," I say, in correction. "I made at least one horrible error in judging a hustler, which is going to cost me much more than I can possibly imagine."

She nods. We had talked about him at our first session. He is why she is here.

"I understand," she says. "But what bad things happened with the others."

Perhaps, in fitting augury, the very first hustler that I brought back to the Columbia-owned apartment which I shared with Mary had given a warning. He had returned after we had finished, somehow worming his way back into the apartment. He stole $20, yet left an $800 gold watch, a college graduation gift to Mary from her parents. I tell Florence all of this. I can tell she's not surprised, almost snorting by her body language a, "See I told you so," quickly followed by an also unsaid, "And I bet there were probably a lot more similar incidents."

Sensing her silent censure, I get oddly defensive. "That's one incident from the late 70's," I argue. "And there's really not been much more like that since."

She looks doubtful. "No fights?" she says out loud. "Didn't you ever get in a fight with one of them?"

"Florence, I've never been in a fight—physical fight—with anyone. Hustler or lawyer—or maybe I should say hustlers of any type."

"Never?" she repeats.

"Never," I say again. I don't know if it's amazement or alarm I see in her eyes. Perhaps alarm for lacking a skill I may yet need to develop.

Visibly shaking herself—causing a reverberation through me—she shifts back to the topic at hand, as she challenges, "So you want me to believe you never had a problem with any of these street hustlers, even if it didn't rise to the level of a physical fight."

Welcoming the shift, I refocus on her mindset—apparently convinced that since hustlers "do bad," they can only "be bad." I feel like I'm about to give a social science lesson to the social scientist, as I ask her, "Have you ever met or talked with any hustlers?"

She admits she hasn't.

"At least, not knowingly," I rejoin, thinking of Robert. I argue out loud that there are many hustlers who, but for their nighttime strolls, live normal lives, going to work, going to school, hanging out with friends and family who have no idea.

Florence nods in doubtful acknowledgement.

"Of course," I admit, "I'm sure some just need money to feed an addiction and will do anything to get it, even degrade themselves."

But I didn't see many of those, I think to myself. Or, in my fevered pursuit to feed my own addiction, I didn't bother to look hard enough to tell. I continue the argument, claiming that, "From my perspective, all, or almost all, looked to me like they had made the choice freely, whatever you may want to say about power and control. If there were any chains around their necks, they were more likely to be the kind that are gold and polished. Does that mean they weren't also seeking affirmation of their worth by selling their bodies? Who knows? But an awful lot of them seemed into it, if you will. And they didn't look any weaker or more pathetic or more pathological than a lot of people I know who don't hustle. In fact, in some ways, I'd argue it's just the opposite—that the struggle to resist the lure of the libido or other dark drives is so intense that the pathologies of those who fail in that struggle pale to insignificance compared to those who succeed. Of course," I add in a none-too-subtle defense of self, "certain segments in society do work assiduously at beating everyone up over those desires."

As if bestowing the blessing of my friendship would raise the worth of street hustlers in Florence's eyes, I tell her how I've actually entered into what could be called a relationship with some of them.

Without saying, I acknowledge to myself that my aversion of thinking of Robert as a hustler—or, more aptly, my aversion to him even thinking of himself as a hustler—gives the lie to any belief that it's A-okay to be a hustler. But then I think, are the dozen or so whom I've invited over the years, not once, but several times into my home, not nice, decent human beings? Or, at least, not worse than any other human being?

Of those I continued to see up until December 12th, I tell Florence of Tommy and Bo. At least those two, if not more than a few others over the years I argue to her, have or had, or came close to bordering on, affection for me.

Of course, I admit to her upon seeing that raised eyebrow, neither Tommy nor Bo would hesitate to play me. A game—if not always enjoyable—always tolerated, because we all kind of knew it was a game and they knew me well enough to keep it within acceptable boundaries. I've known those guys for almost five years, I inform Florence. Yeah, I admit to her, if you do the math, it was towards the end with Pi that I was fooling around with Tommy, Bo and other hustlers.

I met both of them around the same time and at the same place, 34th Street and Eighth Ave. Tommy was eighteen, and Bo was nineteen. And, to me, one more beautiful than the other, though which one would depend on the day I was asked.

I saw them grow up, I tell her. Tommy, more carefree and out for a good time. Always talking about his "shorty"—"girlfriend," I explain to her, having had it explained to me. "I have no reason to doubt that he's more straight than gay," I continue. "But he likes the easy money and he likes showing off his body." I don't bother describing how that body is hard, smooth and charcoal black, with a kind of welterweight tone to it.

Bo, I tell her, has a darker mood than Tommy. His lighter skin tone and the fact his body is more like a bantamweight—a six foot two inch bantamweight with sinewy muscles wrapped snuggly around beautiful black bones—I again keep to myself. I do tell her how Bo wanted to become a rap star, and had even recorded a demo tape which he had played for me. Instead, though, I let her know, he ends up becoming a father and in constant battle with crack addiction, having the addiction, as well as a baby daughter he claims to love, in common with the mother.

Of course, I can't forget that both Bo and Tommy had spent time in jail. I had asked them, mostly to tease my greed for a realized vision of sex behind bars, what it was like. No sex, they had claimed. But what I remember most was the avoidance of the question, with Tommy saying at one point—when I pressed him—that he didn't want to talk about it. With the reality no longer confined to porno videos, I can't bring myself to bring it up. Instead, I simply tell Florence that even now, with a phone left unanswered because Caller ID is powerless to reveal who's the predator and who's the prey, it has flashed numbers and locations with Bo most likely the source. I assure her that I've done nothing, not even the easy acceptance of an offer made over the phone by one I've known for years. No, most nights all I do is fret and drink—and pace—and worry and drink some more. No smoking, though, I almost brag.

"Good, you have to stay out of trouble," she lectures.

"Don't worry," I say with complete conviction.

"Well," she continues, "Whether or not it was dangerous, you have to agree it was not healthy. And I'm not talking about threat of disease, because I understand that you only play what you call games, and don't engage in unsafe sex. But I'm talking about healthy mentally, spiritually, if you will."

"I know," I admit, meaning it. "But, as I've said before and repeat again, I don't, objectify, if you will, everyone I have sex with. Certainly, there were none of those quote, unquote, games with Greg and Pi and …"

"I understand," she interrupts, "And we'll get to them later on. I'm also sure you've formed—what, perhaps, I might describe as bonds—with some of the others. But you have to admit, you were basically out of control."

"No doubt," I acknowledge. "And if I had found that perfect, unconditional love which apparently so many in the heartland have been blessed by, I might have settled down," I say with the sarcasm returning in full force. "Or, I guess, if not a perfect love, sex, at least, should be freely offered— that's it, right?—like it is with Trump and every other used car salesman with a diamond pinky ring who bags a bimbo. C'mon, Florence, who's kidding whom? It's the way of a not insignificant part of this world. Mine is just more upfront and honest."

Less defiantly and knowing my riff really didn't respond to her criticism, I continue, "Look, here I am—or was, I should say—physically healthy, some money in my pocket, and tempted constantly in a place and living a lifestyle where, as long as you're reasonably discreet, few judgments are made.

And, most important," I say in what I suspect is just the beginning of a much longer riff, "We're hard-wired for sex. What is it that's said?—men, so long as they're breathing, think about sex once every sixty seconds or so? Look, we are the descendants of those who sowed their seeds over the widest area and with the healthiest partners." I pause but decide to leave the word 'young' and what she would surely see as an imputed smirk out of it, and to move on to my intended goad.

"Now, the whole gay thing is a twist I've thought a lot about, and can't figure out."

As expected, Florence looks up as if she wants me to continue.

That's all it takes. "At one point," I begin, "when I was young and good looking, it seemed to me as if homosexual desires were rampant. There were an awful lot of guys looking at me in a way they shouldn't have been. Guys with wives, or guys who claimed they wanted wives. So I became suspicious of anyone who reached out to me."

Into it, I start speaking with some passion, telling her how I became so obsessive about the topic that I had almost convinced myself that those early primates who succeeded in that battle of natural selection and so became our progenitors were those who first became aware that sexual desires had to be harnessed for the species to continue.

"And this awareness was not simply intuitive, but actually an antecedent to human consciousness," I pronounce to her. "If you saw the movie, *2001*"—her nod being enough for me to continue—"I think that the spark of light in the eyes of that ape was due only in part to a recognition that the massive animal bone it was wielding could be used as a weapon. The recognition of the need to suppress desires which can only destroy was the other half of that—the Venus component."

I don't bother, however, going into another argument I've made—to myself at least—that in that movie, Strauss' Zarathustra was speaking, through those reverberating contrapuntal tympanis and blazing horns, of both sex and violence. How it was all about an awakening duality which perfected less discriminate killings of the 'threatening other' and more discriminate unions with the 'procreative other.' With that duality—that separation—skins were stripped from those dead animals whose bones were used for weapons to cloak a nakedness previously ignored. How bizarre that now, in our advanced civilization, sexual fantasies of being stripped naked and ravished—or its inverse—flourish from a young age until not-so-effectively repressed by that civilization. More noodling than I am capable of, though, so I say nothing.

As if reading my mind, Florence retorts, with a question mark in her tone, "Destroy?" I realize she's referring to the last thought I had actually expressed out loud when she continues, "Does that mean you think homosexuality is destructive?"

I hesitate. Here we are where I've been before in many similar conversations with some of my gay friends, one of whom wouldn't speak to me for more than a year afterwards.

"I don't see how it can be denied," as I once again become the provocateur. "It's simple. No children. No future. Destructive." And it's not only the future, I think, again, without saying. If there's excess on top of excess, then, as has been made brutally clear, the host is also destroyed. I get the feeling that Florence, too, figures there's no particular value in bringing up that topic.

"And how do you feel about this as a gay man?" Florence asks, as if in challenge.

Okay, good, the standard response, at least the standard response from one with a brain, to get me to admit, if I am well-adjusted enough to recognize my psychological maladies, that I'm filled with self-loathing.

"Actually," I tell her, further upping the ante of the argument, "I feel special—privileged." And, though it's more complicated than that, I do. "Gays," I continue, "Whether by reason of the struggle with their homosexuality or, who knows, maybe their superior genes—how else do you explain Plato, Michelangelo, DaVinci, Alexander the Great, and on and on and on—are, on the simplest and most readily acknowledged level, more creative. And I would argue with little fear of contradiction, more open to dialogue without preconceptions, and generally more tolerant and more compassionate. Personally, I revel in being a part of that unique fraternity."

"Of course," I point out to her, "There's the other side. The dark side. Unable, or unwilling, to admit that homosexuality is a difference with a consequence, many gays suffer from all the pathologies of those in denial, the depths of which can only be measured by how much you want to love yourself. That kind of suffering can cause the cream to rise, if you will. And, if you're lucky and can get past the curdling phase, you come out stronger, better, not cowering in fear of what others think, appreciating that homosexuality is not just equal—it's more, and it's less. In other words, it's different."

Those eyebrows go up.

"'Different', though, is not what most gays want," I acknowledge in response. "Equality is. Without a doubt," I concede, "Gays have reached a point where they are telling themselves, and the world, that they love themselves, and that the world should love them, just as much as straights love themselves, and as much as the world loves straights."

Yep, no longer satisfied with mere acceptance or even equivalence, and forced for so long to face our more modern Neanderthals who measure tolerance by how thick the club is with which they smash all those faggots over the head, equality is now demanded. With power moving their way, many gays are ready to battle for their sugar-plum-fairy vision of connubial bliss. So, not only do they knock that club out of the hairy hands of those modern apes, but they stoop to pick up one of their own.

"For me, though," I tell Florence, "I'm just not sure that this is the next step up on the ladder of higher consciousness. Rather, I fear, it may be a turn on a well-trod path so radical that it leads to an abyss. Where do we go from here? There's no precedent. Are we so much smarter, so much more advanced, than any other society that's ever existed?" I ask. "Or is it simply an appalling conceit of a self-indulgent generation that's never not gotten what it's wanted."

With eyebrows fluttering but before she can say anything, I continue, admitting that homosexuality was far more acceptable in certain earlier cultures. But, as I point out, those cultures didn't survive. "And even in the glory days of those earlier cultures—from the little I know—homosexuals were a breed apart, a special breed I like to believe. And that's the way I think it should remain. We don't need, and probably shouldn't want, boys and girls at the gymnasium showering together to prove that all sex acts are equal. That will be fine when we clothe ourselves solely for protection from the elements. And that, I know, will only happen when Adam and Eve again become one with God and, so united, return to the garden."

"For now," I say to Florence, "Perhaps we should listen to those reactionaries when they tell us they know it's a choice; that one chooses to be gay. Logically, they can only believe that if they know they could have made the same choice, but instead opted for Column A, Heterosexuality. Choice—or no choice? Who knows? All I know is that, as I said before, when I was young there were too many guys looking at me, when they shouldn't have been. Let's keep the 'shouldn't have been' in the equation," I assert, "Making the choice to propagate easier and the choice to indulge more difficult. At least that's my choice," I say with far more finality than I feel.

"Besides," I continue in mock horror as the image enters my mind, "What self-respecting gay man would want a bunch of hairy right wing slobs hanging around the piano at Don't Tell Mama singing Judy Garland songs."

I pause to hear an appreciative harrumph mirroring the glint in her eye. But she's unwilling to quit the battle, as she demands, "I don't know, isn't it really self-loathing to suggest that equality for gays is dangerous?"

"In my opinion, no," I insist, re-engaged. "Not if the reality of that abyss is fully understood by those who most want to reject it." Kind of like that primitive primate in *2001*, but at a wholly different level I say, again only to myself. Problem is, and I let Florence know that I am aware of it, this kind of thinking, without more—and I never bothered with the more—leads exactly to where I am today. Nothing to rein me in—if I revel in my 'difference,' there are none of the boundaries that come with trying to be like everyone else.

What I don't say to her is who cares about the boundaries anymore. Since the world—especially my personal world—seems to be approaching the abyss from many angles, I no longer care. It just doesn't matter.

To bring the discussion home, I end with, "Of course, I could be wrong. Perhaps we've evolved to the point where it doesn't matter who you fuck. But something tells me that, if we had, there wouldn't be two million and some odd cots in what's ludicrously called "correctional facilities" across these fair United States."

With the unsweetened "F" word trumpeting the tension in my voice and the arousal in my color, she finally backs off as I, finally feeling chastened, look away.

"Right now," I finish up, "I'd settle for a little love flowing both ways."

"That's quite a riff," she says. "You've obviously thought a lot about this."

"It's who I am. How could I not?" I respond quietly.

A silent moment passes, and then she says, "Well, as you know, my report is to cover actual events that affected your development, brought you to where you are today. So, though what you say is interesting, let's get back to your life. I realize it's late, but I'd like to finish up tonight."

"Now, still, this thing with the hustlers. I want to make sure I have it all, that I understand it. I mean, I see how what you were just saying ties into this behavior. If we're approaching an abyss, as you say, then anything goes, right?"

"No doubt," I respond.

"Well," she continues, "Where does it stop? Or, in other words, don't you have respect for anything or anyone, even yourself?"

Whoa, I think, powerful stuff, and going to that 'more' I don't want to be bothered with. But, she's asked and what better way then to relate it to the 'actual events' she's supposed to report on.

Respect. A word, though mostly unspoken, that permeates the world of hustlers. You can feel their almost visceral yearning for it.

"As you know," I begin, "Almost all the guys I picked up were Black or Hispanic—mostly Black. They don't take too kindly to being disrespected. And, I got to tell you, I really believe that I dealt with almost all of them with a certain level of respect. Look, I don't think Bo or Tommy, or any of the others would keep coming back if I hadn't. I wasn't giving those guys big enough bucks for them to put up with being 'dissed' by me. I can tell you with some assurance that, at least when they first started out, Tommy and Bo had no shortage of customers. And, I know, they both also had other ways they made money. Believe it or not, they liked, or at least had no problem with, what they were doing. And they seemed to like me.

"To tell you the truth," I continue, "In some ways, I am more in sync with the guys I pay for sex and have more respect for them than the people I work with. I would sooner ask some of those street hustlers to help me out. And that's why you don't see even one of my current colleagues on the list to write letters to the judge. It's not because I don't want the Firm to know. If I had enough respect for any of the people I work with, I know they wouldn't tell. I don't know whose fault it is, but I have no desire to get really close to any of them, and the feeling seems to be mutual."

With both of us nearing exhaustion, Florence insists on some finer shadings of how I spent the last twenty years of working life, which I dutifully supply. Less than half an hour later, with that task complete, she asks, "Okay, now, I know we're both tired, but I want to talk about your lovers. Greg, Pi and, I guess, Robert."

Shedding some of my fatigue, here I supply the finer shadings willingly, with bouts in the telling of sadness and loss, mixed with the joy. To soften the sadness, I wish I could say there is an epiphany in the telling, but I know I always knew it. Faced with an inquisitor, it becomes impossible to hide that those relationships—at least the two no longer febrile—ended because of lack of respect. Mine. I was unable to do what should have been effortless—to have matched my love for them to their love for me.

I wonder, though, to myself, "Is that really it? If I had surrendered, would we have achieved the heartlander's bliss of unconditional love?"

After some missing details are supplied, finally, we finish up. The clock is fast approaching 10 p.m., the session having taken almost six hours. We talk a bit about process—about performing interviews with my family and friends, coordinating the letters they are to send, preparing the report and delivering it to Max. She asks me to touch base with her after I take what I've taken to calling the pervert test. We can then decide, she says, if it's to be incorporated into her report. I'm also to send her copies of school transcripts, the law review and legal articles I've written and those few and paltry testaments to my commendable character, which I have had to wrack my brain to recall.

With words of support and encouragement, which in deference to her seeming sincerity I try to take to heart, she makes her departure into the night.

* * * * *

In bed, with sleep unable to be forced the way eyes can be shut, I remember another. Isaiah. Was my failure even to recall him a sign of how little I understood what Florence and I were talking about?

It was only a few years ago. Never before, or since, have I brought a boy from the streets to Connecticut, my retreat. We'd even gone to a movie and dinner with William. At dinner, the waitress, beguiled by Isaiah, asks his age. Ignoring William's glare, I assert my dominance and force her to guess. "Wrong," I had virtually chortled with the glee of the victor, letting her know that her guess of eighteen was off by a year.

I saw Isaiah a few more times before we fell out of touch, which happened not because of me. Then I saw him again, a year or so later, late at night, again on the streets in the Village. Physically, and in ways less tangible, he had changed, not for the better. It was awkward only for the moment it took me to disengage. By the time I was driving home, probably with another, I had mostly forgotten about him. Until now.

Respect. What do I really respect? Too often it seems respect is offered to get what we crave. For some, it's money. For others, power. For me, well, no one who can dare to look would ever have any doubt.

21

Miracles

Television is what I turn to during the month of April, a month free of trips to 100 Centre Street. Some of what I watch simply helps to pass the time till the next court date or the next call to or from Max or the next fully-formed, fear-filled fantasy of a sure-to-happen fact. Some helps to distract, sometimes in coincidences too odd not to unsettle. Like when I catch glimpses—because I can never bear to watch—of the trials and tribulations of others such as Michael Jackson or the Catholic clergy. And then there are the Iraqis, imprisoned in their own homeland by foreigners, and then abused, with the worst excesses happening, according to *The New York Times*, in the most bizarre and sickening coincidence of all, on or around November 8, 2003.

But on at least one occasion during the month, a show that actually makes me feel good, and which brings hope and some peace is shown on PBS. It's a broadcast of a talk given by Wayne Dyer on "*The Power of Intention.*" Somehow he makes all seem welcome. His message—that if you know who walks besides you at all times then you can never again experience fear—is exactly what I'm yearning to hear. That companion, who he calls "source," "spirit" or "god," he firmly believes is linked to all of us and links all of us to each other.

He warns, however, that it is a link which becomes encrusted with all the concerns of living at ordinary levels of consciousness. But if properly attended to, he argues with the conviction of the true believer, then each of us can create miracles.

Miracles. Just one is all I need.

22

Home

Today I am supposed to sign a contract for the sale of my apartment. It's April 24, 2003. Only two weeks earlier, I had placed an ad in *The New York Times* offering it for sale.

It isn't just the fact that I am getting almost three times what I paid for it that takes away the sting of selling a place that I have lived in for over a dozen years. Nor that I feel that the market is insanely overheated and that it is as good a time as any to sell. It's not even the bulwark against fear, however misdirected, that money in the bank and shedding responsibilities brings, although that's the primary reason that I have decided to sell.

No. There is no sting, because no matter how much of a jewel box it may be, however wonderfully located on the edge of one of the world's great parks, near the center of the world's most vibrant city, truth be told, it was never a home to me. I have realized that for awhile, but never more than now.

Now, I desperately need a place to support me, to give me comfort. Although I can pace and hide and cry there, I just feel in my bones that it is not the place I want to be when all of this is over. And isn't that really what a home is? After the worst trauma in your life, the place you can't wait to get back to.

I guess there's a lot of reasons it doesn't measure up; some of them my fault, some of them not.

Though its stunning views, ceiling mounted Italian light fixtures, stone kitchen counter- top in black—with appliances to match—and Ralph Lauren green bedroom add to the luster of the jewel component, the fact is it's a '60's box, and a small one at that. It lacks any of those hidden nooks and crannies, filigreed molding displayed at the proper height, or those massive creaky wooden floorboards which grace apartments of a certain age and enchant you into falling in love with them.

Even the over-the-treetop view of Central Park has a picture perfect postcard sterility to it, not unlike what the park itself has become. Neutered by marauding, horticulturing doyennes of the Upper East Side, fearful, as they are for themselves, of any pocket of decay or unruliness, the park has become another exhibition of the World of Disney, centered in the new Times Square. Now, each time I look out my windows, the virginal unreality of the park stands in bald accusation of my new un-virginal reality, no longer hidden.

Without doubt, for all those years that I have driven up and slid into what others would kill for—an inexpensive, reserved parking space in an outdoor lot in front of my apartment building, directly off Central Park West—I never felt like I was arriving home.

The cottage, on the other hand, which I have owned for a fraction of the time and in which I have slept even less, shares more space with my soul. In part, because even though not grand by anyone's definition of the term, it does have levels and decks and stairs and stone walls and fireplaces and railings and skylights and a Palladian window. And a view of the lake from a forested perch. In other words, it has that enchantment.

It has something else, too—something even more important—friends and family. They visit often there, almost never here. No, instead my visitors here serve only one purpose. Except, of course, for Greg and Pi and Robert.

Now, on not one but on two separate occasions, a whole group—who knows how many—of uninvited visitors had come bearing neither peace nor goodwill. But what, I guess, should I have expected? I have been not only willing, but eager, to foul my home with the semen stain of strangers. So how can I complain when those who may get their own rocks off by exposing crimes freighted with sex, eagerly grab any excuse to sniff around, fouling it some more.

Nope. There are plenty of reasons for me to leave.

* * * * *

At 2:30 p.m., I sign the contract, send the down-payment check to be deposited in escrow and begin my withdrawal from a City and State that no longer want me, but which won't let me go.

23

Dis-Abel-ed

The results—devastating. They suck the life and wind right out of me. Science at work, it has to be right.

I could make—all over again—the excuses I made to Florence and Lisa and the others on the day after the test: too much booze the night before while communing with Greg, my lover for over ten years whom I hadn't spoken to for over twelve years; too much cleverness by half; led astray by the tester, by the earlier tests … by primordial yearnings.

I had called Greg the night before, because I wanted him to talk to Florence, to ask him, after all these years, to be there for me one more time. It took more than my customary single bottle of wine to screw up the courage to call. Any alcohol would do. So the second bottle was so cheap, it was graced not only by its own screw top but it held twice as much booze as a regular bottle.

After leaving a mournful, probably even pathetic, message on his voicemail, Greg calls me back in minutes—twelve years later. He sounds exactly the same. I tell him everything.

About the picture he moans, "And you're so not a pack rat."

After, he offers, without artifice or hesitation, words of comfort and support and time set aside for Florence and a letter, I tell him how good it is to be talking with him.

"Maybe we should get together for dinner," he suggests just before we hang up and just before I screw the top back on that bottle of alcohol, by then almost completely empty.

* * * * *

The test is administered in the same suite of unpretentious and worn grouping of open areas and private spaces where I meet Dr. Burrell—the well-respected forensic psychiatrist—a week and a half earlier. To get there, I travel to Brooklyn to a small 1950's class B building located across the street from the Brooklyn Courthouse.

For an hour and a half with Dr. Burrell I give him the condensed version of what I had revealed to Florence. When we finish, we talk about the tests. The test he recommends is named after its developer, a psychiatrist aptly named Abel.

You look at provocative but non-pornographic pictures and then press buttons with different numbers in response, I'm told. As it is clearly far less degrading than the plethysmograph test—a fancy name for a test where your response to sexual stimuli is measured not by the intentional press of a button with your finger, but by the unintentional engorgement of another member of your body—I opt for the Abel test.

In truth, not only didn't I fear the test, I welcomed it. It would prove me 'normal,' at least as normal as most. God, if I'd feared the test, I would have prepped for it the way I prepped for the Bar Exam, the LSAT and every other test I've taken in my life that have had so much less significance for it. So certain am I of success that, as I hand Dr. Burrell a check for $1,500, I follow up on his suggestion and tell him, "After the Abel test, I'll come back and take the lie detector test."

Then how did I "fail" it? How can that be?

The first part of the testing on that sunny but cool early April morning is both easy and hard. Easy, rating how you would react in a given situation. Hard, matching colors and geometric shapes like with a Rubik Cube, while under the unstoppable tick-tock of a stopwatch. Devastating, the last question of a word game, a game I should've been good at. In thirty seconds, I'm to come up with a word that describes the similarity between the words "freedom" and "liberty." Anchored into my brain and unable to disengage, I can think of only one word, and that I hold back for something better until the tester prods after the thirty seconds expires. With no time left, I blurt out the word "justice." How inelegant, but better yet, how ironic. Perhaps "license" struck too close to home, so my mind rebelled. "Privilege," though best describing both, can also be used in a way that's less benign. So, I can only think of "justice" and feel the failure for it.

With alcohol poisoning my system and confusion in my brain as to whether these tests were even part of the pervert test—after all, that's all I'd signed up for—the tester tells me we're moving. Some of the very few words she speaks to me not related to a test. Not disrespectful, but disengaged, except for when she asks about my shaking hands towards the end of that particularly difficult part of the "Rubik's Cube" portion of the test, where her tone is more suspicious than concerned. Of course, how can she know that the poison within me is not the one she may have suspected?

So, after taking more than three hours of tests I'd not expected, I'm moved from the small closet-sized test center—with its supplies for the office and a metal card table at which I sat on a metal, folding chair—to what looks like a real, though tiny, classroom, with a teacher's desk up front and several more diminutive desks respectfully facing it. She seats me at none of these. Instead, I'm placed at a desk to the side, as if on probation pending the results of the test. The test—the one I've come to take.

On that desk is a carousel to hold slides, like from the 1950s. She begins with the instructions.

"Look at the pictures of the people and objects flashing on the screen and rate them on a scale of 1 for 'disgusting' through 6 for 'highly pleasurable' on how you would feel if you were to have sex with them," she says. "Press zero if your feelings are neutral."

Not nearly as demeaning as the penile "growth" test, but not a whole lot better I think. With it rated to a 90% accuracy with the "growth" test, at least according to Dr. Burrell, the highly respected forensic psychiatrist, I figure no matter how degrading, as long as it works, it's worth it.

We do a test run and I press a lot of 'zeros,' thinking that the image on the screen is not a sexual object—female undergarments, toddlers, women or men peering into car or bedroom windows. You might as well show me violins, for Christ's sake!

"No," she admonishes, "Pressing so many 'zeros' will result in there being no result." I think what she actually says is, "There will be too many false positives," whatever that may mean. It's clear I have to take a stand. Pressing 'zero' is not a stand.

So, I think, with a too-clever mind addled by left-over booze, now juiced by fear and fatigue, if I press 'one', isn't that too simple? Isn't that a giveaway? That I have something to hide? I'm too clever to be sucked into that. This test must be out to game you, so I'll game it first. I'll press a lot of 'twos.'

Twos. "My God," I think after, "Did I even press a 'two' when the one depicted was a two-year-old?"

What was most striking, though, is that all of the pictures, even the ones of the adults, are curiously asexual. Are they frightened to include pictures of sexy people? Afraid of being accused of titillating the already-too-easily titillated? No porn to catch those who love porn too much? There is only one I remember as actually thinking, yeah, he's close to being sexy—mid-to-late teens, blond, and shirtless, revealing some body definition. But even there, his face, smiling vacuously at the camera, has that sexless, featureless 1950's look to it, just like the slide carousel projecting all those pictures.

For over twenty minutes, I view and rate multiple clones and morphs of the Cleaver family. All of them—Ward and June and Wally and Beaver—and some of their aunts, uncles and cousins too who, though never introduced to the 50's T.V. audience, are all too easily recognizable by anyone sitting in my chair as related to that famous family.

Some, scandalously, are paraded in front of the camera clad only in their bathing suits or, more shockingly, only in their underwear. And, as it would have been if it were actually the Beaver himself, the pictures are more embarrassing than provocative. Even the pictures of the undergarments, unfilled by human form and presumably there to appeal to a very particular fetish, look as if they are ripped from the pages of a 1950 Sears catalogue.

Before completing the test, I knew I had fucked it up. Of those I tell, only Rich had the balls to bellow at me, "You pressed two when you saw WHAT?" But after his outburst, he, too, tries to calm and console. Like Florence and the tester whom Florence, in responding to my frenzy, contacts on my behalf, they all say, "Just wait and see, you never know," but with the tester letting Florence know that I cannot take the test again. No make-ups allowed.

Now, with the test results not in my hand, but only conveyed without-quite-saying in a phone conversation with Florence, now with the results of science staring me down with no remorse and with excuses derided, I cannot escape confronting my truths, whatever they may be.

I say to myself, how can it be? I know my fantasy. It's out there, in the bars, in the clubs and on the streets of New York, hustling late at night—where children are not allowed, a fact which I'd otherwise hadn't even bothered to notice until it became a part of who it is said that I am.

Yes, I had admitted to Florence, age is a factor. Yes, I thrill to the elastic skin and spirit that is attached only to youth. But, as I had also told her and as I had believed in my heart, pre-pubescence is not it. I want my boys to have man-sized parts and hard-packed bodies.

The test, though, this test which is supposedly able to tell, now says otherwise. It's almost who cares about legal niceties when you fail the pervert test.

What will all the Ward and June Cleavers of this world think? How could they see anything other than an irredeemable, dangerous predator, certain to pounce on their poor, beloved Beaver, and reek unspeakable perversities on that pudgy, virginal body?

What do I think? I think it can only get worse. I think that when those who care to peer into the dark corners of sexual deviancy click that mouse and scroll down to the State of their choice, then enter a zip code; I think that when my name, age, photo, home address and sex crime details pop up onto the screen, and when it reads "Convicted: Child Sexual Abuse; Convicted: Child Pornography," that they will be given a warning more true than I had ever thought possible. That's what I think after I hang up with Florence who doesn't need to give me my "score" for me to know what it is.

24

LUNCH AND THE ADA

Incongruous may be the best word to describe it. My next court appearance is, by chance, sandwiched between lunches scheduled with my favorite clients. One on May 4th, with a woman I've liked and represented for almost my entire career. The other on May 7th, with a banker who is my best client by far and is, as Firm legend now has it, the first client I had met when I started at the Firm.

As I'm paying—at least until the Firm reimburses me—and as I like fish, and as I've rarely been in the mood to lunch this year, and as I may not be able to do it much longer, I splurge, getting reservations for both dates at Le Bernadin, arguably the best place for fish in the City. Who knows? Maybe it'll be a good portent for the day in between.

* * * * *

At Tuesday's lunch on the 4th, I can't help but enjoy myself being with Melina, especially now that I've been all work and worry, and no play. So, I let loose, and we play a bit, helped along by a bottle of white wine to accompany food not only perfectly prepared but almost guiltless to boot. The guilt we save for the dessert, when it becomes clear why it deserves an entirely separate chef who has an entirely separate and well-deserved reputation.

With a lot of time having elapsed and with a lot of practice since last December, and working hard to dismiss the results of the pervert test, I'm at ease, almost buoyant, bordering on engaging. We joke and laugh and talk about the future.

No matter how close I feel to her, though—and I probably feel even closer to her than I do to Leigh, the long-time banker client who'll be sitting across from me in a few days at this same restaurant—there is no way I can tell her. Both of them, though they may be the ones who laugh a little louder, stay a little longer, and enjoy themselves a little more at the neighborhood holiday parties, they are still card-carrying members of the country club set. And for that set, the boundaries aren't only on the golf course, and the penalty for being out-of-bounds off the course is far more severe.

Sated, we step outside into a glittery May day. I kiss Melina on her cheek as we say our goodbyes and as I wonder if this will be the last time.

* * * * *

I can't think of anything much more disconnected, within the confines of the island of Manhattan, than the elegant hushed tones and respectful service of Le Bernadin and the oppressive, cold, dead weight of 100 Centre Street.

It's May 6, 2004. I sit as quiet as I can in the courtroom, bright with the glare of fluorescent lights and voices filled with the creaking of justice's wheels.

Lisa is by my side for support, but we say little to each other. I notice for the first time that the name of the judge is Aabak. I notice, because, although the judge has yet to enter, Max has walked by and briefly explained again that he is a good man, independent and fair.

Max expects to get a sense of the judge's position on my case today. It shouldn't take long, he says, as he walks to the seats reserved for lawyers with business before the court.

She's there, too. ADA Strauss. I summon, for the first time really, the courage to look at her. And courage is what it takes. After all, my life, my dignity is not enough for her. She also wants me to go to jail, to be locked up in prison for a term that Max refuses to even acknowledge. How can you want that for anyone unless you hate them? Lisa has said, "To her, you're not a person—you're a sex crime." To me, it seems, that's how people can bring themselves to hate. But, as I've never been hated before—at least not that I know of—nor truly hated anyone else, it's just not something I can understand.

Max has said to me, "There's no talking to her"—that "the path to sanity and justice" is to "work through the judge, and ignore her." Though neither is quite as colorful as Rich, both Max and my brother, the judge, echo him in believing that she, as my brother judiciously put it, must have "issues of her own."

To wonder "why," as Lisa keeps reminding me, is pointless—an impenetrable koan. It goes in circles around an unknown center. Given the consequences to my life, however, to wonder is addictive. The antidote? Well, there really is none. All I can do is repeat as a mantra Lisa's answer—"Because she can;" and ignore the alternative—"Because she should."

Looking at her today, as she busies herself around the prosecutor's table, what do I see? Not the girl scout of Rich's musings, but a youngish woman. One already with a severity to her—not only in features, but in her countenance, marked by a mouth permanently turned down. Noticeably wider at the bottom than she is at the top, she reminds me, lacking only a habit, of a nun, a Semitic nun. Ungraced by that habit, though, and with frizzy curls, too many and surprisingly too wanton, perhaps she's really more the harpy. Yes, that's it—in my imagination, an unkempt harpy, herself a figure to be imprisoned, preferably in the dungeon of some bleak and foreboding castle on a faraway hill.

If she were a man, though, then what would I think? What's the male equivalent of a harpy? But would a man be doing this? Pursuing me with such seeming vengeance? Perhaps he would, if he were also a father.

I shake myself from my reverie as my name is called, having missed the entry of the judge. I proceed to the table for the accused in front of the judge, who calls Max and her to the bench. She says little. Max says a bit more, and the judge says somewhat more than that, all beyond my earshot, but inaptly, looking benign and ending in minutes.

After receiving my summons to return on June 6th, Max signals more than he needs for me to depart. I follow him quietly out of the courtroom, followed by Lisa carrying my bag.

We head toward the elevator bank, but then Max directs us to walk down, so we can talk in the stairway. He looks animated in a satisfied way, as he begins with a similar voice, "As I expected, this judge has done some homework already, and has some familiarity with your case."

Okay, so what, I think, which Lisa verbalizes with a prodding, "Uh-huh."

Max pauses, and then says, "I hesitate to say this, because I'm superstitious, but I don't think this judge is going to send you to jail. Don't get me wrong. He made it clear that this is too serious a matter to plead down to a misdemeanor, so I think…", and his voice trails off, at least to me.

"Misdemeanor" is the last word I hear. Even raising it as something that can't be achieved was beyond imagining. I need no translation that this is good news. What I do need, however, is assurance, so I ask, not knowing whether or not I'm interrupting him, "What about her?"

"She doesn't matter. He makes the decision," Max says with a tone of finality and dismissal. He then fills us in on the process. The judge is aware that we're preparing a social psychological profile and, at the next court date, Max intends to give him an update on the status of the report. By then, Max believes, the judge will have had time to more fully review my file. "I think we may be able to settle this in fairly short order," he adds on another hopeful note.

For Max, the results of the pervert test have already been dismissed from existence. For me, I have a ways to go yet, but I'm getting there.

After an encouraging peck from Lisa, we separate, with the feeling of some achievement, most notably emanating from Max.

On the subway, headed for work, I consider. No jail time. Max's goal from the beginning, maybe his only goal and maybe because he sees jail time as a real threat while it just seems too incomprehensible to me.

Of course, there's also no career—a different life. Am I ready for it?

Then, what I don't want to even think about. Maybe though, just maybe, if so many people are put on those pervert cyberlists, if even those whose only crime is a stirring in the loins at the sight of a naked sixteen-year-old are added, then the shame will be diminished. Maybe even reduced to the point where its honorees are seen as no more dangerous or disturbed than those who leeringly refer to adolescents as 'jailbait.' Until then, though, it's a fraternity of child rapists, with everyone on it branded with the sins of its worst offenders.

But no jail time. Lately, to prepare for that which no preparation is possible I'd been telling myself I could handle it. Now, with the threat diminished, the vision clears. Sure, I've hung out with guys who've been to jail. But this would have been constant, not an hour or two. It would have been in their element, not mine. Beyond that, the whole system seems designed to break and humiliate beyond any requirement for control. And, of course, there's that primal childhood fear, a fear that no medication or spiritual training can placate.

Most terrifying, though—and surely the reason why Max has been so dedicated in trying to keep me out of jail—is there I would be, a white, middle-aged child molester amidst those whose hate must surely surpass even the hate of those who put them there—a white hot flame applied to a seething cauldron.

Yes, it's a world almost inconceivable, one separated from me by a deep, dark, awful chasm—a Tomb—filled with Southern assholes and kicks in the head. She must see that.

Oh how easy we find it to brutalize each other—and how easy the absolution that a label provides.

* * * * *

The following day, with the previous day somehow forgotten, I find myself once again ensconced in the luxury reserved for the privileged. My lunch with Leigh, the banker, borders on the celebratory. But for some odd reason, he orders the lamb.

25

Divining the Stars

"If you think you're going to retire, move to Tahiti and live on the beach, you can forget it," Nick says to me, about a half-hour into our session.

Nick is my sister's astrologer. She didn't need to be told that I had gone to the New Age Expo at the New Yorker Hotel to suggest I give Nick a call and set up an appointment. And I didn't need much encouragement, even after being told he charges $200 a pop.

When I arrive at the Greenwich Village apartment where he stays when he's in New York, I'm met by an attractive, dark-haired 40ish woman who I learn is his ex-wife. That the place borders on commodious is the best that can be said, as it otherwise looks like any one of many in the stable of apartments owned by NYU which was long-ago forgotten.

Before settling into my reading, which he indicates he is going to record so I'll be able to listen to it again and again, Nick tells me a bit about his life. I learn, for example, that he's twenty-two years older than his ex, which he seems pretty proud of.

Good for him, I think. I'll be able to relate to this guy, at least on one level. And I'm not particularly surprised, because Nick, notwithstanding a decent sized bulk, is full of energy, with warm, inviting eyes and a ready chuckle, looking younger than his apparent age.

That he should specifically disabuse me of any notion of retiring to an island paradise is but one of a number of things he says that provide a jolt. Being so specific and so relevant to where my head's been at since this all began, it gives some greater level of comfort in his soothsaying credentials to whatever it is that's on the chart he keeps glancing at.

Yep, no question, some of my innate skepticism is shaken in the face of his uncannily accurate observations. Right off, he observes that I've got issues with authority figures. This, he claims, "is fine, because you need to experience that in order to grow." Juicy as it is, I leave the observation unexplored, in part to avoid having to say too much to him. I've decided to give Nick no hint of my situation, not because of shame, as he is clearly beyond judging, but because I want the reading to be free of any distraction that a revelation of such magnitude might have.

Even more trenchant than his observation about Tahiti, he bears in on transformation and change in my life. It's all about change, change, change. Presenting it, as he does, in such a positive way, it almost makes me eager to suspend my disbelief for an hour or two.

"You're already one of the one hundred million or so people on this earth, who," as he puts it "are on the dance floor." This, I learn, is his way of describing one who's achieved a certain level of consciousness. He gives me no time to agree or disagree.

"You're coming to the end of a cycle of evolutionary growth," he continues, "and it's time to put things in motion, to achieve a new and even higher level of consciousness. The way to do this," he says, "is to take a thought, hold it, and fill it with intense emotion."

Unfortunately, I think, most of my current intensely emotional thoughts are unlikely to bring me to a new, higher level of consciousness.

More pointedly, he notes that this transformation is "death of the old ways of being and birth of the new" and can be a difficult and delicate time, "like a caterpillar when the cocoon is opened, and the butterfly emerges. Its wings are wet and it is easy prey for any predator."

Me as prey. Me as a butterfly. How can I not be enthralled.

To challenge his rosy glow, I tell him that there's definitely change going on in my life, but that it's due to a crisis, which I otherwise leave un-described.

"Crisis is opportunity," he says with unfazed optimism. Then, claiming that he doesn't say this to all his clients, he asserts that I "am incredibly powerful." He acknowledges, though, that such power can be used for "good or bad," but that he sees a "self-healing" going on in my life. And that if I properly engage all of this energy now circling around me, then

I shall do something "to touch the minds, souls and hearts of others."

It sounds as if he means for the better, but I leave the question unasked. To all this he puts dates for the beginning of this cycle and the end of that; some of those dates in the future, and now all on tape for me to check and confirm, including the "major structural change" in my life that's supposed to occur by this coming December.

The other major event in my life which he claims my chart shows is a powerful and enduring love interest. He asks if I'm involved with anyone.

"No," I tell him flatly, though not without a glimmer of hesitation.

He appears flummoxed for the second time. The first was when I told him that it was November and December of 2003 as the time I pegged as the beginning of my life transformation. He had thought it should have happened months earlier, and blamed my not being able to give him my exact birth hour as the cause of the confusion.

This time, he looks again at his chart. "Haven't you met someone special?" he asks.

And, of course, I have. But Robert can't be the one. For God's sake, since that night he'd spent with me three months ago, I've only seen him once—and that, only for a dinner engagement. Nor have I talked to him many more times since. The entire history of the relationship has been tortured.

Too many differences. Too many complications, especially now.

With the observation, however, he again catches me off-guard. "I am obsessed by someone," I admit. "But it's not more than that."

"Okay, okay," Nick says, yet without backing off, as he continues, "It's going to happen at some point soon, though, for this love interest shows up three times in your chart. Once, indicates a possibility of a relationship; twice, a probability; three times, well—just keep your eyes and heart open, and let it happen."

I don't know what to think. He can't be right. Just let it go, I figure.

The tape clicks, signaling the end, and Nick asks if I have any questions. I ask the question I had before I arrived. He answers. We talk about it a bit more. Then I thank him and leave, braced a bit, but also more than a bit disappointed.

There were some specifics, but all this talk of change seems awfully general. At least that is how I am already remembering it as I walk out the door of his apartment onto the springtime streets of the Village. Besides, how come he didn't know of the trauma, I think, accusing him inwardly. And how can he put such a positive spin on the change I am facing? Most tellingly, though, as an astrologer, why hadn't he divined the demonic significance of the Harmonic Concordance on my destiny, even after I specifically raise the event in the Q&A at the end?

Of course, he knew of both the Harmonic Concordance and the Harmonic Convergence, he had told me. But he also acknowledged that he didn't know what either meant, though he realized that plenty of New-Age types had imbued both events with a significance they claimed would be readily demonstrable.

As he had pointed out, none of the consequences predicted at the time of the Convergence in '87 have panned out. Nor was he aware of any that occurred during the more recent Concordance. He did say that both represented an alignment of powerful energies and "that if you feel it has significance in your life, then you should honor it."

That's not what I wanted to hear. I wanted, or expected, him to tell me that my astrological chart gave every warning that on November 8, 2003 the stars and planets and asteroids guiding my life would implode in a vast, sickening suction of gas and matter, to form a Black Hole, insignificant and shunned by all, out of which no light would ever again be able to escape.

That's what I had expected to hear. That would have matched the drama my life has become.

26

THE STREETS AND THE LAKE

It's bizarre. I'm sitting here and can't get over it. My guts are virtually screaming for it.

It's the night before I intend to drive to Connecticut to open the cottage for the summer and the urge to pick up a boy is overwhelming me. Why now after five months I don't know. Other than the one night with Robert and that one "indiscretion" at the gym, I've been successfully denying the drive since December 12th, 2003. There's no obvious trigger, except, perhaps, a re-invigorated, earthy horniness and the bottle of wine I just polished off. What it really is, though, is that with the passage of time, the fear has dissipated—at least enough. Whatever the reason, I feel the anticipation gurgling in my guts.

I virtually float to the car and head to the Village.

* * * * *

Reverting to years of routine, I park the car on the darkened, familiar streets to take a walk to get a clearer look at one of the few boys out tonight. Given the slim pickings, I think that maybe the police have been working the streets more vigorously than the boys during my absence. But I don't care.

I see no police and I once again trust my internal radar to warn me of any danger. In twenty-five years, it has only failed once, and that wasn't a failure to pick out the cops. I squelch any fear that the radar will fail tonight. I just know it won't.

I'm right. The boy is cute, and it's not because I'm grading on a curve out of desperation. I've seldom done it before and, even having sex only once in five months, I'm not going to do it now.

Hispanic, trim, beardless, and claiming to be a college student, he looks safely at the 20-year mark he gives as his age. As we drive uptown, he sounds like he may actually attend college.

Once in my apartment, I don't even consider my control games. I just want his naked body next to mine. He seems almost as eager, as we strip in the living room and, to waste no time, drop to the floor, hugging and kissing and playing with each other.

God, it feels so good, and I've missed it so much.

The play is affectionate enough that we both come and even talk for a bit afterwards.

Sensing it's time, he collects his money and leaves, seemingly alright with the excuse I offer up for not giving him my phone number. I do accept his and promise to call. "Maybe next Friday," I say.

I sleep better than I have in a while.

* * * * *

Driving to Connecticut, I begin the cleansing, convincing myself that I need no convincing to not again do what I did the night before. It's not because of the shame or fear, but because—at least, so I believe in this glorious sunshine on this glorious day—I don't need that kind of release anymore.

The cottage does that for me. It fills a void. I feel a distance from problems and addictions, and a happiness I don't feel in New York. I'm filled with contentment simply by making the cottage look good and inviting, both to me and to any who may drop by. Maybe if I just promise to stay here for the rest of my life ….

I stop, first, at the local nursery to buy a couple hundred dollars worth of flowers. When I arrive, I see that Bill, the handyman, has been by to turn on the water and put in the dock and even, pray tell, the boat. I immediately set to cleaning up the surprisingly little dust and dirt and other refuse which had taken what little refuge my cottage offers during the winter months.

While planting flowers to add a splash of color to the gnarled gray bark of my favorite oak, I get a call from Pi. He offers advice on meditation, "Close your eyes, and think of a golden pyramid enveloping you, offering you protection against all that might hurt you."

Moments after I hang up with him, mom calls. First, she offers words of support that only a mother can offer, "If there were a way, I would have all of this happen to me instead of you." Words I know to be true. Then she offers words of hope, saying, "By this time next year, this will all be over, and you'll be getting on with your life."

The phone doesn't stop ringing as I even get a call from Rich in what's late morning, California time. Eschewing the quiescence which had settled over him since I decided to stick with Max and since he heard the ADA had added child pornography charges, he tells me "What I have to do."

"Except for—what'd you say, ten pix of what we'll call a fella of indeterminate age—the rest of those pictures show that you are not what they are trying to say that you are. You show a jury thousands of pictures…"

"Hundreds," I interject a little too quickly, speared by the goad.

"Yeah, yeah, with hundreds of pictures," he continues with a victorious smirk in his voice, "How can it be other than an odds on favorite that you'd a picked up at least one of those freaky boys with late-bloomin balls." Before I can even venture a guess, he continues, "They exist, as I'm sure you know better than me. It's an actual medical condition, and there's an actual word for it—check it out."

"A word!" I almost snort, but successfully hold back. He knows it. And he knows I know he knows it. Oh, well ….

With homework assigned, he moves on to another lesson—this one, however, I had already learned. "Look, all you need is reasonable doubt. You're a good-looking, successful gay guy who's lived a life filled with sex—lots of sex, wild and crazy sex."

My mind wanders to a Greenwich Village street.

"Played right," he continues to the critical part of the lesson, "you'll look like one lucky dude, and that ADA will look like—what did I call her?"

"A harpy?" I offer quietly, stepping on his line with one of my own as a little payback.

With a flustered, almost indignant, "No," he continues, "Okay, fine, so I won't repeat myself, fucker," as he recognizes a reciprocal goad. "Seriously, though, who's the jury going to want to identify with—a frigid loser or a free-wheeling Lothario, albeit a somewhat twisted one. But not an evil, or criminal, one." Not bothering to pause for a reaction this time, he sums it up, "Jim, a sympathetic jury should be a wrap in this case. So, not only are you not going to jail, you're going to walk away and you're going to return to the productive life you were leading before you were hit with all this bullshit."

Without also reminding me, again, of the importance of the talent of the "wrapper," he insists I have mine—Max—"check it out." He also commands that we order up as many pix as possible of what he calls, "deficient, naked eighteen year olds" so as to provide "pictorial comparisons" to the jury.

While I'm still on the phone, William stops by. Before Rich lets me off the hook, he further commands, "And don't forget—they're scum. Just be sure to pay that detective whatever it takes to get enough information so that your attorney can tear those fuckers another asshole."

After I hang up, I tell William about the conversation. He looks more bewildered than I feel I can manage. So, we end up talking mostly about nothing which, blessedly, is interrupted by Lisa and Leslie. I know they're here to make sure that the cottage, which serves as the waterfront retreat for their own tiny weekend home in the hills five miles distance, is up, ready and running. As they come bearing chicken, store bought potato salad and pre-washed greens, I check to see how much grime and grit encumber the outdoor grill. While I'm scraping off a layer or two, I tell Lisa of my conversation with Rich.

A sibilant "Yes!" escapes as a cheer, as she adds, "I told you to stay close to him, didn't I," happily taking some credit for one of my friends. Almost before finishing her sentence, she shoots me a look which leaves no doubt that it's Max whom she worries may be "deficient."

* * * * *

On Sunday afternoon, before I'm about to return to New York, I get another call—this one from my brother,

Charlie. We talk about everything but. Not because—like Lisa—there's little left to say, but because more like William, he doesn't quite know what to say, or how to say it.

Even if noticeably infrequent, at least he is a brother who calls. The judge and the teacher have known, essentially, since I told Charlie and the chef. Each, other than Charlie, has called once. And then, only after a time.

Thinking about it, though, once has been enough, at least at this point. The support and the bond are there. And the judge has agreed to write a letter of his own, to be delivered to another with whom he shares a title of honor.

With all this, as I pack to get ready to return to the City, I'm not feeling abandoned. For now, the cottage is open and ready to share, at least for one more summer. It's my gift to those who will take a part of their spring to write their own letter to help quiet and convince a stranger with power over another, power over me. To write a letter of quiet conviction, I realize they must convince themselves that I am not also a stranger.

27

Switched Up

It's almost 9:30 a.m., June 3rd, and I'm nervous as shit. Ms. Spear has me on hold, while she looks for Max. The court appearance is scheduled for right now, so why would he even still be in his office, I fume through the fear.

Finally, he gets on the phone and sounds a bit nervous himself. "Look," he says, "I'm on the other line with Calvin. He's showing up in my place today for the hearing. But it seems as if you've got to go to another one of the courtrooms in the building, and I'm trying to find out exactly what's happening, so hold on a minute."

Another courtroom? What the hell does that mean, I think? Just getting here takes enough out of me. Why do they have to put me through this shit at the last minute?

Max gets back on the phone. "It looks like they've reassigned your case, so you should go to the Eleventh Floor, Part 31, Room 1116. You got that?"

He seems to hear my response, though I wonder how. "Calvin will meet you there, and we'll talk after it's over. Nothing's going to happen today, so don't worry."

No time to think, as my legs carry me forward with a kind of frantic energy that an overwhelmed brain makes worse with the threat of misdirection. I get there though, on time, or at least before my name is called by the clerk.

Calvin is already there, out front, waiting. Without Max's calming presence and again, frightfully confronted with my own insignificance, I'm a wreck. Calvin, though a sweetheart, is only a kid, a soothing presence only in the sense that he telegraphs Max's determination that this hearing, too, must be insignificant. Except, of course, for the unexpected, which has now happened.

I enter the courtroom with Calvin and take a seat, not without first noticing how crowded it is today and how most of those present seem more hollow-eyed and vacant than scared.

How do I look to them, I wonder?

Even if I'd wanted to further ponder the crowd, we're called and are up and out in minutes, put over for two weeks hence.

Walking out with Calvin, I wonder to myself whether the brevity of this morning's appearance and the short interlude to the next has anything to do with the change in the courtroom. I don't really care, as I just want to get out, and I know that Calvin is not empowered, in more ways than one, to answer any question of any substance.

Back at the office, penciling into my calendar in my own secret code my next court appearance, I discover that the appearance is the day after I've invited one of my clients to the Firm's Sky Box at Madison Square Garden for drinks, finger food and a concert courtesy of Madonna. Odd. Another "special" occasion married to a court appearance. You'd almost think I was planning it this way—though nothing could be further from the truth. For today's appearance, my "special" occasion is a yacht race in Greenwich for tomorrow. Well, I guess, more fodder for my internal nighttime harangues.

"A concert with Madonna," I think. "Hhm. Wouldn't she be a great one to sit in judgment? She'd understand."

It is then that I realize that in all the frenzy and furor of the morning, I hadn't noticed whether, if along with the courtroom, the judge, too, had been changed.

28

Memories, Memorex and Max

At the yacht race in Greenwich Connecticut on June 4th, my sailboat—at least the one I sat on, which is actually owned and was skippered by one of my putative partners—places second.

At the Garden concert on June 16th, Madonna does a disappointingly mechanical and sexless version of what Madonna used to do best.

And, in the courtroom on June 17th, I confirm for myself that my judge has changed from Aabak to Zyzen. Other than that, nothing is accomplished, and we are adjourned until July 12th.

Other than that.

I don't know what to think about the switch. It's almost like it's a sign, another one of those portents, except this one is deadly serious. There I am with a judge who is going to keep this angry, crazy, driven woman in check. Then "Poof," he's gone! Max's fret about being "superstitious" and not wanting to speculate about what the judge would do, and then ignoring his own warning, sits with me eerily.

Max has played it down, or has tried to. With a tone less than convincing, he said, "It is what it is. We can deal with it. We'll adjust. There's a way to approach everything. If this happens, then I do that. If that happens, then I do this."

Of course, he hadn't even bothered to return my phone call to him from after the last court date to find out if my suspicions about the reassignment were correct. Nothing new there. It has become increasingly difficult to get a hold of him. But he hasn't hung up on me. At least not until today.

It's June 30th, and I wanted to talk to him about the pictures and the tape. Even more so lately than before, that's all I want to talk about, the pictures and the tape. I can't stop thinking about them. So how can anyone—especially my lawyer—expect me to stop talking about them? Especially the tape.

I'm pretty sure what the pictures show, although ten seems like an awful lot. It's the uncertainty of the other part of this. The part that gave them the right to enter my home and remove those pictures. That's what's gnawing at me. All the questions plaguing my brain—of who and what and where and when. Questions that shouldn't be there, because how can I not know? Maybe they are doing this in a way to torture me, by suggesting there may be another truth.

Or do I torture myself? It will all end with the tape. All these questions will end. So we must get the tape, and we must get it soon. That's what I tell Max, or want to. But, instead, he hangs up on me. Until I get that tape, peace will have to be achieved by waiting with a mind made empty.

But I cannot empty my mind of the question of why. Why are these street hustlers—and another crazy woman—coming after me? What do they have to gain?

In this world, of course, the answer is most often money. With criminal conviction comes all of the proof that they need, is how they must see it.

Or are they viewing it through lenses that to me seem opaque? Can one who hustles on the streets after dark, or even one to whom he is dear, be outraged at innocence besmirched when that hustle is greeted; so outraged that no effort is spared to punish the greeter?

Or is the accuser being used again, this time by those given authority to preach that the snaring of one whose use is corrupt excuses that which may be corrupt in their own?

The last I can think is the hatred of the self-hater who, when given the chance, can only delight in the destruction of any who might otherwise be blamed. And who better to blame than one least like the blamer?

That's what it's been like—my mind reduced to the cadence of obsession, an obsession Max refuses not only to engage, but even to humor. I need to get answers, and Max is the only avenue I have, but he has just hung up on me.

He long ago let me know that I'd have to cede control. And, when he observed, "You're not used to that, are you?" I hadn't disagreed.

Is he training me to cede control, by not taking my calls and now, by hanging up on me? Is he training me to absorb his mantra of, "One day at a time?" Or, is it less benign, this disengagement of his?

Mom, Lisa and even my brother, the judge, all know about it, and they keep pressing me to do something, as if I have any power over Max. Finally, the judge says, "I'll talk to him." So I tell Ms. Spear that all those who care about me would like my brother to talk to Max. My side thinks that maybe my brother can get a better sense from Max than I can of what's going on, some idea of the strategy and tactics, including what's up with the new judge and how we might be able to switch again.

And that's almost the way I'm thinking of it, as if it's "my side" and "Max's side"—not a good way to be thinking.

Worse, though, are the questions on Max's competence. He's all there is between me and jail. So, when I sent a set of motion papers to my brother, the judge, after finally receiving copies of those papers from Max's office and when my brother judged them to be "mostly boilerplate, like he had taken it out of the drawer," I fretted some more. And I haven't even bothered to discuss it with Rich. I know what his reaction would be.

I am torn. When you're with Max and either the object of his attention or simply a part of his audience while he's performing, there's no denying his charisma—he's almost magnetic. That, with his intuition, gives him a virtually limitless capacity to manipulate others. And isn't that what you need in a trial lawyer?

Presumably, this will all be grist for the mill when the cottage and I will be welcoming the entire family, who start arriving, then departing, in stages next week. Charlie with my brother, the chef, first; who overlap a couple of days with the teacher; who overlaps for a day with the judge and his family; all overlapping with my mother, who intends to stay for five weeks.

Best of all, Pi is visiting. I found that out, not without an awkwardly hesitant moment or two, when I called him last weekend. I think he fully intended to call to let me know and to meet up with me, but he didn't know quite how to tell me that he's coming with his new boyfriend to do a driving tour of the East Coast.

Truth be told, and after our talk I think he now believes me, I'm very happy he's found someone else, though happier still that he's coming to see me.

* * * * *

As I'm getting ready to leave the office for the day to go to the gym, my partner who owns the sailboat stops by to let me know that as a result of a correction of some semi-suspicious error which had favored a very rich client of the sponsoring bank, we had actually won the yacht race.

While slipping on my suit jacket, I think to myself, "If only it were all so simple."

29

A Gift From The East

It's just like the movies. The blood splatters all over my shirt, and even onto my eyeglasses. My mother lets loose with a shrieking, "What happened?" And I just remember feeling like it was penetrating a lot further than those countless other times it had happened before. Especially since what it was penetrating is what I like to think of, perhaps somewhat wistfully, as one of my smaller appendages.

How can it possibly get in that far? There's just not enough meat. I'm telling the story to Pi and his boyfriend, Jeff, while we are sitting under the stars, across from the lake, finishing up steaks I had grievously wounded myself to prepare to such bloody perfection.

"I must have used half the roll of paper towels, and not the cheap stuff, but Bounty, soaking up the blood," I let them know.

The wound is now wrapped and under control. But it had given both me and my mother a bit of a scare, the tip of a very sharp steak knife plunged—with the aplomb and effect of a professional spearing—right into the thumb of my right hand, just below the knuckle.

The ensuing gusher is enough to cause my mother to not only shriek, but to call the Pulaskis, Dr. Puklaski being the intended callee. But his wife, having suffered a similar experience, gives most of the advice. She strongly urges I go to the emergency room, cause otherwise, "There may be an ugly scar or, even worse, you may suffer from a numbness or tingling for the rest of your life." Advice she herself had apparently neglected to follow, thus suffering the consequences she now feared for me.

I demur, though. Pi is coming. The blood will stop flowing, at least from the wound. People get knife nicks all the time. But Pi visits rarely. I've only seen him twice since he moved back home in 1999. The last time was more than a year ago, well before my arrest.

As we sit at dinner, I say to him, "It was because you were late. Again. I was distracted and worried."

He gives that short, staccato, knowing laugh that goes up an octave, before it ends as abruptly as it begins. I let mom and Jeff in on the inside joke, recounting only two of the more egregious examples of Pi's tardiness. How I had waited until eight at the TKTS booth in Manhattan before surrendering to inevitability and having to hurry myself to the theatre to enjoy, alone, a performance of "Angels in America." I also tell them of the time in London where he disappeared in Harrods only hours before we were to fly back home, so that I ended up angrily/worriedly taking the train alone to the airport, which, somehow, he had successfully arrived at before me.

My only satisfaction is that he always seemed to look sicker about the consequences than I did. Nevertheless, his tardiness never ended—it just became a bit less frequent.

"I told you that we got here late because we got lost, 'cause of your bad directions," he complains in mock exasperation of my complaint, which now, after all these years, can only be mocked. It is impossible to feel true exasperation with Pi, crowded out as it is by a feeling of true closeness, regardless of how far away he lives.

"I wish I'd been able to see Charlie," Pi says.

I feel like telling him he didn't miss much, because all four of my brothers came and went with hardly a mention of the two-ton elephant stalking my every move. Maybe they thought I just didn't want to talk about it, but I think it was the other way around. The teacher, when I pick him up at the airport for the drive to the cottage, does want the bottom line, kind of like the Cliff Notes version. As the drive takes almost two hours, he gets a little bit more than that, including my letting him know, just before we arrive, about the switch-up with the judge. He just shakes his head and says with a conviction I, too, may once have mustered, "Well, I don't see how it will make a difference. There can't be a judge out there who will send you to prison for something like this."

Pi, of course, has gotten the full, unabridged version, often in real time at least as real as can be achieved with a call separated by half the globe.

I turn my attention back to him and Jeff just as Jeff finishes regaling us with a story about his dog, some bad dog food and how he got even with the dog food company on the radio talk show he hosts in Japan.

After I finish telling them the story of my day-long experience with the celebrity soothsayers at the New Yorker Hotel and of my guilty disappointment that certain unscheduled fireworks failed to occur on the recently departed 4th of July, Pi looks at me and says, "I have something for you. Come on. It's in the rental car."

As he and I walk down the stone steps to his car, he lets me know that Jeff is not only a Princeton graduate who speaks fluent Japanese and has some sort of irreverent talk show on Japanese radio, but that he's also written a bunch of English as second language books that have done quite well in the Japanese market. No doubt, the guy's impressive—reasonably attractive in a thin, waspy, toe-headed kind of way. And only three years, rather than my eighteen years, older than Pi.

"I think you know I'm happy for you," I say, "finding someone else. But isn't it kind of tough, with him in Japan. That's still quite a long plane flight isn't it?" I ask.

He explains that, in some ways, it's actually better, especially because, as a "soon to be well known" actor, he has to be discreet.

"Makes it more exciting when we are together," he adds.

As we near his car, the motion detector on the light affixed to a small shed filled with bikes, tubes and lawn stuff senses our presence and two bright floodlights flip on. He takes the opportunity to inspect my face.

"Yeah, you look pretty good," he says, with a tone that seems to be struggling against doubt, as he places two fingers of each hand on either side of my face just where my chinbone meets my earlobes. He then pushes my skin back aggressively enough that my neck and the lower part of my face take on a tautness it hasn't had in years.

While shaking my face loose, I retort, "You mean for my age?"

"Well, not bad," he confirms, with that short, sharp laugh, whether at my inelastic skin or his overgenerous evaluation, I'm not sure. "You've lost some weight, so your cheekbones and chin stand out more. It's good," he says.

"It's the pacing," I say to him, as if in full explanation. He nods in understanding.

I thank him—tentatively—matching the tenor of the compliment. Then, I add, "And, of course, you know that you look great," confirming what he already knows.

"Of course," he responds, again with the laugh, a laugh as knowing as the tone of his voice.

And he does. He looks fantastic. He was cute at seventeen, when I first met him, but now he's cute and handsome in a way that either eludes or would look perverse in a thirty-year-old white guy.

"Here," he says, as he opens a small, elegant black leather travel bag sitting in the back of the rented SUV and removes what looks like a black enamel ring box.

"Nice," I drawl, commenting on the bag.

He ignores me, as he knows that I know that—even if not yet "well known"—he earns a good living.

"Let's go over to the lake," he says, as he begins to cross the small, quiet street separating the cottage from the lakefront, while carrying the ring-sized box.

He seats himself on the edge of a lounge which is on a part of the dock that extends into the gentle chop of the water. The night air indulges like an expensive comforter as I sit on the lounge next to his. Opening the box, he takes out what looks, in the bright moon and starlight, to be a pale, thumb-sized minaret.

Vanity forgotten, he looks me straight in the eyes and says, "It's a statue of the Buddha, made from the Bodhi tree. I'm going to tell you what to do, and if you do what I say, then everything's going to be okay. I know it."

I don't even bother to resist the tears as I turn my head away from him. I can't get away from it, no matter what, and my emotions are always just below the surface. Here Pi is, who's loved me in the past, bringing his love back again for a little bit, and for a little while, to help. It feels both good and bad. Good that he's doing it, and bad that it has to be done.

He's heard me cry over the phone plenty of times lately, so I'm not embarrassed. But I want to help him to help me, so I wipe away the tears and turn my face back to him.

"Hold your right hand out, palm upward," he instructs.

With my thumb still swathed in a home-made tourniquet of torn T-shirt and scotched tape, I do as I'm told. As he holds the miniature Buddha over my outstretched hand, he quietly, almost silently, recites some words, whether in English or not, I can't be certain. He then asks me if I feel it.

"Feel what?" I ask.

"The tingling in your hand. Do you feel it?" he repeats. "You have to believe in the Buddha—the power of the Buddha." I believe enough in him and his concern to say that I do.

"The most important thing is to really believe, and to sit quietly and meditate. I'm going to give you a mantra to repeat three times when you wake in the morning, and before you go to sleep at night. And you should do it while you're holding the Buddha next to your heart. Do it for forty-five days, and if you do it, and do it with the right heart, then at the end of forty-five days, things will change for you, for thc better."

While he writes out the mantra, he turns a face I still love toward the evanescent light of a complementary moon. His eyes seem focused on a distant place as he almost chants,

Na Mo Ta Sa.
Pa Ka Ra Toe.
Ah Ra Ha Toe.
Som Ma Som Put Ta Sa.

I repeat the words, with Pi at my side, three times, and notice as I hadn't before, the tingling emanating from my wounded thumb.

30

HEAVEN, HELL AND THERAPY

On July 15th, I check my cell's voicemail during the intermission of *Hairspray* that I'm attending with Pi and Jeff on the New York City leg of their East Coast tour after their stay at the cottage. I get what I always am looking for whenever I check it, a message from Robert. This time, he doesn't just want to talk or have dinner. Instead, he suggests that he come by later.

I immediately call him back and he agrees to meet me after my planned post-theatre dinner with Pi, a dinner I'm having alone with Pi, Jeff having graciously bowed out so Pi and I can spend some time together. Alone.

Hairspray couldn't have been a better choice to begin the night. It's pure delight, with the rare power to make you almost forget all that is unpleasant. That spirit flows into the dinner with Pi, where we talk with optimism about everything we hadn't yet talked about in our lengthy, long distance calls and our time at the lake. We surprise even ourselves, not with the easy intimacy which had never disappeared, but with the continuing curiosity of even the smallest details, a continuing curiosity borne of our continuing deep affection.

What I used to have with Pi, though, the other kind of intimacy, is now reserved for Robert. As I hold and hug Pi outside the nouvelle French Bistro on 43rd and 9th where we had dinner, I can't help but wonder why Robert has chosen to call this night, of all nights. It's not because of Pi. He doesn't know Pi is in town. It's just too weird. Here I am with Pi and Robert on the same night. Surely, it will be a night to remember. I figure just accept the simple and pure magic and beauty of it. It is owed to me.

Only three days earlier, on July 12th, I had the other side to confront, the ugliness. Another court date. No Max, just Calvin. Lisa was there too. Another extension was granted to complete Florence's report. Though granted, I could tell that Judge Zyzen is getting impatient and that there are not going to be too many more extensions allowed. Max, obviously, knows this too because he schedules a rare meeting at his office for the day after that court appearance. On his agenda, not the tape. I decide not to raise it—it can wait. Instead, we discuss whether to go to trial or to accept a plea. Again, the plea. But this time, indirectly, it seems to me he's letting me know that Zyzen, unlike Judge Aabak, does not appear as ready to accept a plea that doesn't involve jail time.

So much, I guess, for the wisdom of the teacher.

Sitting in his cramped, dingy conference room, which substitutes as a storage closet and which is filled with Max's musky black-man scent, he says to me, "People go to trial for one of two reasons. They're either innocent, or they're prepared to gamble. Innocence, I leave that to God. On the level of us mortals, a decision to gamble can be made for a number of reasons. The plea deal offered can be so heavy-handed that you figure the punishment for a conviction after trial couldn't be that much worse. Or you feel, for whatever reason, that the prosecution is going to have trouble proving its case, and you're prepared to risk it. Here, we have a prosecutor who's just not dealing. So you gotta figure that she, at least, believes that she has a good case. Frankly, though, I'm not so sure. She's too angry, too wrapped up in this. That clouds the vision."

"Of course," he continues, "You also can't discount the pure greed for career advancement. A conviction on as many counts as possible—and she sure has loaded on the counts—added with a jail term—preferably one that is also as long as possible—is a plus in their book. Regardless. Also a plus is that you're not exactly the typical criminal defendant. They get to assuage their consciences, if not show the holy voter, that they're really equal opportunity avengers. But all this can blind someone to the reality of a trial, prompting wishful thinking on their part that it'll be easier than it may well be."

There it is. Though I've always known that that's the way it is, that there are sides, opposing positions, with the State in one corner and me in the other—not to engage in a Socratic dialogue of good and evil or sex and violence but to come out swinging—I just never thought they'd come out swinging, and swinging so hard—at me. She's in charge now, however, calling the shots for the State ever since Aabak disappeared in a puff of smoke a month and a half ago. And I can hear her thoughts ringing in my ears: "If you want to engage in that Socratic dialogue because you think that sending your sorry ass to jail is an overreaction, then try it with a jury. But, though your lawyer may think I'm blinded by my zeal or 'issues,' I know the rules of evidence. They are what are sacred to me—'just the pix, Ma'am. Oops, I mean, just the facts. Well, whatever, I'm ready. Are you?" That's what she's thinking.

Because she can.

Prompted by what's going on in my head, I say out loud "When are we going to see the pictures?" Max needs to see what I've already seen. And, as I need to know what he already knows, I follow that question with another, one I've asked and dropped before, fearful that even talking about it will make it occur. Yet, I quietly ask the next before he answers the first, "How much time is she demanding?"

"Soon," he answers to the first question. And, like every time before, he says to the second, "It ain't going to happen. So let's not even go there. We're going to show them just how wrong that decision is. We're also going to slow this thing down, way down. Among other possible benefits, that might give her time to turn her laser beam of doom on others."

"Not this one," I think. Not her. But Max still seems to have some hope. It's tough for me, though, to know what he really thinks. I feel certain that he sees me as reckless and not predatory. But, if we end up in a trial, just how good will he be in convincing a Manhattan jury what to think. And with even one "Guilty" on those seventeen counts, I know it's the judge, not the jury, who decides on the punishment. And this judge … well, this judge isn't yielding—to Max's charms or anything else. So, considering tactics I had hoped could be ignored, I ask out loud whether there are "clever lawyer-like ways" to get the jury to decide without really deciding.

"There are certain things we can do to get the issue in front of the jury," he answers elliptically. I drop it, still not prepared to face the fact that, reckless or predatory, either may put me in jail. A difference with the same consequence is no difference at all.

He then tells me, as if I didn't know, "She's intending to rely on the pictures to inflame the jurors, to get them to hate you. I don't like stooping to aphorisms, but here, a picture may truly be worth a thousand words." Almost as if in a reverie, he adds, "But there are interesting constitutional issues regarding the pictures…. "

A split second of momentary euphoria, of legal battles won and life preserved based on the highest legal principles. Then he states what I also already know—that the State has the burden of proof in establishing the age of the child in child pornography cases. I can almost hear Rich in my head, 'Fuck the Constitution. Let's talk late-bloomin balls.' But, as I'd already mentioned to Max Rich's advice on the pictures—and as he had looked insulted—I don't raise it again.

Snapping back to the practical, he says, "So if we move forward to trial, we have to decide whether to seek a severance," as if the decision to go to trial has already been made. "That is, a separation into two trials—one dealing with the charges related to the pictures and the other dealing with the charges of the prostitute. Legally, I think we're entitled to such a severance, and I am inclined to request it. I'm not sure this judge will grant it, though, which, of course, may give us grounds for an appeal. But, in any event, I want to think a little bit more about it, and so should you."

Adding my piece, I affirm, "Well, as I said to you before, maybe we should just let the jury see who I am, everything about me. You know, let's show them all the pictures, not just the ten she selected; everything the cops took from my apartment," wanting to believe that there is a difference between a sybarite and a pedophile.

He looks at me and interrupts with eyes alight, "That would be a Max Rosario move. They want a trial about sex? Let's give them sex. See if we can't get those twelve people to confront their own inner demons. And then see how comfortable they are judging others."

He's beginning to sound like Rich and, though I like this warrior instinct, I'm really beginning to wonder whether it's a chimera. Not wanting to confirm that, however, I interrupt by returning to a topic he just brought up and that remains unpleasantly unsettling. "So, what about this judge?" I ask.

"We've just got to deal with him," he replies. "What I know most about him is that he's a political hack. And, unfortunately, he's kind of a dumb political hack."

Apparently sensing my gloom deepen, he adds, "But as I also said to you before, I adapt. I'm just going to put on my political hack hat and deal with him that way. There's always a way of dealing with these guys." He doesn't, however, look too certain.

Though left unsaid, it is clear that a trial has become inevitable—a ferocious prosecutor and a timid judge. No choice but to fight back—unless I'm ready to be totally fucked, the literal meaning of which I don't even want to think about.

My mind wanders, searching for a reed to hold on to. Though I failed once, maybe I should try again—prove I'm no menace. Lisa's strongly in favor, though more for my own psychological well-being than for any benefit it may have on my case. I raise it just before Max looks like he is going to dismiss me.

"Though it may not help, it can't hurt," he responds.

However passive, it is there. Then, for some reason, I ask a stupid question. He arches an eyebrow as if contemplating whether I'm suffering a sudden attack of idiocy.

He decides, however, to simply confirm that, yes, "The more respected the therapist, the better." Then, he dismisses me.

I know why I asked the question. I was looking for a reason not to call that other, perhaps the only other, "'well-respected forensic sex psychiatrist" in the City.

* * * * *

The day following my meeting with Max, with no further excuse, I call. And, in another of those odd pairings, on the same day as the day of theatre with Pi and Jeff, dinner with Pi and an unexpected evening with Robert, I meet the "other" shrink. And, in that meeting, he alludes to a test I can take.

I feign ignorance. But I am sincere in telling him I am looking for therapy, not testing. I am also searching to see if he will put his impeccable credentials behind my normalcy, without the test.

"No," came back the answer, but in many more and far more nuanced words. Well, actually not so nuanced.

After talking with him for the requisite fifty minute hour, I have to believe that any status he has as a therapist rests on whatever expertise he may have on administering, grading, interpreting—or whatever it is he may do with—the pervert test. Because when talking to him and expecting him to respond as a human being, he simply seems flummoxed. Not a bad guy, just kind of out of touch for a sex therapist, strangely lost in his texts and his tests. Easily well into his sixties, he may simply have lost interest.

Whether he knows he can't handle me or just doesn't want to bother, he extols the virtues of his partner in therapy, Madeline Rutkin, and suggests I meet with her. So, I schedule an appointment for Wednesday, July 21st, to meet the partner of the second "well-respected forensic sex psychiatrist" who has failed me.

31

En-Abled

Within minutes of taking to her couch—chair, actually—the type becomes clear. Hip, Upper East Side, never to be matronly and never to be without an opinion firmly expressed. Jewish, of course; with kids, of course.

Being my contemporary, her kids are all likely safely past the age-of-consent. And, even if not, all are surely trained to be savvy enough to be safe from the likes of me. In fact, she'd probably not only happily let me take them to the zoo—though she'd prefer the Met—but would be thrilled if I engaged them in a deep philosophical discussion about homosexuality and rites of passage, followed by a refresher on Jesuitical misconceptions of objective reality.

That's what we're talking about—homosexuality, not objective realities—when she says to me, "I've got a book you should read."

This, in response to my less-than-fully welcome acceptance of unfettered gay liberation. Unlike her partner and the earlier celebrity therapist and, to a lesser degree, Florence, all of whose professional reaction to my rant had been difficult to gauge, Madeline has positively bristled.

"I'm always willing to be convinced otherwise," I say in counter-response.

"Good. Because this book contains a whole, long history about homosexuality that's really a fascinating study, and it may very well change your opinion."

I guess to her, living it ain't as good as reading about it.

"Getting back to you," she continues, "after listening for … what? Forty-five minutes? It's pretty clear to me that unless you're lying, and I can usually tell when someone is, you're no pedophile. But you can certainly be classified as what we call a hebephile, which is someone who is attracted to adolescents."

I remember this discussion and vaguely remember the term from my session with the first celebrity doctor. He had said, "A lot of observation and testing have revealed that a large majority of people are attracted to adolescents. The clinical term for that is …."

She then confirms what doesn't need confirmation for me by adding in so many words, "It's simply a fact that our society doesn't quite know how to deal with this. And, unfortunately, treating adolescents as children doesn't do them any good either."

"Unfortunately?" I could think of a few more potent words than that

Moving to another track I'm not sure I want to be on, she then says, "There was a test years ago of a group of Czech soldiers." Mercifully, she doesn't go into any more detail about the test itself. But she does continue, saying that, "A substantial percentage of those soldiers even appeared to be attracted to those who were clearly underage. Now, you may ask"—without my doing so—"what is clearly underage? All I can tell you is that some countries have pegged the age of consent at fourteen, at least for male-female sex between partners of similar ages or with parental consent. Many make the distinction at the onset of puberty." Then, telling me something I'd known since the time I myself was just past being one, she adds, "That's how Webster's defines 'boy' and 'girl', and it's certainly a clear delineation."

And she certainly has gotten into it in greater detail than either celebrity therapist No. 1 or No. 2. Listening to her, though, I'm not sure that this is helping me. She confirms my feeling in her next breath.

"You can't give up sex. It's an important component in maintaining a healthy mental attitude. Some people with desires similar to yours have simply left the country to travel to places where attitudes are more tolerant."

Yep. I don't need this. Not that I want to deny or squelch my sexuality, but I really don't need any encouragement. If she could give me a pill to magically transform me into desiring only middle-aged women, I wouldn't want it. Yet, at this point in my life, I hardly need someone who sympathizes with my desire to partake of the glories of male youth.

Still curious as to whether any battle against one's desires wouldn't turn into a rout, I ignore her efforts to empower me and ask her, "Is there really any effective therapy to alter the object of one's desires?" quickly adding, so that she doesn't have further ammunition to think I'm just another self-loathing gay man, "You know, in the case where somebody is attracted to children."

With a less than assured look, she says in a tone matching that look, "There's some evidence to suggest that if, during masturbation, one practices consistently to change the subject of their fantasy at a point just before climax, that they can actually reorient their sexual preferences."

For a moment, I'm intrigued. But that moment passes quickly, as I am pretty sure that such a result is as likely as someone switching their preferred high by simply thinking of a cigarette while sucking on a crack pipe.

"I think that particular therapy is especially pointless, however," she continues, "for homosexual men, even homosexual men attracted to teenagers."

Teenagers. Yep, on one thing she's right. Whatever Dr. Abel may say, I'm no pedophile, at least no more so than anyone else with a sexual bone in their body.

Walking out the door of her office a few minutes later for what I know will be the last time, I suddenly realize with regret that we hadn't talked about addiction. Certainly that's something she can't consider mentally healthy. Of course, if the treatment is similar to the other one she described, there probably would have been little point.

Ahhh… but there would have been a point about my getting the name of that book on homosexuality, as I remember another thing I'd forgotten.

Oh, well, I guess I'll just have to keep on living it.

32

Two to Six

"Two to six."

My God.

"That's what she wants you to serve. Two to six years. Which means it would have to be in State prison, not in a City jail." Finally, Max has revealed it. I'm not sure why, after this third or fourth or fifteenth time that I've asked him. But he does and, right now, I wish I hadn't asked.

"Six years of my life," I utter. In prison. Then, the list. Can it be?

Because she can.

"Almost no one spends the full time in jail," he responds as if in comfort, then quickly adds, "Look, let's not even think about it. It's not going to happen. I let people know when it's possible, to prepare them. And I haven't done that with you yet, have I?"

Hasn't he? Okay, I want to believe that. So, I push it away. Go back to where I was before I asked the question. Did I think it would be that much time? Not now. Can't think about it. It's Friday, July 30th. Max, Lisa and I are walking back to his office after another court date which accomplished nothing other than to set another one for September 9th. I've got all of August, my birthday month, to me.

For whatever reason, Zyzen didn't give the same evil eye he had given at the prior court appearance, when his impatience with the delay in delivering Florence's report clearly showed through. Perhaps he's just looking to take the month of August off, too, and couldn't be bothered with trying to hurry things along. Or maybe he knows I'm turning 49 in a week, and doesn't want to appear churlish.

Max, instead, is the churlish one, as he again says of the judge, "It's too bad we got switched. Zyzen is such a hack. With Aabak, this would have been all over by now."

This time, it's Lisa who says, "Okay, enough about the judge. There's nothing we can do about it," virtually throwing back into Max's face what he normally says to us. Though difficult to follow, there's little doubt that his advice has always been right. It's the only advice that makes any sense. As the old proverb goes, "I need the serenity to accept the things I cannot change." Blah, blah, blah.

Already, two changes I thought I'd successfully made have recently become undone. First, I started smoking again—slowly in the beginning, with a cigarette or two bummed from my compliant secretary. Then, after feeling too much like a mooch, buying a pack. Then, not stopping from buying packs.

It is while I am smoking one of those cigarettes at home that I say, "Why not?" to my other addiction, so successfully repressed but for one lapse—not counting Robert's two visits—since December 12th of last year.

I answer the phone even though the Caller ID leaves little doubt that it's coming from a public pay phone. Can he still be calling after all these months? Just over seven, to be precise. And he is. It's Bo.

"Where you been? I been trying to reach you," is about the extent of his wonder after so much time, although he repeats it two or three times.

I don't even bother to express my wonder that he's been so persistent, after what I know, or could have made a reasoned guess, have been scores of failed connections. So I deal with his wonder by saying that I've been, "dealing with shit"—and some equally obscure versions thereof. That's all I need to say to get past that, and on to what each of us want.

It was eight days ago today. One day after Madeline Rutkin, the sex therapist, expresses her concern that I not give up on my sex life. And, seven days after Robert proves to me that I probably never will, Bo adds the coda to that proof. And, maybe, the coda to the proof of the subtle awareness which passes between two people who connect. Without a word said, he seems to sense it is likely to be our final encounter as he engages me in a way he hasn't before, in a way that leaves no doubt as to his willingness—desire—to submit.

No question, with all this time passing, the fear factor has lost a little of its power to the libido factor. Now, though, meditating on "Two to Six" will likely have an affect those books, and the attempts at meditation those books recommend, haven't yet had.

Max's "She's been foaming at the mouth for me to see them" brings me back to the incongruous reality of a warm sunny day in lower Manhattan. At a typical New York pace, we cut across Broadway.

"I'm going, too," Lisa confirms with Max as we reach Vesey Street. "Has the time been set?" she asks.

"No," Max responds. "I'll let you know."

They're talking about the pictures, about going to look at them—all ten, making up ten counts of the indictment.

Bo is in at least ten. But none that make up the indictment, of that I'm sure. I wonder what he'd think if he knew those pictures are now sitting in some private little safe of ADA Antonia Strauss. He'd probably get a kick out of it. Certain as he is of his attributes, first he'd laugh, then he'd smirk offering to let her feast her eyes, knowing that even she wouldn't be able to resist looking.

"As if looking at some pictures is going to make any difference, going to get me to agree to send you to jail," Max says, shaking his head in disbelief at either the ADA's outrage or her innocence or her chutzpah.

Maybe not if they were pictures of Bo, I think. But they're not. They can't be, or we wouldn't be having this conversation.

Well, we'll just have to wait and see, the three of us. And after that, we'll all decide what to think. Now, all I can think about is "Two to Six."

33

THE PICTURES

The time has arrived. The exact time is not set until the late afternoon of the day before. I receive a call from Calvin in Max's office, telling me I should meet Max at his office the next morning, August 4, 2004, at 10:30 a.m., so we can walk together to the ADA's office to view the pictures. The pictures, which have become more important than the original charges. Before the pictures, it was no more than three counts and no time in jail. After the pictures, those three counts morphed into seven and, tacked on with the ten counts of possessing those pictures, are two to six years in State prison.

Wakening early from a fitful sleep, I catch the C train at the same station I go to every weekday morning. But today I travel to the Fourteenth Street station where I transfer to the E train on the same platform. I arrive at the Vesey Street building housing Max's office on edge and thirty minutes before the appointed time.

I stop at a nearby deli for a cruller and a coffee, sharpening that edge, and wait for the seconds to tick by and for Lisa to join me to offer support and perspective of that which only I, the authorities and the participants have previously seen.

I enter Max's office five minutes early and Lisa arrives shortly after, looking ready. We are all subdued as we walk through the heavy August heat, chattering idly and receiving the unnecessary warning from Max that nothing should be said and no reaction given.

Even now, I can't help myself. So I ask again when we'll be able to listen to the tape. I need to know even if it's only to know that I need to remember.

Unsurprisingly, he bristles, but this time only slightly. He states simply that he will inquire. With both of us recognizing the significance of the task we know we have ahead, further discussion of some other task is postponed.

As we approach our destination, I realize with a jolt that the building we are about to enter is the same one where I had been taken that December morning, to spend time pacing in the second cell of that day, and where a viewing of a different sort had taken place—the viewing of me in a lineup, a viewing by those who wanted me punished.

My guts cringe, but I say nothing. Given a visitor badge this time, we step into the stifling, crowded car of the only operative elevator of three.

The elevator door opens and we walk an eerily familiar corridor echoing with the sounds of bureaucrats at work. Max directs us to a waiting area, an area unchanged, it seems, for decades. The chairs we settle into look straight from the Sixties, with curved, oxidized aluminum arms and legs, and faded orange and white—and in some cases, torn—naugahyde seats and backs.

Lisa pegs it perfectly, saying it reminds her of our Catholic grammar school, as I think that there, too, God patrols the corridors, keeping them safe and meting out unforgiving discipline to any of those who stray.

"Robin egg blue" is what Lisa comes up with in describing the untimely color of the paint adorning the cubicles stretched before us, as well as the color of every alternate tile to the dingy white of every other tile of the checkerboard linoleum floor.

It isn't long before she shows up, shaking only Max's hand, ignoring Lisa and me with what must be a practiced indifference. She leads us down a private corridor, then stops, as Max alludes to Lisa's presence.

"Oh, yes," she says vaguely, as she turns to face Max with a look somewhat less vague. Not one to miss a perfect pitch, Max says to Lisa and me, "Give us a minute."

Lisa and I return to the waiting area to wait some more. "Perhaps we'll have to get a court order," I joke lamely after several minutes pass.

Eventually, Max returns, and the three of us walk out into the public corridor. He is uncharacteristically tongue-tied and obscure, as he begins by saying, "The reason we have not yet been shown the pictures is that they are old."

What, pray tell, does the age of the pictures have to do with their not having been shown to us, I wonder.

He pauses for too long, leading me to speculate internally, seizing on the bizarre and extravagant hope that perhaps they are so old, they had disintegrated and are no more.

But that's not it. Whatever it is, it's not good. It's clear from his eyes that he is searching for words which will not alarm me. He shifts and says, "You were right."

Now, even more confused, I wait for an explanation. As he continues, it is clear that the pictures are not too old to see, but that, as I already know, the pictures depict a scene from long ago.

He is saying I was right, because he remembers what I had told him that Saturday morning in December, when I first met him, and what I have repeated to him once or twice since—that of all the boys I have engaged, and of all the pictures I have taken, there is at least one that should not have happened. Though it matters not a wit, only three in the world know just how long ago it has been. And only three in the world know the circumstances of how it happened.

In that era, over twenty years ago, and with nothing quite like it since the days of Giuliani, hustling boys of all shapes, sizes and ages were out, about and abundant.

I had seen those two boys at least twice before I had engaged them. Once, late at night, plying their trade in a car parked alongside the Hudson River. The two were companions and traveled together. So, the one who shouldn't have tagged along and posed with the other for pictures which should long ago have been discarded.

Unique in more than one, life altering way, I remember. With accents unlike all others, how can I forget? Portuguese, I was told. Not from Portugal, but from the one country in that other, more exotic America where Spanish does not overwhelm. Maybe that's why I kept those pictures.

Max starts down the corridor in the opposite direction of where she had first led us, apparently deciding that the pictures will complete and explain his otherwise bewildering story. I follow this new path without further question.

Who were they, in New York for the summer, to visit? … a brother? a cousin? For sure, a relative of some sort living near those Greenwich Village piers. And wasn't it I who first talked of money. In fact, one of them was almost dismissive as I handed it over—as if its value was best revealed in displaying how little value it had.

We arrive at a big wooden door. Max checks the number affixed alongside, hesitates, then opens it. The room we enter is large, well cooled and furnished by chairs, sofa, desk and small conference table of a style and vintage certain not to shame the décor of the waiting area we have just departed.

She is already there, with a large, brown envelope cradled to her breast, looking less severe but no less serious than she has during those multiple court appearances before. In her own element, without the formalities, and about to reveal what she believes to be her ace-high hand, she seems relaxed. Another enters the room; presumably, an intern. Betrayed by his own youthful look, but betraying no emotions, he is introduced only to Max and then takes a seat in the dated sofa older than he.

She sits next to Max, opens the envelope, withdraws the contents of my fate and fumbles.

"I'm not sure which of these are the chargeable pictures," she says, with the evidence in her hand. "I think it is these," as she hands certain of the pictures over to Max. He looks first. Then, in neglect of his own advice, he passes them to me face down, as if in shame or horror at the scenes depicted.

Turning them over, I see not the original Polaroids, but oversized copies, seemingly computer-enhanced to starkly highlight each detail. Otherwise, no surprises—at least, not to me.

Is it ten that she hands us? I don't count to confirm. But the number of boys I'd already known, and any more than the one boy or any one picture of that boy simply adds to the excess—on her part and on mine.

One encounter, unsatisfying in the part and with the one that now counts, from decades before, back to haunt and condemn. No sex acts, for what had we really done? But nudity and, in one, their erections proudly displayed. And, in two others, a youthful me, clothed, but clearly reveling in the nakedness of the one fully ripened, the one with the dark hair and the dark, hooded, expectant eyes—whether teasing or demure, it's impossible to tell—made all the more bewitching by a shy, not-quite-innocent, but still angelic smile, all shown to such dazzling effect in these pictures enhanced by inhuman hands.

But of course, it is not his picture that is clearly condemnable. It is those of the other—a round, pudgy cherub, with vital parts still so flimsy as to be unable to engage even the imagination.

I still remember how I had treated him. Kindly, at least during the time we all shared. Certainly, though, it could not be masked that he was the third wheel—not really wanted, other than as a useless appendage of the one who was. There, only to facilitate. And if he wasn't aware while we played, he was made cruelly so, when a week or two later, he called and asked if he could come to visit again.

"Was the other with him," I had asked?

"No," he had said simply.

I doubt my response back was as brief. But it would have made no difference, because there was no longer any doubt.

If a lesson unkind, was it not also worthwhile? Approaching his own middle age, would he not now agree it is best to learn early that it is beauty that commands, and if you aren't lucky enough to be graced by its blessing, then you will likely suffer more, or at least differently, than one who is?

Now, of course, it is I who am to suffer, to atone for the suffering I may have caused him. So be it. Certain that the one who is most intent on inflicting my suffering would forever fail to fully understand this different yet equally essential violation of another, I imagine myself, with some small satisfaction, preparing an indictment of my own and serving it upon her as I push back those pictures which seemingly so outrage her, but which no doubt empower her beyond any earthly power I will ever attain.

There are a few other pictures in the brown envelope—some, more than likely, included by design. Amidst a few more naked boys of indeterminate age are others, more disturbing, showing scenes of bondage of a type and with "victims" sufficiently youthful as to inflame most anyone's heart. The point or purpose, presumably, to let us know that if given leave by Judge Zyzen, she intends to do exactly that.

Not content to fire only this one additional shot across the bow, she notes to Max that there are "hundreds of others" he is welcome to view.

"And the tape of the conversation?" Max queries, whether to shift the focus or to appease me, I don't know.

"Whenever you like, you can come and listen to it, except not next week, as I will be out on vacation," she replies.

Max, with sincerity too real, commends her for taking time off. She actually almost lightens a bit, smiles a bit and says only to him, "Yeah, I've been working pretty hard and can use it."

We get up. Lisa and I turn and leave, walking past the intern, as I wonder what he had seen, what he knows. He could have been one of the many that I had interviewed for a much better-paying, but far less powerful, position, and for which he would have been duly respectful and appreciative. But not here, not now.

Max shakes their hands and follows us out to the elevator lobby. There, Lisa gives me a reassuring, almost confident look, as if to say—if that's all they have, its not enough—at least not enough to put you in prison.

I had not told Lisa much more about the pictures than what I had told Max. But her imagination of what could have been is apparently more active, or at least more fretful, because she seems relieved, whereas he seems subdued, pensive. No reassuring looks or words from him.

Lisa must sense this, too, because her first words to him after we exit the building and feel free to talk, is would they really send me to jail for this?

He hesitates, again too long.

Frustrated by this, Lisa, even knowing Max has already been told of the affliction and that millions suffer from it, doesn't hesitate to remind him of Rich's "deficient" teen defense.

He straightens himself and brings his large hand to the bridge of his broad nose and says, "Of course—at the right time, I'll do whatever makes the most sense to do."

But it almost doesn't make a difference what comes out of his mouth, as he seems to be adjusting right before our eyes. Lisa and I both know that he doesn't like to lose, that he has a sense of what result is fair and right. But now, perhaps, he is reconsidering what it means to lose, what it means to be right in the circumstances. Perhaps he is again assessing the risk of what he said, and what I would like to forget, after the previous court appearance—of the possibility of "being punched in the face" if we decide to fight.

For me, I had expected to be any one or all of outraged, shamed, panicked or despairing. Instead, at least during the viewing and as I stand now with Max and Lisa, I feel an almost curious detachment.

I remember those pictures. They are a part of my history—a distant, small part, that now looms larger than anything I could possibly have imagined, the unreality of it, perhaps, sustaining my detachment.

Not yet able to come to grip with the fact that—regardless of whether the scenes depicted are forced and trashy, or willing and playful—they are forbidden, as at least one of those who played and posed is a victim, by order of the law, cloaked with a status he cannot refuse and absolved of any choices he made and may have repeated prior to being repeated with me.

Still, I grapple with the final irony that I am the one to be caught in the repetition that matters, the one that is on film, where those who were filmed are not evanescent and obscure nor remote and unobtainable, as in all those movies, videos, books and ads that are known so well and that are seen so often, because they seldom fail to sell.

There, not only the State but many defenders of the virtuous young hesitate in their ferocity, recognizing that they would be forced to convince those who get to judge and decide—the great unwashed masses—that the fetishization of youth and beauty, and the guilty titillation so poorly masked which it provides, may be as repugnant as the act they deplore. Instead, a nauseating hypocrisy pervades—tolerated or ignored because it sustains so much.

Be warned, though, if you dare to remove that which serves to insinuate, if you dare to strip off those briefs, then, even though you may have a reality more pure, it shall pass from the acceptable to the unacceptable, on its way from the guilty thrill of the hypocrite to the criminal reality I now face.

Playful? … Shameful? ….

Either way, a risk—so much at risk.

So, then, "Why?"

Because I could.

Or, so I thought.

With that, there they are—the soiled bookends of that part of my life now so scrutinized. Pictures of one from an evening long ago, and the story of another from a more recent evening, who would adopt those pictures as his own. And, of course, all of my life stories in between, some of which are accompanied by pictures of their own.

With the rawness of the images giving such potency to the imaginings of those who seem to love nothing more than to police those imaginings, it can only be said, "too much." Too much sex, too much youth, too much beauty—too much which would render all those who are uncomfortable with too much, unable to judge anything other than that too much has passed, too much that is unacceptable for me not to pay.

34

The Narrative

"What's the narrative gonna be?" Florence asks.

"Well that makes sense," I say to myself. All pictures need an accompanying story—sometimes to explain, other times to excuse.

I haven't seen or spoken to Florence since April, when she let me know, without ever really saying, that I'd failed the pervert test.

We're together again, face to face, courtesy of Max Rosario, at Max's office on Vesey Street. It's August 25th. Max called this meeting, and then kept us waiting over an hour. At this meeting, we're supposed to decide what to do with Florence's report, the draft of which only I, of the three of us in Max's cramped, stuffy conference room, haven't yet seen.

From Max's characterization of the report, though, I do know that Florence apparently focused on what a good lawyer I am. And what a shame it will be for me to lose my license. For Max, this is a non-issue, as the loss of my license is a given.

How can I not agree? Its clear Max believes that the report needs to be refocused on something it might help to achieve, something like keeping me out of jail.

In a way, the attention in the report on my career makes sense. Other than sleep and the pursuit of "entertainment," work completed the circle of my typical day. I have no wife and kids who will be bereft or impoverished if the State packs me off to prison, nor any worthwhile causes or even hobbies which will suffer in my absence. So what else was Florence to focus on?

All that time and all those letters from all those people, including six who were clients thinking they were recommending me to another possible client. Except for those six, I've read none of those letters, not even mom's. If Florence focused her "narrative" on my job because the letters that most moved her were those from my clients, then I'm not sure I want to read any of the others. I'm not sure if that's being hard on them, or being hard on me. Maybe it's just the impossibility of the task, asked to write to one who is to judge whether someone you care about—and to some of them, care about a lot—is to go to prison for sex crimes.

I don't answer Florence's question, and neither does Max. There is no narrative. She was unable to find any excuse, at least any excuse anyone sitting in judgment would buy. Dangerous predator or reckless sybarite? It's the same. Everyone hates a child molester, especially one that doesn't have an excuse that even a bought-and-paid-for forensic social worker can find. Another test I've failed.

We decide to shelve Florence's report, a report I haven't even yet read but nevertheless know what it will never include.

35

Moving On

Today, October 1st, I move out. Twenty-five years after moving in, my life on Central Park West is coming to an end. And no one's in sight, other than the three guys working for the moving company I've hired.

I do, however, run into one of my three neighbors I've kind of gotten to know over these many years. Not well enough to have ever visited their apartments—other than one of them, once—or them mine. No, just well enough to exchange some pleasantries and, with two of the three, some minimal personal information.

"The Bronx," I tell her, "I'm moving to the Bronx." She looks up and away as if to hide her embarrassment for me, eking out an "Oh." I turn to one of the moving men as if I have something to say to him and she moves on.

Yep, today I'm moving to the Bronx. I've worried that it would be worse—a tenement hard alongside the elevated subway tracks coupled, eventually, with medical insurance offering even less protection, if any at all—homelessness and disease linking arms in a finale fit for the Grand Guignol.

Maybe, though, Nick the astrologer is wrong. Maybe, Tahiti—or someplace in the more exotic America—is in my future. Assuming they let me in. Diseases are ignored in places like that. And who needs shelter in paradise.

There certainly would be a bit of irony if that should happen. Me, hanging out with all those beautiful, tanned, hard-bodied Dominican or Nicaraguan or Costa Rican boys—boys made pliable by being even more impoverished and needy than the country of their birth. That couldn't be what ADA Strauss wants for me. Could it?

After all, what else will there be to do once I'm let loose? If exile it is to be, where better than a candy-land, where the sweets are numerous and too inexpensive to pass up. Who knows? Maybe that's it—maybe subconsciously that's what I really wanted all along. Fuck ADA Strauss. It's me.

For now, though, it's the Bronx. Well, not really the Bronx—Riverdale. To an apartment eerily similar to the one I'm abandoning, but without the memories or the baggage. This one overlooks a tree-bedecked Palisades, rather than Central Park; in a building that is equally ugly, equally institutional-looking.

I gotta admit I am happy, though, that I have a decent place to live. And, with the application package including an authorization for the landlord to check my criminal history, I wasn't sure if I would. But, they took me.

As I stand on my terrace on a gorgeous day, taking in, for the last time, a park and a skyline I had fallen in love with a lifetime ago, I realize that my separation from Manhattan and all it represents is now complete.

Tommy and Bo and all the rest of the boys were given no forwarding address. I'll miss that odd honesty I had with them, an honesty borne of something primal which we were all willing to share.

Robert, too, is gone—to Europe, to dance. Maybe, though, given that it's only for a year, somehow—depending on what's up with my life—we'll keep in touch when he returns. After all, with him at least, it was a good summer. Whether of his own volition or ordained by Nick's stars, I don't know. But there were days and nights together in August. And there was a party I threw at the Lake for the dance troupe he performed with at Jacobs Pillow in Lenox, Massachusetts. I can't believe I got up the energy to do that. But it worked out good.

Greg, coming through once again with his letter to the judge and a sympathetic ear on a few phone calls—most notably after I failed the pervert test—is back with his lover. After twelve years, that's where he belongs.

And then there are the others.

Walter dissolved right away, as soon as there was even a hint of trouble.

Two more followed not long after. They had helped "round out" the list of friends to write that letter to the judge. "Of course, we'll be there for you," both of them had said.

After dutifully writing, each had called once in the last ten months. Once.

The third to "round out" the list remains in touch. I knew he would. He's got that kind of heart—big and open. But, right now, I need a talker … and a thinker … and an arguer—and he's none of those.

Agnes, who had been there when I needed her most on that early Saturday morning long ago, who had found Max, decided the money was more important than I was. Each contact I had with her—however slight or inconsequential—was charged against the retainer I had given her. I stopped calling. And, eventually, I asked her to return the balance of the retainer. With the check, her letter stated in full, "This concludes my legal representation of you in this matter. Good luck with everything."

Lisa, of course, remains. Though she'll never leave Manhattan, she'll also never leave me. Not while I still need her.

* * * * *

While standing outside in the sun in the Bronx, one of the movers, as he finishes unloading the last of the boxes from the truck, asks me about the private school. "What school?" I respond. He points. With a discreet entrance at the other end of the massive building I now call home, I hadn't noticed it before.

Whatever pleasure I had been taking from the beautiful day, time off from work and the unexpectedly pleasant surroundings evaporates, as my stomach churns into an unpleasant queasiness and a weight settles on the top of my eyes. Though I've just arrived, hastily shoved into a corner in the back of my mind, I suspect that it may not be long before I have to leave.

Nothing I can do about it now, I realize, as I hand the movers the cash, including a sizable tip for their services and turn my attention to unpacking.

36

Arguing Lawyers

"When confronted with the fact the boy was fourteen years old, defendant, in substance, responded, 'It doesn't matter.'"

So ends the third paragraph of Antonia Strauss' answer to Max's letter, a letter Max had sent to request that the court "consider mitigating circumstances" that would make "a custodial sentence inappropriate and unreasonably harsh."

Max had filed his letter with the judge the day before the September 9th court date, which resulted in a postponement to today, October 8th, 2004.

No mechanical voice waking me this morning, warning me, my move to the Bronx apparently enough to confuse and win my release, at least from the machines. She's not confused or gone, though, with her reply to Max's letter delivered yesterday to the court and to Max. This causes another postponement. We are to return on October 29th. Dismissed from court, I'm now trying to read and digest her response, to see just why she thinks I should spend up to six years of my life in jail.

Many things she writes jar, and some continue the confusion, but then I read the final paragraph of her response. "In fact, the sentence for each of the counts could legally be run consecutively to one another, resulting in a maximum exposure of 31 to 63 years of incarceration."

My god, in her mind, for what I have done, six years of my life is a bargain.

Even in the bright, warm October sun bathing the sidewalk a few blocks from my office building to which I have escaped to read her second and more personal indictment of me, I feel cold. A wave of nausea seeps more deeply and pervasively into me than can be attributed to the stinking black soot and smoke emanating from the belching bus traveling cross town on 50th Street.

Here I am reading that the stinking black soot and smoke emanates from me. I sit on the utilitarian street furniture usefully set out nearby, and breathe. I give myself ten minutes and read it again, with slightly less clouded comprehension.

In Max's letter, which he had delivered to the court in lieu of Florence's report, he makes it clear that he is not addressing the truth of the charges but, instead, is presenting an argument to keep me out of jail. He notes that I was a hardworking and responsible student and remain so as a professional, citing the letters from Rich and my clients. He also notes that I am a surrogate father to my younger sister, citing Lisa's letter.

That's it.

With nothing left good to say about me, he switches to what's not bad. He points to my lack of criminal history. Then he mentions the "adverse collateral employment consequences" any felony conviction will entail, especially to one licensed at the grace of the State and especially for a felony conviction for a sex crime involving children.

Perhaps believing that to embellish would be to diminish, he writes simply, "The defendant's character and the nature of the crimes charged make the defendant unusually susceptible to prison abuse."

"Prison abuse." Almost three pages of his eight are devoted to "prison abuse." And no where else does he cite legal precedent to make his case.

'In substance,' ADA Strauss responds in an eerie echo, 'It doesn't matter.' No, to her—in her six-page, double-spaced re-indictment—the allegation that I "touched the fourteen-year-old boy's penis and squeezed his buttocks," are reason enough to send me away for a good long time. Regardless.

Of course, though, it's really about the pictures, as she rages that they make it "clear that the defendant has been engaging in acts with boys and young men for many years."

"Young men?"

"Acts?"

Those "acts," I guess, will have to be left to her imagination as, except for two of those pictures in the set of ten that counts, I'm not even in any of the other pictures. Not one.

But, of course, there are the "boys."

"Boys"—a word that I, too, have used carelessly in the past. Now, because I didn't care, she, in her screed to prove how much she does, will surely be given a pass if not a plus for her own careless use.

Were others also 'boys?' None so easily defined or, for sure, the counts in that first indictment would not have stopped at seventeen. If measured, though, by days from birth alone then, in my selection from the mix of beauty offered up in the bars, in the clubs and on the late night streets, I fared no worse than did chance. For they were out there, those 'boys', mingling with the 'men.' And now the bill is presented by a captain with eyes no longer diverted.

With her eyes wide open, she fumes at the "more than 200 Polaroid photographs of naked males;" and of "genitals," especially "genitals" which are "exposed, often in an erect state." Then there's the trove they uncovered containing "a dildo, anal plug, black leather whip, leather straps and handcuffs." Last, but surely not least, is the video, the one shown to the "complaining witness," with its scene of a "young male … tied to a pole, while another male, wearing a mask, masturbated."

With that litany of excess, how could any who judge sort out the what, the where and the why—or the who—of the "issues." To her, handcuffs and straps and phallic gavels are unseemly and degenerate when used as toys in sexual games of pretend. Instead, cheered on by a society intent on denial and suppression and punishment of that which is primally feared, they are to be used as the favored instruments in a deadening, real game to humiliate and degrade.

Sex. And reason. And an objective reality that exists only to vitiate.

Of the one frightening reality more certain than most, she virtually scoffs. It is "simply absurd," she writes that one such as I is "automatically in danger and therefore not a good candidate"—candidate, she calls it—"for incarceration." But not so absurd, apparently, for her not to acknowledge that any risk of "prison abuse" to me can be reduced by "placing defendant in protective custody, if needed."

"Protective custody." Words seen before in newspapers and magazines applied to criminals who are famous or criminals who are despised. Now, chillingly, they are applied to me.

What would it involve? Greater isolation? Greater confinement? How much isolation, or confinement, or "prison abuse" can I take before I'd rather be dead?

Beyond the fear, her words also continue the confusion. There's that "fourteen-year-old" boy's penis, jumbling telephone warnings and teen ages in my mind. What am I not remembering? Did Treat's mother say fourteen, and not sixteen? No. I'm almost as sure as my mind is now capable of being. Perhaps she lied to get me to admit, thinking I'd admit to sixteen, but not fourteen. That makes more sense and, according to the ex-cop on my side, the other side can say almost anything, including threats to extort, in the quest for an admission.

And there's that other strange, short—thirty second—call about my "paying" and about him being "only fourteen." Friends of Treat, Pablo and Lydia before the plan to extort was fully hatched? Who knows? The tape will answer it, though. Then I'll know. The tape that Max hasn't yet bothered to obtain, and which I know better than to raise with him again. "All in good time," he will say, with an incongruous impatience at my impatience. All in good time.

Also, there are details which provide some spur to a mind that can't remember—or has blocked it out—or has melded it all into one.

For one, the videotape. I remember it well. But did I share it? Did Pablo and Treat watch a video with me? I've surely shown videos, but did I with them?

For another, and most important, when did I ever say, "It doesn't matter" in a phone conversation with a trick who supposedly has just told me he's only fourteen? I can't imagine it, so how can I have done it?

But that, according to ADA Strauss' response, is when I said it. In the conversation she and the police recorded which is on that phantom tape.

Again the thought arises, maybe Max should be fired. Maybe I should get somebody who will push this through—who will, at a minimum, get that goddamn tape. Lisa's ready to fire him, backed up by Mom and, in the distance, my brother, the judge. And, of course, for Rich, Max was never good enough.

Then there's Nick, Lisa's astrologer. Lisa had gone to him for her annual "checkup." At the end of her session, she tells me that she asks him if he can check my chart again. He does. And, in a reality too unreal, he stops, looks at her and says, "He's in trouble, isn't he? With the authorities?" Lisa froze, even in the retelling.

"Hmmm," Nick had said, as he looked at the chart again, "It doesn't look good. The only thing that can help is a good lawyer. A really good lawyer."

So we look. How can we not? Though I, frankly, am a somewhat reluctant looker.

One wants $500 just for the consult—I pass him up.

Another, a young woman who reminds me of the ADA. That might not be so bad if she weren't also a bit too green, not seasoned like Max, and certainly not as intuitive. Another pass.

The third is a nice and truly impressive guy. He, however, comes with a big price tag, $525 an hour. No fixed price fee from him. And beyond the 'but' of the money, there was the 'but' of the experience. Too long separated from the downtown criminal defense bar, I decide.

The last lawyer Lisa finds—as, mercifully, she's unaware of Rich's connection to Roy Black—is a seasoned veteran who actually had a case opposite Antonia Strauss. More oddly, he had as his client in that case another lawyer, one who was addicted to surfing the web for pix of the unformed young. The client-lawyer went to jail for three months. And the lawyer who represented him tells Lisa, with no uncertainty, that it's "impossible to deal with Antonia Strauss," that he's "never dealt with a prosecutor quite like her in his thirty-five years as a criminal defense lawyer." The only path to avoid crucifixion, he says, is through the judge.

With this confirmation of Max's words, both Lisa and me feel better that Max hasn't fucked it up, that he hasn't been unavailable to ADA Strauss when he should have been available, or has paid too little heed to her when she wanted his attention.

All these names of all these lawyers Lisa obtains by reaching out not only to friends but, if usefully connected, to college classmates long ago left behind, including one who happens to be an ADA in the Manhattan DA's office and another who happens to be a sex crimes prosecutor in D.C. No stone is left unturned—a whirling dervish. That Tasmanian devil from those cartoons of long ago, spinning wildly to win.

A sister who loves me more than I deserve.

In the end, who knows which lawyer is the right lawyer. But it is clear that there is one, filled with the conviction of a prosecutor, who is not letting up. She wants me in jail, no matter what. And I'll need all the help I can get. Now, though, as before, I just feel in my bones that there is no lawyer quite like Max, no one else to whom I want to entrust my fate.

Only time will tell if he measures up as the "really good lawyer" that the stars demand.

37

TOTAL LUNAR ECLIPSE

October 27, 2004 begins like most other days since December 12th, except for the expectation, as this time it's a hopeful one.

At the office, the Schick matter—for which I will "book" the biggest one-time fee of my career—is wrapping up. Documents are to be completed, and the loan funded, if not today, then certainly tomorrow. So, I focus on another deal for a new client brought to me by an old contact, one I had accepted reluctantly and without pleasure. It's just so odd that I'm getting more new clients and bringing in more fees than I have in any of my previous twenty years at the Firm.

Enduring the new, extended commute, I arrive at the office just before 10 a.m. Emails and voicemails greet my arrival, focusing my attention and forcing me to hurriedly consume my bagel and tea, and ignore the news on *The New York Times* website.

Today is also the scheduled date for a court appearance. This one, a small claims matter I had commenced months before because I was pissed at being charged for a repair by an installer of an expensive window shade at my prior apartment. I shouldn't have bothered. I should have let it go. But I didn't, and now I've got to go to small claims court.

With everything on the Schick matter other than the funding completed, and with good progress on the new deal, I leave the office just before six and head to the court downtown. Once there, I notice that across the street is the criminal court. I can't help but look at it from the third floor window as I wait for the doors of this courtroom, the one in what to me is the aptly-named civil court, to open.

My case is settled in a way that's fine by me. They get nothing, and I get nothing, a result I could only pray for in that other court.

I leave and decide to walk to the nearest subway station for the line that is closest to my new apartment, to determine if it's convenient to take that train to my next court appearance—the one in criminal court, on Friday, two days from today.

Before I get to the station, I decide, instead, to just walk, something I've been doing a lot since December 12th. I head north to SoHo, but first stop at McDonald's.

After eating without any of the mindfulness demanded by those books which now serve as my primary companions—'course how else can you eat a Big Mac meal—I cross Canal Street and turn north up West Broadway. As I pass familiar trendy shops and restaurants, none have any reality other than as backdrops to my obsession.

I reach Houston Street and look up to see if that which filled me with expectation earlier in the day has begun. No evidence of it, however. The total lunar eclipse which I know is to take place tonight, the first lunar eclipse to be seen in New York City since November 8, 2003, has yet to begin.

If that had been the only coincidence, I probably would have ignored it. But there's more. According to some of those who follow the stars and the planets and their impact on our lives, the lunar eclipse tonight presages the beginning of another astrological event of some minor significance—The Grand Quintile—to occur tomorrow, where stars and planets are to align in a certain way that, according to those believers, should not be ignored. But what's eerie, is the claim that it has a direct relationship with November 8, 2003, the day of the far more recognized Harmonic Concordance, and the first day of the beginning of my new life. That which was conceived on the day of the Harmonic Concordance, they say, will be given form or birth on the day of the Grand Quintile.

What does this have to do with me? Am I going crazy? It's just that there have been so many weird coincidences. Of course, isn't seeing those coincidences, in and of itself, a sign of craziness?

So what, I'm crazy. Who cares? It's better to be crazy than to be filled with despair.

In a way, what the stargazers say is already true. My next court appearance is the beginning of the next phase of the process. No disposition with ADA Strauss or the judge has been reached. Unless I want to simply accept going to jail for up to six years of my life, we have no choice but to proceed to a trial. My rebirth.

I continue up into Greenwich Village, figuring that it would be appropriate for the lunar eclipse to commence once we are both in sight of my old haunts, where it all began—the Ninth Circle and Uncle Charlie's.

I reach Christopher and Greenwich. Expectantly, I look up over the gothic spires of the former woman's prison at 10th Street and Sixth Avenue. But it is not to be. Fitting, perhaps, because, of my old haunts, one is now a cheap Italian Trattoria, and the other, an Irish chain restaurant specializing in beer and whiskey. Besides, what kind of good omens ever occur in sight of a prison, even one that's been liberated?

I consider calling Lisa and Leslie. Knowing, however, that my commute will take at least an hour, and succumbing to my addiction to be alone, I walk down fluorescent-lit steps and head towards the train for the Bronx.

* * * * *

Too many stops later to count, and only two stops before the end of the line, I am deposited on the gritty and worn streets where 231st Street intersects Broadway. I cross Broadway under the El to connect to the bus which will carry me to the more rarefied atmosphere of Riverdale. Mercifully, the rancid aroma of spent grease that occasionally wafts from the local Popeye's is nowhere to be savored this evening, perhaps in honor of the moon's performance. Less mercifully, the bus takes a long time to arrive.

When it finally pulls up, I embark and travel up the hill to my apartment. Upon alighting, I notice that the eclipse has begun.

I head toward my new home, not with the intent of ignoring what has begun, but with the intent of dropping off my briefcase and heading back into the chill night air.

In my mailbox, there's an unexpected envelope from my mother. I open it. It contains an article from her local newspaper, entitled "*Beyond the Storm, The Sun Still Shines.*" I read as I ride up in the elevator. The article begins, "Where there is life, there is hope."

As I walk down the hallway and enter my apartment, I continue reading. Then I begin to cry. Again. Lately, it seems it's gotten worse. Or maybe it's just because of the day, a day that teased me with the possibility of hope that this event of supposed cosmic significance now occurring outside will serve as some sort of guide to my own path of understanding. If there's a God, I pray, let him be reflected in something real and in something connected, in a way that I can convince myself is intimate, to me.

I regain my composure and go back outside. The looming presence of the thirty-story behemoth containing the apartment I now inhabit obscures that which is then taking place in the eastern night sky. I head north towards the stone, brick and stucco single-family homes sitting incongruously alongside my building.

On the cusp between that which typifies the City and my life of the last twenty-five years, and that which conjures up the neighborhood of my youth, I look skyward and see the arc of the shadow as it expands, ever so slowly, obscuring the moon. Perhaps never before in my life have I gazed so intently, wanting desperately to become part of a phenomenon of nature bearing hints of the divine and, with that, the possibility of redemption.

Please, God, let this have meaning beyond another example of nature's former mysteries, now dissected in such excruciating, scientific detail as to rob it of its power. Please, God, please let it reclaim its power.

I begin again to cry. It's just not working. Notwithstanding its beauty; notwithstanding any coincidence I want to imbue with significance beyond the ordinary, I fear that it has no power to alter the course of my life.

Still, though, it is beautiful, even awesome. If not the same as a miracle, it, too, can offer some sustenance to the soul. So, I calm myself. Seeing the moon as if for the first time, I stand transfixed while the shadow grows, enthralled in the realization that its cause is the path of the earth crossing in front of the sun and in the observation, however flawed, that the part of the moon not yet obscured seems almost to throb with greater clarity and dimension. Does it take, I wonder, an imagination unhinged to fully absorb the scale of what is occurring and our place within it?

Slowly, but inexorably, the eclipse expands. I feel the need to pass over into the other neighborhood, the one of single-family residences, the one of my youth—to try to recapture if only for a moment, just a little bit of what I have forever lost.

So, I head further north. Like what is happening above, it is unsettling. Near-steps from my building with its 600 apartments housing the city's mosaic mix, is a neighborhood of single souls joined together in family units. The houses are stately, with the warmth and wear and tear of real lives lived within, unlike the manicured perfection of the mansions of nearby suburbs where, it seems, the gifts of nature are transported and cultivated to form unnatural barriers to all who pass. Not here. In fact, some of the homes I now pass lay a grade or two below street level, and can be seen by all. Best of all are the encircling trees—trees which must have existed even before the predecessors to the current residents came and developed, and trees which will likely continue beyond the passing of those residents who now live within their midst.

At one such home, I stop and look up towards the still dense foliage enlivening one of those trees. Through the cloaked vibrancy of autumn leaves at night, the moon peers, itself now fully cloaked in a gauzy filament of shadow and mystery.

Whether in rebellion or warning, the wind increases and the chill seeps into my bones.

I head back to my apartment and shortly after I arrive, Lisa calls. I get to talk about it all, all over again, not just in my own head, but with someone who loves me. Before we hang up, she says to me, "Don't give up hope. It's only the beginning of the birthing process."

But, I think, without faith, how can hope be sustained?

38

"A ... What!?"

Two days after the lunar eclipse, I wake to the news that the Boston Red Sox have won their first World Series since 1918.

It's October 29th and I'm scheduled to go to court. Again.

Transferring at the wrong station, I end up taking the train to the station downtown for which I had searched two nights earlier. Late as a result, Lisa, already at the court, is worried and has left a message on my cell phone which comes to life as I exit the subway. Though I arrive fifteen minutes after the appointed time, nothing has happened. In fact, and not unexpectedly, my lawyer hasn't yet shown up, nor has anyone from his office.

Lisa and I enter the courtroom together. Not having received a call from Max and knowing that he calls in advance of anything of import, I assume this court appearance, too, will pass without significance, notwithstanding the moon and the stars.

In fairly short order, Calvin and an older attorney from Max's office enter and confirm that, as Max is trying a murder case in the Bronx, ADA Strauss has agreed to a postponement.

I half-jokingly ask Calvin if I can leave too.

"No, no," he answers urgently, not appreciating any of the jest. I should've known better. I don't need the sound of urgency.

After three or four other cases are disposed of by the judge, my case is called and I, once again, pass through the gate to the table set aside for the accused, opposite that of the prosecutor. Calvin and some substitute ADA approach.

In the middle of what I expect to be peremptory, Judge Zyzen barks, "A *what*?" One of my lawyers must repeat what he has just said as Zyzen barks, somewhat less loudly, but sounding no less perplexed, "A conference!?"

I look up, confused. The next court appearance, I learn, is for a conference, not to schedule hearings for a trial, as I had expected.

"Yes, judge, a conference," the older, presumably more experienced, of my attorneys repeats, unperturbed. "As the ADA agreed," he adds pointedly, and the substitute ADA says nothing. Faced with the apparent joint position of opposing counsel, Zyzen merely sputters. A date is set, three weeks later –the 19th of November.

Outside the courtroom, my older advocate takes note of the judge's reaction, explaining—not at all well—that the ADA has, "with wrinkled nose," agreed to the conference, the purpose and substance of which are clearly beyond his ability or willingness to explain.

Just as well, I figure. Let Max explain, in his good time and in his own way. I'm in no hurry—one day at a time.

But the one thing I can't forget, I ask about, "So, what's up with the tape? Has anyone listened to it?"

"No, but we will before the conference," he says, continuing, as if in explanation for not yet reviewing this last remaining crucial piece of evidence, "It was just handed over to us at the last hearing." He fails, however to note that the last hearing was almost a month ago, and the tape no more than minutes long.

"Can I go back to the office and listen to it?" I nudge, already knowing the likely answer.

Calvin and the older attorney look at each other as if the ball has just been lobbed to the other. But the older attorney can't escape his seniority, so he takes a swing, saying, "I'm not sure if it is available," suggesting it may be with Max.

Again, just as well. I should probably listen to it with Max at my side.

39

The Conference

Arriving at the courthouse, Lisa happens to be entering as I approach. My insides settle a little as I kiss her and we make small talk about her just-completed trip to Mexico which, but for some lost luggage, had gone well.

Once through the metal detectors, we proceed to the eleventh floor. Both Calvin and Max arrive shortly thereafter—the both of them, and almost on time, clearly not a throw- away court date. My insides start churning again. Solicitations and pleasantries concluded, Max turns to me and says I look awful, and that he could see the tension in me as soon as he rounded the corner from the elevator lobby. I smile weakly and take a few breaths to try to relax. "That's better. You've got to keep your spirits up," he commends.

He then tells us he's made the decision to seek to sever the pornography charges from the prostitution charges.

"This judge, as I've said before, is not on our side. And though I think it would be clearly incorrect from the precedent we've found, he may not grant the motion for severance," he says, adding "But then we'll have grounds for an appeal."

Probably more bad news than good. But, for some reason, I feel pleased that he is considering fighting on, if necessary.

"This is what's going to happen today," he continues. "As you know we have scheduled a conference which will take place at the bench with me, the prosecutor and the judge. We are going to go in there to make our case, essentially work them over to convince them what is the just and right result in this case."

He makes a few faint jabs in the air, as if in a fight, then flashes that half-smile full of empathy and warmth which he uses to try to relax the un-relaxable.

"She is still insisting on a prison term of two-to-six years," he adds to make sure that I do not underestimate the difficulties. "So, today, we're talking to him and leaving her out. We'll make some proposals."

I'm about to toss out some of my own when he drops the bombshell.

"For example, if there were to be a custodial sentence, rather than at State prison, it could be at...," without hearing the name of the place that isn't a State prison, but where I could be jailed.

How can this be? Us, talking about jail time. It has been Max who has said to me at various times and in various ways, "You don't want to go to jail." "Let's not think about jail time." "It's not going to happen." "It doesn't make any sense." "If jail were likely, I would let you know, to prepare you." How many times and in how many different ways, did he say it? Four? Five? A dozen?

So, then, he's preparing me? Why now? Why here?

He has stopped. He sees that he has lost me and he waits for me to return. I look up.

"Listen," he says, "Nothing has even been offered, let alone decided. But possibilities have to be explored, if for no other reason than to get a handle on exactly where this judge is coming from. I'm just saying that I want to let them know that if we were even to consider incarceration, State prison is out. The facility I'm proposing is a medical unit at Rikers. It's safe, secure and supervised, and it's in the City—so I'll be able to check on you." He pauses, looks above my head and continues, "Also, you may not know, but some sentences involve weekends only."

My head shakes back and forth. I force it to stop. As if in reassurance, he adds that we will decide together on whether to accept any offer.

"How much time," I force out.

"I don't know. Let me see how it goes with them. Six months—no way a year."

Again, he reminds, "This is a process," as he ushers us into the courtroom, continuing to talk, with what I know I've heard before, as if in a stream of consciousness.

As part of that stream, I watch Lisa listen as he says once again, "All who come through this, whatever the outcome, are disgusted by the amount of time it takes."

So what? I'd rather be entering the courtroom once again than entering a jail cell. Let it take as much time as possible, I think.

Lisa and I take seats directly behind Max and Calvin. She puts her hand on mine, whispering in my ear to remind me to take it one day at a time. That nothing is yet decided.

Jail. It can't be. Not for what I've done. Not for one like me. In all this time, Max hasn't warned, and he said he would. If there were hints, they don't count. Not for this. He so made it seem as if it were impossible. No longer. It's now on the table to be discussed. With that, does it not become inexorable?

Judge Zyzen appears. Cases are called and defendants charged, most escorted in handcuffs from the locked door behind and to the left of the bench. Handcuffs and locks that now loom larger.

A clerk calls my name, but he is off to the side and is not the regular clerk. When Max goes up, he is told that my prosecutor has not yet arrived. How incongruously courteous, I think—to let him know. And how unnecessary, it turns out, as it isn't five minutes before she is circling the files, piled thick, on her table.

My name is called, so those lawyers whose names are not called approach the bench. One of them, intent on trying to put the one who's not to be heard in context—to humanize, familiarize, "put flesh on my bones." The other, to prosecute, and imprison.

Strain as I might, I can hear nothing. But I can see. It is Max's show. Fingers extended to point beyond; hand into hand to confirm what all should know; and arms outstretched to unite in compassion, if not understanding. A virtuoso in body language—combined, I am sure—with passionate and heart-felt words.

But the body language of the others is equally telling. Her eyes cast down, towards her notes, lips pursed, face grim and tight, and with her head in virtually constant motion, from left to right. More discouraging, his—the judge's—head moves in tandem with hers. Occasionally, though, he pauses, removes his glasses, and leans back in his chair. During those moments, she musters and takes the stage, likely unleashing her most devastating arguments about my serial predation, so as to harness him, bring him back to the fold, undermine whatever strength he might then be summoning to make an independent or compassionate judgment.

Twice during the several-minute discussion of my fate, he summons the courage, or curiosity or compassion or whatever, to glance my way, but he does not look into my eyes. For if he did, I am prepared to look back. What harm, I figure. I'm not sure if my eyes would show fear, defiance, supplication, penitence, confusion—or even emptiness. Most likely, a combination—but for sure, some link to our common humanity. Perhaps that is what prevents him. To punish frightfully by locking one away in a place you know—for that one, at least—is likely to be an inferno, can only be done when there is no common link; can only be done to the evil, the corrupt or the dead. Or, worse, can only bc done by one who is himself evil, corrupt or dead.

The show ends. We're told to return on December 2nd.

In the corridor, Max confirms what the bodies have already conveyed. Whether for my benefit, or borne of a distress made no less raw from twenty years of criminal practice, he briefly rails against a system where judgment and punishment are wedded to process and rules, a system that is unable—if not outright hostile—to fashion what may be a better, more humane result.

"The problem," he acknowledges, "is that better results are irrelevant to almost all, when one is charged with sex crimes against children, because no one is prepared to consider any facts or circumstances, other than those conclusively proving absolute innocence."

"Children"—the word echoes as never before.

"To look deeper is to risk having to look deeper into oneself," he continues. "It is tough enough to do it with sex, but it is virtually impossible to do it with sex involving a minor. The prosecutor is firmly with the vast majority of people in the way she is dealing with this."

Because she should.

"But what about the judge" I think? What about his plan to circumvent her by appealing directly to him? Max has stopped and is uncharacteristically pensive, so I pose the question.

Standing in the hallway, he repeats what he has said before, but which now has far more devastating force—"A political hack," adding, unnecessarily, "He's just too afraid."

Giving text to the few times the judge paused and pondered, only to be set upon by the prosecutor, Max tells us that whenever his argument for a less draconian punishment seemed to be getting a more sympathetic hearing, she would say, "Just let me show you the pictures."

"I wish she would," Max adds, "just so we could get past that."

Incongruously, Lisa asks, "And the list?"

"He is on it, no matter what," Max dismisses without a pause.

Facing jail, I long ago accepted the list.

"What about probation?" I ask, hopefully raising something that hasn't really been discussed since before my indictment.

"We talked about it," Max says. Then touching my arm, as if in jest—but only half-so—he adds, "You'd be on probation for life." Continuing, he says "She's inconsistent on it, saying first she's dead set against anything other than jail, and then saying it'd have to be a very long probationary period."

"But look," he says, half-hopeful himself, "Even if it were a long probation, first, who do you think the probation officer is going to focus on? You, or Mr. Jellyjams over there?" pointing to a young black guy in street clothes sitting on a bench and eating a sandwich who, for all any of us know, could be an officer of the court in good standing.

"Second, in no time you'll just be phoning in. And third, you can get a release from probation."

He doesn't have to convince me that probation is better than prison.

He then says, "No matter, I'm just going to continue to work at it, to let them see that they are dealing with a real person, not some bum or beast, and that you've got a real lawyer," adding as if in afterthought, "Besides, if we can't work it out with this judge and we have to go to trial, it could well be a different judge who tries the case."

A ray of true hope. "A different judge?" I interrupt, to get confirmation.

He nods and continues his thought. "And I imagine that the new judge would ask why we are all here, why this hasn't been settled. So we may well have another chance," he finishes.

I ask the obvious. "Is a different judge likely to be better?"

"He can't be any worse," is the reply.

For the second time this morning, bad news that for some reason makes me feel better.

"Look, I've got another appointment I've got to go to," he says just as the word "tape" escapes from my lips, confirming that he hasn't yet listened to it. He does, however, add, "I'll give you a call to arrange a time for you to come and listen to the tape with me." Without hesitating for questions, he looks directly into my eyes and says, "You have to get strong. You have to strengthen your spirit. Quit smoking, this time for good, and quit drinking beer."

"Wine," I rejoin, grateful for the concern and the change in the topic.

"A decision cannot be made if you feel broken," he continues, "because then—no matter what—it will be the wrong decision. Now go do what you were planning to do today. And, buck up."

"What's supposed to happen on the next court date?" I ask.

"Our ADA is supposed to complete an assignment. One I know she'll fail," Max concludes at the same time that he's heading off to his "other appointment." So, neither Lisa nor I get to ask what the hell that means. Instead, we just look at each other, but say nothing.

"What difference does it make," I think.

Calvin accompanies Lisa and me as we walk down the courthouse steps. At the bottom of the steps for the second time that day, I see members of the Falun Gong, meditating, while displaying their pictures of torture and abuse in China.

I ask Calvin if he has ever meditated. He says that he did in college, several years earlier.

"Often people turn to meditation and spirituality in times of trauma," I remark.

"It wasn't like that for me," he says. But as we continue to talk, he corrects himself, recalling that, in fact, he became interested in meditation after two friends of his died violently. One of them by suicide. "He seemed Okay the last time I saw him—which was only a day or two before," Calvin says. "There was some sort of trigger. And it was over." He tells us his friend was found with a briefcase, containing only a Bible and some pot.

40

Because She Can

On Thanksgiving, I have dinner with Lisa, Leslie and a friend of theirs at a small country-style restaurant in the Village. The week before that, William treats me to the theatre with tickets to Le Cage Aux Folles. In turn, I treat him to dinner and the information which, up until then, I had been unable to share with any other than Lisa—that the prosecutor wants me to serve two to six years in State prison.

Today, December 2nd, it's another morning in court. This morning, from what Max told us at the last court date—the day of the conference—is the prosecutor's day, the day for her to turn in the results of the "test" Max mysteriously referred to and never explained. Except to say he knew she would fail. As for the tape? Well, I couldn't be bothered to push it. And Max never called.

Other than court officers and clerks, and a couple of stray lawyers in the front row, the courtroom is empty when Lisa, Leslie and I enter. Lisa had seen Max in the lobby, so I know that he's in the building. As usual, he'll show up when he has to.

Unlike almost all my other court dates, time passes with very little activity, and no one seems to care. About forty minutes after my scheduled appearance of 9:30 a.m., the judge walks casually into the courtroom, seemingly content simply to socialize with anyone but us.

The three of us stiffen. After a few minutes, Lisa leans over, saying it reminds her of when Monsignor Boticelli would enter the classroom in our Catholic grammar school. They do kind of look alike. With his broad, fleshy, mottled nose, drooping eyelids and incipient jowls already well-veined, Judge Zyzen has a face only a cartoonist could love. But, unlike Judge Zyzen, Monsignor Boticelli could only scold, call you a sinner and send you to hell after you're already dead.

This time, I make no attempt to catch his eye. It seems both pointless and unnecessarily challenging. Whatever boldness I had is gone.

As he chats with the attorneys and court personnel, passing within feet of one whose freedom he is to decide, I think to myself what can possibly be going on in this person's mind. Does he just do it so often that certain types of people do not exist for him? Does he think his presence in this setting, with my fate in his hands, does not disturb? Or is it the opposite? Is he flaunting his power and trying to intimidate?

Within less than ten minutes, Antonia Strauss strides in with enough purpose to look neither left nor right, as she heads straight to her table laden with folders—one of them, perhaps, containing the test, complete and ready to be turned in.

Max's continuing absence now makes me feel stripped naked. With Lisa and Leslie clearly feeling the same, it's decided that I should leave the courtroom and call his cell.

With task complete, I re-enter and re-take my seat. Just before Max finally enters, the judge takes his seat, seemingly unconcerned with the hour delay. Confirming that the few others in the courtroom are either wandering voyeurs or destined to come later on the calendar, my case is immediately called.

Max and I pass through the gate and he and she approach the bench. They begin. From the gestures and occasional words heard over the din of the inconsequential babble of the court officers standing behind me, oblivious to my straining ear, it is clear that she is giving no ground.

At one point, I hear her say that if Max's arguments were accepted, then "No one would go to jail." At another, she complains that Max "doesn't even return my calls," as if giving further sanction to her disdain for my life, a disdain so in evidence by her pursed lips, narrow eyes and strenuous shakes of her curly locks, which are not nearly as locked into place as her unchangeable mind.

Listening intently, or trying to, I can hear that the discussion turns not to whether but to where, I should be incarcerated, if I were to accept a plea. Then, from what I can tell, it turns to the risk I would face in State prison—Max's "ace in the hole" in that letter the prosecutor dismissed with her own "it doesn't matter."

My stomach settles lower. A phone is requested. One is moved from the desk of the clerk to that of the judge. The lawyers and the judge consult. The judge dials a number, talks some, hangs up, and then dials another number. He mentions a name into the mouthpiece and asks, "Is he available?"

The following fifteen minutes or so are spent waiting, waiting for whoever is attached to the name I didn't hear. Or don't remember even if I did hear. Presumably, it's the name of someone with authority to assure the judge that it's okay to send me to jail. That's what it must be.

It's then that I realize that this was the prosecutor's test, her test, to prove I'd be safe. A test Max said she'd surely fail. And either she had, or she'd handed in an incomplete or Max wants to prove her wrong. And the judge, now, is seeking his own answers, apparently not willing to rely on hers alone, or feeling the need for his own absolution before sending me to hell. The silence is broken by the judge's voice. But I cannot hear his words. He talks to the one on the other end of the line, for maybe a minute. "Thanks," the judge says, and hangs up.

Has he found one to give him assurances? Has he been told that, of course, the prisons of the State of New York are safe for all who pass through their steel doors, to serve whatever sentence the court hands down, for whatever crime that person has committed?

What else would one with such authority say?

It's over.

Because she can.

… should.

….

It's over.

41

The Heart Stops Reluctantly

Somehow—numb—I make it back to the office. With tasks to complete and calls to return, I find myself for the next few hours able to function in a world apart, so very far apart, from that which I have just left.

With almost no sense of it, the day winds down. My thoughts turn wholly to my other world, just beyond my office door. In parting this morning after being directed to return January 4th to schedule hearings for the trial, Max had said I should not worry, that worrying is his job, his burden to bear—and that he will guide us through.

Having just spent the latter part of the day doing the same for others, but for matters inconsequential, I redirect that focus to my life, to matters beyond my imagination.

How is it possible to come to any answer when confronted with the unimaginable?

My thoughts return to those I've had before and hinted at to others. Now, though, now I really wonder if I can bear it any longer.

I need, somehow, to take charge. First, I need some further guidance—or some further understanding—of what may await. I think of the only sources readily available.

* * * * *

Barnes and Noble is crowded with holiday shoppers as I look for the section dedicated to stories of prison life.

The first book I select, absentmindedly, tells of an early twentieth century barbarian who raped, pillaged and murdered his way throughout the southern states, acts not only continued, but ingrained, during his time behind bars. Unsettling, but I tell myself it's of an almost ancient, uncivilized time. It must be—it has to be.

The next book I grab is the story of a now-famous musician and his early, dissolute life. By chance, the book opens to a page where he describes the cockroaches crossing the small, filthy floor of his cell as one of the few joys he had while in jail, because they offered company, and a diversion from the deadening monotony and intermittent violence he otherwise experienced.

Unknowable. Locked in.

He writes that he keeps his prison-issued shoes in his closet at home to remind him of a place he "never, ever, ever, ever" wants to visit again.

Even after, an indelible stain.

From months ago, when discussing the options, "You don't want to go to jail," was what he had said. An outcome now seemingly ordained. What other option can there be? Is another now less unimaginable than that which I now face?

There would be no more trees .... Not even a window to view them from.

It's over.

I gotta come to peace with what I decide—a decision I've hinted at to others I love that I could accept, trying to give them that peace I now need for myself by telling them "No matter what happens, I will have accepted it." Did I mean it? "No matter what?"

With movement and thought made awkward by a growing separation, with the decision in the beginnings of being made, I head toward the medical section.

Looking blankly at first, eventually I focus. Then I find it, briefly thumb through it looking less blankly, and then purchase it—a book I've heard about, called *Final Exit*.

Outside, under the street light in the cold, I open the book and look again. I begin to read.

Reading, I realize there's all sorts of options once a decision has been made. Reading more carefully, I discover that the best way, absent a sufficient quantity of recommended drugs, requires only sleeping pills, a painter's mask, an ice pack or cold compress, a 19 inch by 23 inch oven bag and a large rubber band.

I begin to shake but I continue to stand in the cold, reading some more. I walk back and forth and then I walk on.

* * * * *

With the pills prescribed by a doctor's visit from months before and with less than $20 spent at a nearby Duane Reade and Gristede's, I have all that I need. With another $20 spent, I purchase a favorite bottle of wine.

What else is there to do?

"Abuse." An abuser. A white hot flame....

Just do it.

As I ride what seems to be an empty subway back home, my mind doesn't stop working, and it focuses again.

None of the many words I've read, none of the spiritual mind tricks I've tried, none of the ad-nauseum conversations I've had offer any refuge sufficient to keep me on a path so seemingly bleak. What else can be said or done that has not already been hollowed by repetition and proven barren with no deliverance.

I have no one that I love, or that loves me, as much as life itself.

Other than my mother. As close as I've gotten to unconditional love.

All, other than my mother, will mend with the help of others they love more dearly, and as they turn to face the challenges of their own life. Only for my mother will it tear a hole in her heart. But can it be much worse than a thousand slices, slowly inflicted, as a son she has borne, raised and loved is taken apart, first mentally and spiritually, then taken from her physically, to suffer the unknowable.

And, of the others?

Pi—a world away, who's last words to me, when I told him I wasn't prepared to flee, were that I had to be strong.

Robert is only a dream.

William's anguish is visible, as much for my pain as for his realization that there is nothing he can do or say to relieve it.

My brothers, I know, will be shattered, as I would if I lost one of them.

My father might cry a heartfelt tear for a heartfelt minute, and then return to an existence absorbed in nothingness.

Other than my mother, my sister will suffer the most. And my act will be most cruel to her, for all she has done to prevent it. I pray that with Leslie, who has grown to love me too, they will actually grow closer in their shared grief and a need to shape a remembrance, untainted by the bitterness it deserves.

All the others, who I thought were good friends and good people, have now disappeared or failed to connect to my soul.

* * * * *

At home but two minutes the phone rings. I ignore it. Instead, I dampen and toss two washcloths into the refrigerator. It stops ringing, then rings again. I pick it up.

It's Rich.

He knows I had a court date today and wants to hear the results. Surprisingly composed, I give him the truth in all its unvarnished ugliness.

There's a moment of silence before he swings the discussion to tactics and strategies and questions that need to be answered.

I'm tired and barely engaged. Even honed as they are with the razor edge of his sharp intellect, we both know that his arguments are hollow when a judge will not listen and a jury, with sex as its subject, is unlikely to reason. So, after a minute or two, he says, "Jim, I know that in the end, the system will realize you are a good person and that everything will be okay. You have to stay strong and believe that."

I say nothing, feel nothing. Why did I answer.

"How are you holding up?" he asks.

I can't help it as I swallow a sob, silently I hope, for if I weaken too much and he senses it, he will get me to reveal more than I want. Of one thing I am committed, to keep my options open without interference from anyone.

He offers more words to strengthen me. Summoning some strength, I tell him I'm fine, that I am prepared for anything, and, using those words again, I tell him that whatever may happen, he should know that I have accepted it openly and willingly.

Though I've said it before, I realize in these circumstances, that I've said too much.

"You're not thinking of doing anything stupid, are you?" he demands.

"No, no, no," I say, again with the conviction of one committed to decide his own fate.

"Because I just won't permit it. I want you around so we can see each other grow old. And so you can see my kids grow up, breathe the air and enjoy life, which will happen when this is all over. And it will be over."

A long, subdued "Shhhhh" unfolds from deep within me. "Shhhh…," I repeat, feeling some relief myself which gives me the strength to say, "Everything's okay. Don't worry."

"What are you going to do now?" he asks, with a plea in his voice. "Call Lisa," I lie, knowing its likely affect.

I can almost feel his relief, living as he does for the love of blood ties and, with all that I've told him before, knowing Lisa does too. Calmed, he promises to call again soon. We hang up.

I read again Chapter 22 of *Final Exit*, entitled simply "*Self Deliverance Using a Plastic Bag.*" Knowing that I want to organize my papers for those I leave behind, but knowing also that I want to acclimate, I figure I'll just begin the process.

So, I open the box with the masks and the box with the plastic bags. Then, I retrieve the remaining Valium and Ambien from my bathroom cabinet of somewhat over twenty pills in all, about equally divided between the two.

It's approaching 9:00 p.m.

I slip the rubber band around my neck, and then remove it.

I sit.

I need to speak to my mother. I need to let her know I love her. That much I have to do for her. And, I'm calmer now. I'll be able to handle it. So I call.

She answers. Her voice is quiet, almost disembodied, as if the separation has already begun.

We make small talk as she tells me that Lisa has informed her of what has happened in court. Whether Lisa has put a positive spin or whether my mother does not want to show me her alarm so as not to further unsettle me, I cannot tell.

It's enough.

As always with her at the end of a call, but hearing it differently, she tells me she loves me. Less common for me, but now given in more than simple fulfillment of a purpose, I, too, tell her I love her. Then, as if in reassurance, I promise to keep her informed.

We hang up.

Can that be it? Are my last words with her to be so ... ordinary?

I sit quietly, again, for some more moments. To come back, I actually shake myself a bit. I look for a pad. I need to do more. I write a note. I read it again. I speak of her strength and ask her to seek relief from her grief by filling herself with the love of others around her and to remember the good times, though noting they were "all-too-few." Finally, I tell her to hold no bitterness. "With all that has happened," I write, with some belief in what I am writing, "It's as if I'm being beckoned to the other side. So I go, expecting welcome and then peace, something I know I will not find if I were to remain."

What more can I say?

I breathe deeply to find the strength to continue. I go to my personal files stored on shelves in my bedroom closet and quickly locate the statement of my three accounts and the folder with the Deed and other important papers for the cottage in Connecticut, as well as tax information and my monthly bills.

I write down the necessary information to access the accounts. I also write down my desire to be cremated, with my ashes spread at the lake. Completing that, I realize that I have not yet located my Will, the most important document, which I know I had signed in 1989, leaving everything to my mother.

Searching, I find the folder for the Will, but without the Will inside. I know I cannot do this, have everything organized, but no proper method for everything to be disposed. "It can't happen this way," my heart virtually screams out. It has to be as neat and tidy as Chapter 22 promises the end can be.

Vaguely, I recall having had the Will, at least at some point, in my office. I can even remember where on my credenza I had last seen it. It can't be. It must be here. I pull all the files off the shelves and rifle through them feverishly. Too feverishly, I realize. I'm not seeing anything. Going through more slowly a second time, I find it. It's alongside warranties and bills for merchandise purchased long ago. Simply misfiled or not, it doesn't matter. I have found it and there is nothing else to distract.

Other than the rubber band, which I again place around my neck, I put all the required aids near the chair where I intend to sit, as Chapter 22 recommends sitting, not lying down.

The pointlessness, if not the un-endurability, of continuing on any path other than the one I've now chosen envelops me.

I retrieve the note I've written my mother and seal it in an envelope, then place it on top of the files I have assembled. I take a seat on the couch, look out at the darkened hills of the Palisades and begin to cry, knowing that the tears I shed, she will share, when faced with what little is left. And then I cry more tears at the pitifully small words, lacking in any inspiration or grandeur, almost as if in mockery of my life and its events. So full of … nothing.

I sit quietly, again, calming myself. With that, the inevitability of what is to come returns.

I get up from the couch and move to the chair surrounded by all that I will need. I empty the contents of the bottle of Valium and Ambien on the small, nearby table. As instructed by Chapter 22, I first perform a test. I check the bag for holes, then don the painter's mask which is supposed to prevent the bag from being sucked into the mouth and nostrils. I then slip the bag over my head and tuck it under the rubber band and sit for a minute, as instructed, before removing the bag. With the test complete, I put on a baseball cap to prevent the plastic from matting against my forehead and eyes.

I finger the pills, silently asking God or whatever source that gives us life and death to take me quietly and quickly, to bar intercession. Realizing I've forgotten the cold compresses to be pressed against the back of the neck as an antidote to the heat of the bag, I get up to retrieve them. The movement upends the small table on which I have placed the pills and the tumbler, with a sip or two of wine remaining in it. Nothing is broken, but a few of the pills are dissolved by the spilt wine. I put right the table and place the remaining pills on top, wipe up the mess and refill the tumbler.

No more time to waste. Holding the washcloths chilled by the refrigerator, I retrieve first the mask and then the plastic bag, where they lay on the couch. I pick up one or two pills at a time and flush them down with the wine. Finishing them and with the cap and rubber band already in place, I cover my nose and mouth with the painter's mask and slip the bag over my head, securing it under the rubber band but continuing to stretch it just a bit with my fingers, allowing air to enter until I am ready.

Despite all of the months of pleadings and prayers and attempts to surrender all and let go here on Earth, I see no visions or signs, I get no sense of peace or union with that which must connect and course throughout us all. But it is separation and bleakness which is driving me, and it is that to which I surrender.

I remove my fingers and the bag settles securely against my neck. I press one of the washcloths to the back of my neck to try to cool my head, as my face, locked inside the plastic, dampens with the heat and moisture.

I feel my heart in my chest slowing down, pumping harder, as the changed quality of the air being sucked into my lungs invades, then imbues, the life blood flowing through me.

Now, no longer life's blood, but a blood sapping life.

Time passes. How much, I can't tell. It has to have been less than minutes. The pounding inside my chest and head continues to slow and thicken. I feel the separation and wonder, even if I should survive, has my brain already been corroded? With that thought, my mind's eye sears white, quickly punctuated by small black circles, evenly spaced, which explode into an expansive darkness.

"Not yet ready," my brain screams, as I again slip my fingers under the rubber band to pull the bag from my neck so that fresh air can enter, telling myself in some deep, not fully conscious spot that all I need is the fortitude of another glass of wine.

I try to get up—but barely able to rise, let alone walk—I fall.

42

The Aftermath

How to explain the unexplainable? Only with words that are inadequate. Then it passes.

I don't know if I woke up on Friday or not. Is it in a dream that I see myself walking to the nearby drugstore, buying over-the-counter sleeping pills—and trying again? Did I fail twice? I don't know.

I do know that when consciousness fully returns on Saturday morning, I am on my bed. Getting up, I tentatively walk into the living room. There, confronted with the proof of its reality, I remember what I might also have thought was otherwise a dream. I had fallen on the rattan coffee table with its glass top that now lay shattered on the floor, alongside the broken body of the table.

The rest also comes back. I had crawled into the kitchen and remember the struggle of that effort, but not the reason why. Is it to get more wine, even as I know I have no strength, other than to crawl? Even as I know that consciousness is slipping away?

And what of the fear? The fear I thought I had dispelled, until it comes roaring back in those final few moments as I pulled the plastic bag away. Is it not fear that I feel as I crawl into the kitchen? Do I not remember wanting to wake, as I sank ever-deeper? Is that not why the sturdy glass front of the oven also lay shattered on the kitchen floor? Is that not why I am able to make it to my bed with almost no recollection of how? Is that not why the blood drawn from all that shattered glass has caused no more harm than a red stain of blood on my blue oxford shirt?

I don't know. And now, it has passed. A weekend, too, has passed. And no one has missed me.

It's Monday morning. With a commute given clarity by a heightened awareness and by time slowed to a harmonic rhythm, I am back in my office. I sit, wondering. Have I failed? Or have I yet to understand how to measure success.

43

THE CALL—ON TAPE

"Det:	Today's date is November 13, 2003. The time now is 23:57 hours. This is Detective James A. Dropt, Shield ****, Vice Enforcement Division, Sexual Exploitation of Children Squad. This recording is being made on Panasonic Recorder 94777 on a non-serialized audio cassette tape. It is being made in connection with an ongoing investigation of a male-white, uh, uh… in connection with a, uh, sodomy case. Uh, uh, this will be a recording of a telephone call from New York City Police telephone number 212-741-**** to the subject's telephone number of 212-662-****. Uh, the person placing this phone call will be a complainant witness, uh, age, uh, 14. Uh, complainant witness, for voice identification, just state your first name and date of birth.
C/W:	James W*****, December 29, 1988.

Det: Uh, James, uh, do I have your permission to record a telephone conversation between yourself and, uh, a previously-named subject?

C/W: Yes.

Det: At this time, I'm going to pause the recorder, attach it to the phone line, uh, prior to James placing the phone call, uh, I will activate the recorder.

(Dial tone, dialing sounds, ringing.)

S: Hello?

C/W: Hello?

S: Hello.

C/W: This is James, you remember me?

S: James?

C/W: Yeah, remember you picked me and my friend up?

S: You and your friend?

C/W: Yeah, remember we came to your house?

S: Downtown I picked you up?

C/W: Yeah.

S: Uh-huh.

C/W:	Yeah, well, we came to your house. You don't remember?
S:	Eh-hum, how, how long ago?
C/W:	It was like Friday.
S:	Friday?
C/W:	Yeah.
S:	Oh, so just recently?
C/W:	Yeah.
S:	Less than a week.
C/W:	Yeah…
S:	Uh-huh.
C/W:	You came and picked me and my friend up.
S:	Ok, yeah…
C/W:	So you remember?
S:	Yeah, now I remember, yeah.
C/W:	Uh, so what you doing?
S:	Haha, I'm just getting ready to go to bed. It's midnight.
C/W:	You getting ready to go to bed?
S:	Yeah.
C/W:	So, do you want to come pick me up?
S:	Downtown?
C/W:	Yeah.

S:	No. No, no, no. I'm too tired.
C/W:	Oh, you're too tired?
S:	Yeah, yeah. I'm just about ready to brush my teeth and go to sleep.
C/W:	Oh, you're about to go to sleep? Oh, that's bad. So when can you come pick me up?
S:	When?
C/W:	Yeah, I need some more money.
S:	Oh, ho, ho. Well, you're downtown now, right?
C/W:	Yeah.
S:	You can get some money downtown…
C/W:	Yeah, there's people down there, there's people down here.
S:	Oh, yeah? Kinda crowded?
C/W:	Yeah, it's alright.
S:	You're friend with you tonight?
C/W:	What kinda car you drive again? That shit was so fucking nice!
S:	It's a German car.
C/W:	Yeah, it was nice. What type a car is that?
S:	Volkswagen.

C/W:	Oh, Volkswagen. Oh, so, what are you doing? So you gonna come pick me up?
S:	Um, maybe next… , well, I'm not going to be here this weekend, I don't think, so…
C/W:	Oh, you're not going to be there this weekend…?
S:	Well, that's the plan. I'm supposed to leave tomorrow for Connecticut, yeah…
C/W:	So, did you enjoy sucking my dick?
S:	Did I do that?
C/W:	Yeah.
S:	Oh, yeah.
C/W:	Yeah.
S:	I picked up two of you, huh?
C/W:	Yeah.
S:	Your friend was skinnier? Oh yeah, yeah, yeah… that's right! Your friend was Spanish!
C/W:	Yeah.
S:	Right, right, right. I remember.
C/W:	So did you enjoy sucking my dick?
S:	Um, I guess if I did it, I must have.

C/W: Hahahah.

S: Where are you, on the street?

C/W: Yeah.

S: Uh huh, no… no activity?

C/W: No, do you remember, or are you just talking to me?

S: No, I remember. The Spanish boy, and you're Black.

C/W: Yeah.

S: Yeah, is he, is he going to school with you, with you, at the…?

C/W: What?

S: Eh… I'm just trying to remember where you live.

C/W: I live in Brooklyn, remember?

S: Oh, okay, yeah. Well anyway, no. I'm… I'm going to sleep now. I gotta work tomorrow, and then I'm probably going to go to Connecticut for the weekend so… I may be back Sunday. You can try me then?

C/W: Do you, do you want me to come over?

S: When?

C/W: When? Today.

S: Tonight?

C/W: Yeah.

S: Nah, I'm going to sleep now. I need my sleep. I'm tired and I gotta get up early.

C/W: Don't you know that I'm only fourteen? I forgot to tell you that.

S: Don't I know that you're what?

C/W: Only fourteen.

S: Fourteen years old?

C/W: Yeah.

S: Oh, please…. Ha!

C/W: I am. You don't believe me?

S: No. I don't believe you. But that's okay. What difference does it make?

C/W: Haha. Alright.

S: Right.

C/W: So when are you going to come pick me up?

S: Well, you have to call me Sunday.

C/W: So I have to call you Sunday?

S: Yeah. I should be back by 9.

C/W: Alright.

S: Okay. Have a good night.

C/W:	Alright. So… so, I'll talk to you later.
S:	Okay. Bye.
C/W:	Bye.
Det:	The time is now 0003 hours. Detective Dropt putting an end to this undercover recording."

The night before, I had called Max. I knew he had finally listened to the tape. Ms. Spear had left a message on my cell's voicemail telling me so, and telling me to come down to his office at noon the following day, to listen to it with him. I got that message as I walked to the gym. So I stood outside its doors, knowing I couldn't continue until I knew.

He was impatient. "When you come down tomorrow. I'm busy right now," he says, as he hangs up on me. I call back, pleading, "Just answer a couple of questions."

"Okay," he says, clearly not wanting to. I don't know why, but I start with my lies, as if they will reveal the truth.

"Did I say I own a Volkswagen?" "Yes," he answers.

"Did I say I was going to Connecticut?" Again, "Yes."

"That's it," I had thought. "It must be."

Armored against a possibility I did not want to fathom, I then asked, "Did they record all of it? Even the extortion?"

For whatever reason, Max wouldn't do it. Answering my question with, "When you come down" he hangs up on me again.

And now, there's no longer any doubt. I have just left Max's office, where—with Lisa and Leslie at my side—the tape which I've waited so long to hear was played. And where, in that playing, it was confirmed what I don't want to believe—that my thirst for pleasure had so overwhelmed that regardless of the doubts and the reasons for those doubts, I had refused, if not actually been unable, to know the truth.

As I walk north in the general direction of my office, I realize that I have lived a life that made any lies I may have told myself not only believable, but inevitable. A life lived so greedy for more that, if I remembered all that I did, then, perhaps, even I would have had to stop. So, instead, I stopped remembering.

Now, as I replay it in my mind, I remember the call I have just heard. Now that denial can no longer be sustained, now that those whisperings to myself and to Lisa, Pi and others most supportive, that "Something else may have happened that weekend...." Or, "I'm not sure I remember everything...." Or, "How can it be that dates and ages and details don't match up...?" Now that all of those whisperings are given substance, I begin to remember.

What's added to those whisperings, triggering a haunting, hesitating recall, is the name 'James.' A name previously unrevealed, even in the deepest recesses of my consciousness. Walking in a daze, ignoring all around me, I search and think with a memory no longer in fear of the recollection.

James. My name, but not what I have chosen to go by. Yes, he had sat in the backseat of my car. It was there where he had told me his name and I had thought, "How odd." The formal name I have always rejected, assumed with such quiet comfort by this street kid, this young black boy. "Boy"—a word, like so much else, carelessly used.

"Was he really that young?" I think. Fourteen.

"I forgot to tell you that," he said on that tape.

Yes, he had. But if he had told me, would it have made a difference?

Yes .... Wouldn't it have?

For sure, though, it was another reason I hadn't believed. As, most perversely, my lie to myself was given its greatest weight by another remembrance. This one, however, has remained vivid since the day it occurred—a remembrance of Treat, Pablo's brother; the three of us in my apartment on November 8, 2003. A remembrance I know I would not have forgotten if it had also occurred with James and his companion on November 7, 2003. A remembrance that helped convince me that Treat was James.

Whether because of a simple and innocent modesty, or knowing adolescent shame, before completely undressing, Treat had taken refuge under the covers of my bed. Even though it is a hand grown jaded, mine was too quickly withdrawn, with what was surely too little concern of giving offense.

Only once before had the inadequacy of the passage of time in a young life been so starkly confirmed—that once, with the one whose picture is now linked in a way unimaginable.

With that remembrance of Treat, and with a phone call of threats from a self-proclaimed mother and the numbing fear and obsession born of those threats, any doubts as to whether it was the 7th or the 8th or whether he was fourteen or sixteen or whether there was a video or not, were trumped. Yes, those memories had made it easier to convince myself that any confusion was caused by the lies of Treat and Pablo and a scheming mother, and not mine. Or was caused by their forgetfulness in the midst of excess, and not mine.

But, as the details return, I realize there is more—really less—that has made it too easy to forget James. Crossing streets with unseen numbers, it comes. He was tall, taller than me. As he watched, he had objected to the game of submission and control shown in that video. Hadn't he? In fact, hadn't he objected so soon and with such finality that, for anything beyond his name, his height and the video, my memory has not failed me? That there had been nothing else to conjure a memory with sex as its subject?

"Did I do that?" I had said to James and the detective whose name we share on that audiotape—an audiotape no longer, and yet in some ways still, a phantom. Or did James and his companion say to me after watching a few minutes or less of that video, "We don't get down like that?" A choice they made which averted another, which for James, at least, was forbidden to be made. And, accepting that choice, did I not roll from one side of my bed to the other to get up and follow them out of my bedroom where that video was playing? And, after writing down and handing one of them—James it must have been—my phone number, did I not then pay them for nothing more than time spent and watch as they left through my apartment door?

Isn't that what happened? Is that not why I not only went out again the next night but, again, picked up another set of two, Pablo and Treat? Something I don't remember ever doing before. Something, if for no other reason, my thrifty nature would rebel against unless passions had been teased, then left unfulfilled.

Yet, even now, I am not completely sure—and I don't know why.

In the end, "It doesn't matter." Or, to use the less poetically useful words I actually used with James, "What difference does it make."

Were those words a dismissal of the importance of his innocence, as the prosecutor would argue? Or, as my lawyer would argue, were they a dismissal of the importance of his truthfulness as he makes known his innocence? As the one who uttered them that night now so long ago, they seem more an expression of the powerlessness to currently alter what is or what has been. And the pointlessness of reliving it, especially when, as made so obvious by the tape, it all seemed so uncertain.

That James was in my home, however, there is no doubt. And that, alone, will surely be enough, even if there were nothing else. For who would believe a claim of "nothing else" from one whose life defined "too much," from one whose life included too many admissions that "He was there."

In a way, it's all so stunning. Never before, in almost twenty-five years of excess, had such a thing happened. In the course of one week, the second week of November 2003, I had received three phone calls. I remembered two. One, vivid and threatening. The other, recalled just before it was almost forgotten—a brief, pointed warning—"He's only fourteen. You will pay us, or you will pay." A third—forgotten until today. And, in two of those calls, I had told at least two of the same lies, making it easier for me to continue to lie to myself.

How ironic, remembering and fearing the one who threatened but did nothing, while forgetting the one seemingly so unthreatening, who's done it all. And both of them coming into my life in one twenty- four hour period, as if in testament to the power of the cloaked moon on that November weekend.

Then, of course, there are the other two. The two in the pictures—pictures, unfathomably, never discarded. And, from so long ago. So long, in fact, that of the handful of two's I've been with in my life, they, more than likely, were the very first.

As I reach the point where the massive office towers of Sixth Avenue begin, I wonder at the wonderment of it all. Yes, three had called, and, in their own way, all had warned.

Now, with all the consequences for my failure to heed those warnings—all the consequences for the rest of my life—all I can do is ask, "Is this meant to be? Can this be anything other than God's will?"

Or so I've got to believe. And isn't that how it begins.

AFTERWORD

"How do you prepare for something like that?" my brother, the judge, asked as we sat on the porch of my cottage in late August of 2005. A month earlier, after a three day trial but before the verdict was rendered, I pled guilty to the charges set forth in the indictment. In three weeks, I was to enter prison to begin serving a sentence of one to three years.

Without even thinking, I responded with what many would consider a rhetorical question of my own, "Do you believe in God?"

For me, since December 12, 2003, that question has been more than rhetorical. By the time I went to prison, I was steadily on a path to belief. A "jailhouse conversion?" one might ask. Even if it were, does it matter? "Only," I would hope a sympathetic skeptic might answer, "if it isn't 'real.'"

A skeptic myself, mine was never going to be a belief in a personal god who gets involved directly in our lives, meting out justice to punish the wicked and favoring this one over that one. No, it just seemed more reasonable to believe, even if more difficult to grasp, that god would be beyond the easy reasoning of a desperate, "I want to believe" brain.

My brain, and my heart, only began to seriously focus on whether life has purpose or meaning—another way, at least to me, of asking whether there's a god—after my suicide attempt. That's when I began the process of "letting go" of the expectations and demands of the ego. To, in Pi's words, "surrender to that which is." Nearly as challenging as the process itself, is trying to describe it. Prior to going to prison, I made an attempt in an unsent letter to Judge Zyzen. For those who are interested, I include that letter on my website referred to on the back cover of this book.

Helping to sustain me for the two years I spent in prison was a belief that there's 'something more' and that I could best approach it by being something less, by "letting go." For sure, that faith didn't go unchallenged, as I faced experiences I never before could have imagined in a place almost perfectly designed to challenge anyone's faith.

But for me, in fact, my faith deepened while I was in prison. Cut-off from the distractions of everyday life and, for most of the time at least, successful in fending off those remorseless challenges to faith, I was not only able to continue but also to fortify a near-daily practice of sitting quietly and focusing on that still center at the core of the heart. It was a practice I had begun, tentatively, not many months after my arrest in December, 2003. And it's one I continue today.

Though, no doubt, still a ways from a "transcendent" meditative experience—at least if unaided by illegal substances and a Central Park setting—nevertheless my mind's chatter does reduce during those sittings. Moreover, I believe that the dimensions of my heart have expanded as a result, allowing me a glimpse of a reality more inclusive.

As might be expected, I also got to read a lot more than I ever read before. I focused not on the news of the day—which was virtually all I read when I was a lawyer—nor on "best sellers" or other light fare which might help pass the time. No, it was not only my heart but my mind which needed sustenance. And, for that, only the thoughtful knowledge of others would suffice. So, I read books written by and about prophets and sages … and scientists.

Not as easily dismissed as Nostradamus and more modern soothsayers bearing uncanny predictions are the sometimes "spooky" wonders of nature. It's fascinating to read how the scientists, in their various theories to explain those wonders, include what they themselves call "imaginary" numbers in their mathematical "proofs" or posit nearly infinite pockets of hyper-inflating universes. These, according to the prevailing theory, are stitched together by an elusive boson named Higgs brandishing multi-dimensional superstrings and a threadbare cosmological constant.

An heroic effort it is, matched by other scientists with other theories. All though, at least to me, seem as forced—as convenient—as any traditional religion. Perhaps, appalled at the excesses of those religions, scientists have cut off their noses, missing that which, in their own explanations of space and time, virtually reeks of spirit.

What better word than spirit, I would ask, for what they tell us are omnipresent, elemental waves of unlimited potential which, when "observed," mysteriously collapse into that which the scientists said they could not be—particles, particles as "dark" and evanescent as the reality they shape; particles which "entangle" in ways defying our notions of time and space itself; particles which, in an instantaneous explosion of primordial light, were born of a singularity of infinitely compressed unity. From there, they go on to say, a series of (those incredibly convenient) chance events give shape to a universe so perfectly and finely calibrated that we are its fruit—we, who are also composed of, and who are in a yet to be fully-fathomed cosmic dance with, those all-pervasive, transformative waves. Or, as I prefer to think of it, that life rendering spirit.

In a thrall to their 21st century slide rules, most of those scientists then go on to declaim that our very ability to consciously reflect on this mysterious, magical universe is simply another of those convenient "oops" of nature, a "punctuation" in an otherwise steadfast, yet completely random, evolutionary equilibrium.

And of this wondrous universe itself? Well, somehow or another, those slide rules reveal, this something that we are, arose from nothing at all.

I, for one, find all that no less fantastical than a Santa Claus character reigning from a heavenly throne, even one who impregnates—whether immaculately or not—a teenage virgin from a remote time and corner who is to beget Him a crucifiable yet resurrectable Son to atone (oh-so-doubly-conveniently) for the sins of the Father's other less closely related but no less dearly loved children.

Between the extremes of an arid nihilism and a twisted, cartoonish paternalism, it's almost easy, if not downright sensible, to believe what other, more reflective thinkers have proposed: that we are here, in part, to experience the very dualities of the existence which so bedevils us—the pleasure and the pain, the love and the hate, the good and the bad. And we are here to experience it not abandoned and alone but rather on behalf of, and in union with, that "not nothing-at-all" or that "something more" or, as those thinkers like to remind us, the n/one which is ineffable. If that is true, then our very ability to consciously bear witness to, and by our "observation" to interact with, both poles of that creation means we are blessed, as through each of us god perceives and experiences and creates. In such a universe, we would be the dark, evanescent quanta shaping the mind of god. After all, is it not said, "As above, so below; as below, so above."

But whatever one chooses to believe, our evanescence is undeniable. For, in less than an eye-blink of a boundless time, we are gone. It seems to me we can approach death kicking and screaming, filled with fear and apart-ness. Or we can do so in a way that all those great, but so easily dismissible or twistable, prophets and sages have taught—through love.

Through love, we surrender our-selves to all that of which we are a part, and so open our hearts to our return to that infinite unity which gave us birth.

If the promise of some blissful, metaphysical re-union is too obscure to bother to heed the prophets' teachings, then what about the existence we are creating right here on earth? In more ways than one I hope, my life is vivid testimony to the truth of the scriptures so many consider sacred when they speak of karma or of "reaping what you sow." What do we reap when the scales are tipped away from love and compassion and toward hatred and fear? Even if the "fight-or-flight" emanating from fear and separation has been necessary for our survival, who doubts the grace—the power—which flows from love? So, perhaps, another even more profound reason we are here is the challenge of evolving towards something which seems more whole, more perfect, more divine.

How difficult it is, though, to convince ourselves of this path when the pay-off for meditation and prayer seems so ephemeral in this "show-me" world and where few can summon the intellectual courage to challenge the "show-me" scientists. If not the miracle I once so desperately sought, at the least, we all surely want something tangible to prove those scientists wrong.

For me, in addition to the expansiveness of a stilled heart and the logic of an emancipated mind, is the "proof" offered by the pure and simple magic of my life, especially those odd coincidences, what Carl Jung called "synchronicities." I believe they are one place where the elemental "I" crosses paths, in this world, with the elemental spirit.

Think about it—here I am where no one else would ever want to be, and yet I feel blessed.

That's not to say I face no challenges. In a way, tougher than any of those in prison, have been the challenges I have faced since I was released from prison. And that's not because I am now both an ex-convict and a registered sex offender. Rather, it's because I am, once again, encountering the distractions of everyday life, including all that is so seductive and flattering to my sense of "self." Merely by writing this book and hoping that others will read it, I realize that ego has prevailed. And, inevitably, magic will be stripped from the events I describe, whatever excuses I make to myself about the promise of a different type of magic.

Perhaps, then, it's another of those proverbial blessings in disguise that, forever labeled as I am, my ever needy and ever greedy, all-consuming ego shall forever be comfortably held in check. That will be true, of course, only if I do not judge others when others judge me, which may be especially difficult should that judgment of me be other than what one might expect.

In the end, all I can do is struggle as best I can with the complexity of what it means to be human. Fortunately, that includes celebrating those magical intersections with spirit—whether it be three phone calls in the second week of November, 2003, two of which are likely to forever remain mysteries. Or the events which occurred over a December weekend in 2004, which may also be considered "mysterious," but mysterious in a way I celebrate. Though he had missed that month's natural force of historic destruction, Nick, in another of my life's stunners, had not missed mine. "Death and rebirth;" "massive overturn;" "structural change" are words he used to describe the trajectory of my life through the end of that year and are words frozen in time on the tape of our May, 2004 session.

I remember that December weekend as being one where time itself had slowed down, everything was slowed down. Eating. Thinking. And, even breathing. With my attention focused as never before.

Wayne Dyers' "*Power of Intention*," a show I allude to in Chapter 21 and which gave me such comfort in a time of turmoil, was rebroadcast by PBS that weekend. That was followed by a rebroadcast of the last interview Bill Moyers had with Joseph Campbell in a series of interviews, entitled "*The Power of Myth*." The one on that night was called "*Masks of Eternity*," and it focused on God, religion and the quest for spiritual fulfillment. Also on television that weekend, I watched a movie called "*Awakenings*" and another called "*Normal*," the theme of which was the total transcendence of one's ego.

In between were phone calls not only from my mother and Lisa, which were common, but also from Pi and William, which were not. And they, too, were of a theme, as represented, most dramatically, in my conversation with William.

He had called my cell phone, even though he had my new home number in the Bronx and even though he knew I rarely used my cell phone on weekends—though it happened to be on that night. Clearly, he had wanted to register his concern but to avoid a direct connection with me, and with all the messiness that my life had become. Not ten days earlier, in a far more dramatic and permanent attempt, I, too, had sought to avoid that messiness.

But taking hold on that weekend, amidst a spirit that felt almost palpable, was a belief that I had been diverted from that path by a source of strength which went beyond my own. Nurtured by what I "happened" to watch, and to whom I "happened" to speak and even by how I "happened" to eat, think and breathe on that weekend, a growing belief enabled me to begin to loosen the powerful grip that fear had on my life. By confronting William's continuing fear with that new found strength, I took my first, tiny steps into the light.

It was a month later, as I was trying to figure out how to end this book, which was threatening to become unwieldy, that I realized the events of that weekend would serve perfectly. What better way to end than by retelling the story of when fear began to be replaced by faith.

And there's more, for with the loosening of fear's grip, I also achieved the internal peace to finally stop what I had failed to stop so many times before—behavior which is a narcotic to so much which we wish to avoid. As I write this in November of 2008, I have had not one cigarette, and have had nearly as little booze, since that December weekend in 2004.

Was it tough to do? Not at all. Their purpose had simply vanished, and so I could simply stop.

The final goose-bumping coda for me, however, was when I also realized that the weekend had ended on a day on which it had all began—December 12th. One year to the day of my arrest.

So, do I then say, "Aha, there's the 'proof?'" Not to others, I don't. But, when combined with everything else I've tried to describe and much I have not, it's enough of a hint for me to have faith.

Of one thing I need no faith to know for certain—that the first question asked of me by Lydia Cepeda on that early November morning in 2003 is one I can now answer better. And it is an answer which, I would argue, is as "real" as one can be in an imperfect life.

Hopefully, on each of my tomorrows, if asked that question again, I will be able to say the same anew. For so long as that holds true, then I believe my only possible path is towards that which is more whole, more perfect, more divine. And with that, whatever else may come in my life, it truly doesn't matter.

James P. Cornelio
New Preston, CT.
November, 2008

ACKNOWLEDGMENTS

As challenges continued to mount, two of those whom I considered far more intimate dropped away, but another stepped up. He opened not only his heart but, when Lisa's home was deemed unacceptable as a residence for me because it was too close to a school, he also opened his home. Without that, I would not have been released from prison. To the many warnings, including one from a cop who told him neighbors will get "strange" when they learn he's sheltering a "sexual predator" in their midst, he shrugged and said to me, "That's what friends are for." More than for his home, I owe him for his example. And I've already learned enough from him to know that the only way for me to ever truly repay him is to live what's left of my life with that example as my ideal.

As with friends, so it is, only more so, with blood. I've not done my job unless readers are wondering how much more she can possibly do for me. To say again with a heart which happily invites charges of repetition, no matter what troubles she was facing in her own life and no matter how unavailable I was to share those burdens with her, she has been there for me. Together, we pushed and pulled and lifted and cried and, sometimes, even laughed. And, when nothing else was more important, she offered a sympathetic ear and a wisdom I could trust. I love you Lisa.

And, finally, there's my mother. How can a child not ask, "What did I do to my mother as a result of all of this?" As I hope I reveal in my story, my mother is a strong, independent woman with love to spare. But, still, the events I brought down on her head took and twisted her heart in a way no mother should have to bear.

In one of the many, many conversation we had as we tried to comfort each other over the past several years, she said to me about God's justice, "Jim, what I think is that He keeps sending us back until we get it right."

What I intend to do for so long as this earth remains blessed by her presence is to make certain I do everything I can to convince her that with the lessons I've learned in this lifetime that maybe, just maybe, I've cut out at least a few of those return visits. No matter how far short I may still fall, that, I know, will be enough for her.

"Blessed is the man on whose tomb can be written, 'Hic jacet nemo.'" [Here lies no one]

- Ananda Coomaraswamy

Made in the USA